An Actor's Craft

This inspirational guide for advanced acting students brings together multiple ways of creating excellence in performance. David Krasner provides tried and tested exercises, a history of actor training, and explores the complex relationships between acting theories and teachers.

Drawing on examples from personal experience as an actor, director and teacher, *An Actor's Craft* begins with the building blocks of mind, body and voice, moving through emotional triggers and improvisation, to a final section bringing these techniques together in approaching a role. Each chapter contains accompanying exercises that the actor should practice daily.

Combining theory and practice, this thought-provoking and challenging study of acting techniques and theories is for actors who have grasped the basics and now want to develop their knowledge and training further.

AN ACTOR'S CRAFT

The Art and Technique of Acting

DAVID KRASNER

No portion of this publication may be reproduced, copied or transmitted save with written permission or in accordance with the provisions of the Copyright, Designs and Patents Act 1988, or under the terms of any licence permitting limited copying issued by the Copyright Licensing Agency, Saffron House, 6–10 Kirby Street, London EC1N 8TS.

Any person who does any unauthorized act in relation to this publication may be liable to criminal prosecution and civil claims for damages.

The author has asserted his right to be identified as the author of this work in accordance with the Copyright, Designs and Patents Act 1988.

First published 2012 by
PALGRAVE MACMILLAN

Palgrave Macmillan in the UK is an imprint of Macmillan Publishers Limited, registered in England, company number 785998, of Houndmills, Basingstoke, Hampshire RG21 6XS.

Palgrave Macmillan in the US is a division of St Martin's Press LLC, 175 Fifth Avenue, New York, NY 10010.

Palgrave Macmillan is the global academic imprint of the above companies and has companies and representatives throughout the world.

Palgrave® and Macmillan® are registered trademarks in the United States, the United Kingdom, Europe and other countries.

ISBN 978–0–230–27552–2   hardback
ISBN 978–0–230–27553–9   paperback

This book is printed on paper suitable for recycling and made from fully managed and sustained forest sources. Logging, pulping and manufacturing processes are expected to conform to the environmental regulations of the country of origin.

A catalogue record for this book is available from the British Library.

A catalog record for this book is available from the Library of Congress.

10 9 8 7 6 5 4 3 2 1
21 20 19 18 17 16 15 14 13 12

Printed in China

CONTENTS

Acknowledgments   vii

Introduction: What Is Acting?   1

PART I: PREPARING MIND AND BODY

1 Preparation: Breathing, Relaxation and Concentration   **21**
Exercise 1: Breathing Awareness   25
Exercise 2: Relaxation Awareness   27
Exercise 3: See-saw Breathing   30
Exercise 4: Concentration and Personalization   31
Exercise 5: Mirror Exercise   32
Exercise 6: Observation and Imagination   33
Exercise 7: Concentration in Motion   34

2 Vocal and Physical Dynamics   **36**
Exercise 8: Vocal Range and Flexibility   37
Exercise 9: Chekhov's Movements (Plus)   40
Exercise 10: Creating Images   42
Exercise 11: Swinging Side-to-Side   46
Exercise 12: Animal Imagery   50

3 Personalizing: Sense and Emotion Memory   **53**
Exercise 13: Sense Memory   54
Exercise 14: Eating Soup   55

Exercise 15: Packing   59
Exercise 16: Emotion Memory 1   60
Exercise 17: Emotion Memory 2 (Breathing)   62
Exercise 18: Waiting   63

PART II: PASSION AND INSPIRATION

4 Secrets and Sources   **77**
Exercise 19: Photographs   89
Exercise 20: Repetition   95

5 Physicalization and Analysis Through Action   **103**
Exercise 21: One Action/One Objective 1   107
Exercise 22: One Action/One Objective 2   116

6 Actions and Six Basic Actions   **119**
Exercise 23: Six Basic Actions   125
Exercise 24: Mirror/Action Exercise   128

7 Improvisation and Jazz Acting   **132**
Exercise 25: Nursery Rhyme Exercise   145
Exercise 26: Come to Me   147

PART III: PERFORMING THE ROLE

8 Living Through and Interstitial Scenes   **151**
Exercise 27: Interstitial Scene   166

9 Lying and Denial   **167**
Exercise 28: Entrance with a Lie   177

**10 The Role: Psychological Gesture, Homework and
    Rehearsal**   **179**
Exercise 29: Stepping into Character   185
Exercise 30: Psychological Gesture 1   186
Exercise 31: Psychological Gesture 2   187

Conclusion   **193**

Brief Biographies of Key Acting Teachers   197

Bibliography   203

Index   211

ACKNOWLEDGMENTS

I want to thank the support I've received from Emerson College. Four acting teachers, in particular, have been inspirational: Milton Justice, Polina Klimovitskaya, James Luse, and Robert Ellermann. Milton's work with Stella Adler has been an invaluable resource for me; Polina's insights into Vakhtangov have been especially helpful; I have often turned to James's expertise on Michael Chekhov; and I'm especially grateful to Robert, who is, without exception, the greatest living Stanislavsky expert in both theory and practice. I am pleased to see that Robert is finally getting the recognition he deserves. Every conversation and exchange with all four has guided me and produced deeper, more insightful results. Kate Haines at Palgrave Macmillan has been a wonderful supporter of this project since its inception, and Keith Povey and Elaine Towns have offered excellent copyediting advice. I want to thank especially the six anonymous readers of this manuscript; their suggestions were extremely helpful. My lovely wife Lynda and beautiful daughter Matildé have shown tolerance for my compulsive work habits. I owe much to the three principal teachers who taught me acting: Paul Mann, Kim Stanley and Barbara Loden (and I am pleased to see Barbara's 1970 film *Wanda* at last receiving the recognition it deserves). The greatest compliment I can give any teacher applies to them – that their passions, ideas and examples continue to engage and inspire me. Finally, I owe a deep gratitude to my students; this book is written for them.

DAVID KRASNER

INTRODUCTION

WHAT IS ACTING?

The aim of this book is twofold: to provide exercises for the advanced actor, and to illuminate the origination of various techniques related to actor training. The book combines theory and practice, offering a descriptive account of acting technique and a prescriptive way of achieving artistry in acting. I draw on examples from personal experiences as an actor, director and teacher, creating a book intended for advanced students and veteran actors seeking to improve, as well as instructors who will, I hope, find it useful when defining their goals. This is not a basic primer textbook; there are many practical acting workbooks for beginners. Readers will find a recommended list of introductory acting textbooks in the bibliography. The book is for instructors and students who have a fundamental background understanding and wish to advance their training and knowledge further. It is meant to clarify exercises, define similarities and differences in acting theories, and bring together the multiple ways of creating excellence in performance. Past and current acting teachers will be referenced throughout. The section Brief Biographies of Key Acting Teachers at the end of the book lists the instructors and their methods.

The chapters are arranged sequentially to provide a stair-step approach to the development of an actor. While the chapters can be read individually, the sequence allows readers to progress through a series of ideas and exercises. The arrangement of chapters is divided into three parts: the first concerns the development of mind, body, voice and sensory and emotional availability; these are the building blocks of acting. The second part examines emotional triggers – ways of stimulating the actor's imagination and passion, as well as the importance of improvisation in training; these exercises prepare actors for work on a role. The third part concerns playing roles and how to approach a part. Each chapter contains accompanying exercises so that the actor can begin practicing. The exercises can be done alone or in class, but are to be practiced daily and executed like scales in the same way that musicians, singers and dancers practice.

It takes multiple skills to become a good actor. Acting, according to acting teacher Robert Benedetti, "is not one skill but a constellation of skills" and training actors "is complicated by the fact that each of these skills involves a different mode of thought and activity" (Zen in the Art of Actor Training, p. 88). As the title suggests, An Actor's Craft is not all-encompassing – hence the indefinite article "a" not "the." Acting is a subjective art with multiple ways to execute it proficiently, teach it successfully, and define it aesthetically. Being a good actor requires skill, craft, experience, passion, vision, sensitivity, vitality, spontaneity and a host of other attributes that are both exhilarating and highly demanding. The ways of achieving them will be examined here by offering a comprehensive approach that empowers performers to become creative artists capable of making significant contributions to the art of acting.

I believe acting can be taught. Not necessarily from a book, of course, but much can be gained from a book. Acting is an art, and actors are creative artists. Acting is a profession like any other, requiring discipline, a work ethic and professionalism. Actors are artists because they invent something out of imagination and inspiration. Like other artists who interpret, make choices and engage in creative acts – in the actor's case, the creation of a human being – actors invent characters that did not exist before they embodied them. Likewise a painter who creates on a canvas, or a musician who creates on an instrument, actors create from themselves. Their instrument is their body and mind; their blueprint is their life; and their creative activity emerges from their ideas and passions manifested in gesture, voice, actions and behavior. There is no *formula* for quality acting; creativity is not mass-produced but rather actors discover it, refine and reinvent it. Technique – the way of working – is a means to several possible paths of creativity and not a recipe for success. There is a lucrative "industry" of actor training, particularly in the United States, that requires "certification" to teach a prescribed technique – as if learning to be an actor is a timeless art form fixed at a particular juncture of history, successful only if one pursues a paint-by-numbers approach and validated solely by designated gurus. The implementation of such guru-ism – the worship of teachers as deities – has done significant damage to the credibility of actor training. Ideas and techniques involving the instruction of any art form evolve over time; every teacher modifies his/her descriptions and methods; and no single way of doing art creates certainty of excellence. To think so, and to suggest so, implies that actor training is a one-size-fits-all method suitable to all simultaneously. But acting, like all the arts, is not a medical prescription ("take two of these pills tonight and you'll be talented in the morning"). Actor training is based on *ways* of working, not *the* way of working. As individuals vary, so methods of improving vary.

"Technique" (and there are many techniques that will be examined in this book) means the process through which the actor marshals all the elements of her toolkit – imagination, relaxation, concentration, emotion, vitality, interpretation and so on, and presents them through gesture, voice, image, subtext, mind, action and specific relationships to the other actors onstage. Art, playwright and director David Mamet says, "is about the spontaneous connection of the artist to his own unconscious – about insight beyond reason," and the "only purpose of technique is to allow the artist to bypass the conscious mind" (p. 91). Technique is a way to free the artist, not shackle her with rules and regulations; it must inspire actions and behaviors that emerge from interesting choices; it must liberate, not restrict; and it should encourage creativity, not inhibit it. Anything passing for "technique" that fails to inspire the actor "to act" is untrustworthy and should be discarded immediately. Technique enables the actor to enlarge and expand her creative, imaginative and physical embodiment of the role. It must be organic; it is always a process and not a result; and it is neither a label nor a fetish ("I study this and that technique, therefore I'm an actor"), nor something an actor does to "show off." Instead, it is a functional process – a tool – for improvement and clarity. Technique is a part of the organic process: *You are your technique* because your technique is absorbed into who you are. As with an athlete, an observer knows the player's skills were derived by technique, but when it comes to the time to hit the ball or make the shot the technique is absorbed into the player and only the activity in the moment matters. A tennis player might need to improve her backhand technique; she practices a technique that succeeds in improving her skills. It is the same with acting: if the actor is not emotionally connected to herself or to a role, if she is not sufficiently listening and observing her fellow actors, if she is not pursuing actions and objectives and so on, the actor employs techniques to improve these shortcomings.

The study of acting, as the founder of modern acting training, Konstantin Stanislavsky reminds us, is a living organism. It transforms in different situations, adapts to changing circumstances, and must therefore be modified to address individual needs, strengths and weaknesses. When discussing his system of training, Stanislavsky said emphatically that it is "not a cookery book. When you prepare a particular dish, you merely look in the contents, look up the appropriate page and that is that. The 'system' is not an all-purpose reference book but a whole culture which must be cultivated and nurtured over many long years. An actor cannot learn it parrot-fashion," but rather must "make it part of his own flesh and blood, make it second nature, become one with it forever so it transforms him for the stage" (*Actor's Work*, p. 612). What works for one actor may not necessarily work for another; and what works at one point for an actor may no longer apply as that actor takes on a new role, evolves as an artist, or grows as a human being. The director Peter Brook reminds us that "talent is not static, it ebbs and flows according to many circumstances" (*Empty Space*, p. 104). Roles, performances and ensembles change, demanding that we create and recreate ourselves. American acting teacher Lee Strasberg, following Stanislavsky's observation, put it best when he said that the actor works in "two spheres – the actor's work on himself and the actor's work on the role." During the course of training, "one aspect of the actor's art may be emphasized temporarily at the expense of the other, but before a complete and convincing image can be created on the stage both must be mastered" (Introduction, *Diderot's Paradox*, p. xiii). The work on the self and the work on the role are equally demanding, requiring time, energy, focus and attention.

A fully trained actor should have at her disposal multiple tools, and as each challenge arises, new tools apply. This book emphasizes tools aimed at improving concentration, sensitivity, variety of actions, emotional availability, responsiveness to other actors and so on – concerning self-development and creative growth. I shall analyze several roles in this book, and each role requires different things from different actors. To cover every role in the history of theater (plus television, movies and the internet) is impossible. Furthermore, to suggest that there is only one way of performing a role implies that actors are merely spokes on a wheel – any actor can play the role as long as she applies the "rule" or technique so that the wheel spins. Conventional wisdom, for example, suggests that Stanislavsky's technique works only for realism, the Polish director Jerzy Grotowski's technique works only for the avant-garde, elocutionary techniques work only for Shakespeare and so on, as if acting is an assembly line ("All aboard the Stanislavsky assembly line when you do Chekhov and be sure to get off when you do Shakespearean verse"). There is no "one way" to perform Chekhov, Shakespeare, Ionesco, Tennessee Williams or any playwright: different theaters, directors, ensembles and condition of the actor at any given moment influence the performer, creating differing situations and alternating demands. To maintain that an acting "technique" or a training method is applicable only to certain roles, genres or playwrights and not others is antithetical to the actor as a creative and empowering artist. Stanislavsky is very clear on this point, saying "my method gives no recipes for becoming a great actor or for playing a part. My method is the way to the actor's correct state of being on the stage. The correct state is the normal state of a human being in life" (quoted in Gorchakov, p. 119). Embodying a role with interest, passion and dynamism is our aim; I acknowledge the absolute importance of analyzing a role. However, I leave the work on a role to the individual actor as they grapple with each play and apply different interpretations as they arise. What I offer are multiple means of artistic development and I encourage each actor to use what is appropriate for each situation – as each role is attempted, new concerns and ideas emerge.

The aim of acting is the enlargement of human understanding. We engage, in a public forum, the consequences, actions, emotions and relationships occurring among humans. Our objective is communicating ideas about the human condition, to educate an audience about human relations, and to provide insights into human beings. When I observe good acting, I am compelled by the actor's behavior, I am moved by her passion, and I am galvanized by her attention to detail, her relationship to the other actors and objects onstage, and her ability to surprise me. Like great painting or music, I want to see and hear the actor with all my attention because the actor enables me

to understand more of what it means to be a human being. I am led
by the actor's desires and feelings for the role and the interesting,
unique and wholly unpredictable performance. The actor is not seeking my approval or trying to "sell" the notion of a good performance to
me; rather, she is leading me toward her ideas about the role, which in
turn leads me to greater understanding of humanity. The actor is an
artist who brings something special to the stage or screen – a vision,
emotion, concept and energy that is unequivocally engrossing.

Stanislavsky asserts that actors "have the opportunity, through
the ideas that you dramatize on the stage and through your characterization, to educate your audience and to make them better, finer,
wiser, and more useful members of society" (quoted in Gorchakov,
pp. 40–1). I am therefore interested in a certain type of acting: three-
dimensional, emotional, physical, intelligent and socially aware. The
actor should be believable, subtle, exciting, vulnerable, surprising, taste-
ful, empathetic, compelling, ensemble oriented and willing to show
all sides of her personality. The actor conveys depth and restraint,
artistry and ideas, and a willingness to reveal a human being in all
her complexity. Actors must be psychologically astute, emotionally
courageous and brutally honest in their self-examination. And that
is not all: an actor should have a resonating voice, physical dexterity and a flexible body capable of assuming many shapes and forms.
I want to watch an actor who is colorful, exhibiting a wide range of
feelings and actions; it is not enough to be truthful or to be able to
say four lines of verse on one breath; the actor must have a broad
imagination and a range of actions and emotions that sustain my
interest over a two to three hour period. The actor must have a ruling idea about the performance; more importantly, in executing the
ruling idea, Stanislavsky insists that "You must do everything in your
power to make the idea exciting, colorful, strong, and important to
the audience" (quoted in Gorchakov, p. 42). During the time an actor
is on stage or screen she must discover her life through the course of
the story; the audience travels with the actor through the narrative,
watching the actor experience, grow, learn, rise, fall and emerge at the
end changed by the journey's events. This is what is meant by "living
through" the role: the actor has lived through and experienced something spontaneously, influenced by the story and deeply affected by
the unfolding events.

I want to be surprised when I watch an actor, because the actor
understands irony, combines humor and pathos, rage and compassion,

grasps the contradictions and absurdity of the human condition, and adds a creative spin to each role. Actors must develop a keen sense of imagination and fantasy; simultaneously, they must be present in the moment, relaxed and accessible to immediate and multiple reactions, and exhibit depth and intensity of emotion. Actors must have at their immediate disposal a highly active and evolved sensory apparatus; they must be, in other words, responsive to their individual taste, tactile, olfactory, visual, and aural experiences. Actors *discover* in their performance: by discover I mean an actor allows the events to unfold in real time as she experiences them, using improvisatory skills to become surprised by what she sees and hears. Stanislavsky's pupil Michael Chekhov observed that "To create, in the real sense, means to discover and show new things" (*To the Actor* 28) and his other pupil Evgenii Vakhtangov said that an actor must "agitate from the essence," by which he means that an actor must be inspired (agitated) to perform not for accolades or the desire to impress the spectators, but rather moved to present the human condition completely, organically, and with the full understanding of themselves, the play, and the role. "The conditions of the life of a character," Vakhtangov maintains, "must be known as well as you know your own mother" (in Cole, p. 145), and this knowledge allows us to see and hear a fully-formed human being. I want a performance *to endure* in the mind and imagination of the audience, to change the spectator in some significant way. Likewise music or painting, I want an actor's performance to resonate deeply in the spectator. An actor is an artist and should therefore work accordingly: attentive to details, focus on specific choices and actions, cultivate powers of observations, be a student of the human condition, and make decisions about what to enact based on study, passion, inventiveness and willingness to share her own life experiences.

This is a book about acting for every medium. I believe acting for the stage and acting for the camera are not as radically different as many suppose. "Acting is acting, whether in film, theater, or television," writes the acting teacher Harold Guskin. No matter the venue, he says, an actor should discover "the way to free himself from Acting, playing it moment by moment, letting his instinct and his emotions take him wherever they go, trusting the script to sculpt the character" (p. 137). I prefer acting for the stage largely because there are no barriers between the actor and the audience; the raw emotions and physical presence of the actor are a powerful and immediate synergy that cannot be replicated in film or television. The stage also demands a living recreation at every performance and this recreation exercises craft, stretches creativity and improves acting skills. Strasberg has often been accused of teaching acting primarily for film, yet in this observation he strikes the right note for stage acting: "the real problem for the actor," he says, "is how to create in each performance the same believable experiences and behavior, and yet include what Stanislavsky called 'the illusion of the first time' " (*Dream of Passion*, p. 35). Choices that work for a large Broadway theater may not work as well for the screen; an open-air theater and an intimate space place different demands on the actor; yet, as acting teacher Milton Katselas contends, "that doesn't mean the acting is fundamentally different. The work is the same, the degree of emotion is the same. The story is the same" (p. 147). Furthermore, there are wonderful film and television scripts that challenge the actor. The acting teacher Lawrence Parke says, and I agree, it ultimately boils down to this: "Good acting is good acting, whether in theatre or before the cameras of motion pictures" (p. 274).

There are, of course, differences; namely the camera's ability for close-ups as opposed to the need for projection in the theater; the need to express the work physically and viscerally in the theater as opposed to the dictates of subtle facial expression on film; and the continuity of the stage as opposed to the potential discontinuity in the shooting sequence of film or television. But these are technical adjustments for the actor, and too many non-actors make more of these differences than reality dictates. Critic Robert Brustein, for example, remarks that Marlon Brando's "brooding intimacy was, from the very beginning, perfect for movie roles" (p. 90). On the contrary: from the beginning, Brando's theatrical training and muscular physicality worked splendidly not only onstage but also in films such as *A Streetcar Named Desire* and *On the Waterfront*. One could argue that he was too physical for film; his animated body language projected perhaps more than the camera required. But there is little doubt that his acting was theatrical and visceral. He mumbled occasionally, but that behavior (really just a bad habit) has been exaggerated by his detractors. His brooding also increased as he disengaged from stage acting entirely. Still, his theater training surfaces remarkably well in his films and his work is a paradigm of terrific acting – indeed a model that is still worth emulating. A more significant and perceptive remark about Brando, and acting in general, comes from the actor William Redfield, who compares Brando to Laurence Olivier (they were often compared from the 1950s through the 1970s, considered representatives of the best in American and British styles, respectively), noting that during the mid-twentieth century, when the American Method was asserting its presence, what American actors "wanted all along was Olivier's training, will power, and intellectual application grafted onto Brando's muscles, sensibility, and passion. For passion, in Brando's dish-shattering hands, was a thrilling sight indeed" (p. 10). This description defines excellence in acting: training, analysis and will power combined with raw emotion, risky choices, spontaneity, imagination, action and passion.

What is "Good Acting?"

The American acting teacher Sanford Meisner wrote that "Good acting is humanly alive and theatrically vivid" (*Theatre Arts on Acting*, p. 45). This is a good starting point for a definition of "quality acting." Still, everyone will have their own view; this is why we are engaged in a subjective art. I acknowledge quality acting when it compels me to watch and listen; and I acknowledge inferior acting when it leaves me bored and uninspired. Bad acting works on the surface; it is predictable, obvious, shallow and seeks audience accolades. Good acting achieves multiple levels and various nuances; it surprises, revealing varying facets about the human condition – in other words, passion, detail and depth. Bad acting is general and one-dimensional; good acting is specific and three-dimensional. It comes from a deeply personal place in the actor, is well-thought-out, consists of actions, expressed eloquently, tastefully, simply and artistically through the actor's voice and movement, and conveys feeling, humor and pathos. A good actor connects to other actors onstage, giving generously to them in the spirit of care, devotion and concentration. A bad actor is physically tense, forcing arbitrary emotions or actions, and largely ignores other actors; a good actor is relaxed, concentrating and breathing fully, and living through each moment specifically as if it is the first breath of her life. Good acting never tries to force itself upon us, but rather offers a way of perceiving the human condition with thought, wit, ease and ideas. Good actors willingly risk being disliked, repellent, even scorned; as the playwright and director Bertolt Brecht suggested, it is not always necessary to seek empathy and love in a performance as it is to obtain understanding. Good acting can derive only from hard work, discipline and long hours of rehearsal. It demands rigorous attention to the detail of one-self and the role. In good acting, the actor can be silent or read from a phone book; either way, the activity is so engaging that her mere presence in performance is mesmerizing and the result of watching is transformative.

Three qualifying points need to be stressed. First, the script has *nothing* to do with a good performance. *Acting does not depend on what the vehicle is but rather on how it is being executed.* Good or mediocre scripts should be judged on their own merits. Many sub-par scripts seem excellent when first presented by good actors, only to be recognized for their inadequacies when performed again by others; and many fine scripts are relegated to the garbage bin because they were first exposed to the public by under-par performers. *Acting is creating a three-dimensional and truthful depiction of a human being, not the creation of literature*: "What the author has given you in the form of a written play is *his* creation, not yours," Michael Chekhov writes, "he has applied his talent. But what is your contribution to the writer's work?" (*To the Actor*, p. 27). Certainly, a superior script – with vivid dialogue, intriguing story and imaginative relationships – is desirable and should inspire actors. But literature has its own stand-ards, and acting has others, and it is a mistake to confuse the two (though many do). Frequently, an actor can indeed learn a great deal by working with an inferior script. Good scripts can sometimes make the acting easier by providing all the requisite details; the actor sim-ply follows the script's narrative or characterization and provides suf-ficient energy and enthusiasm to support it. Bad scripts make us work harder – and in turn we often learn more – because we are obliged to fill in details the author has left blank. Because of the actor's work – regardless of the text – I leave the theater or film fundamentally changed by the depth, variety and dynamics of the performance.

Second, shock value has nothing to do with good acting. We are often compelled to rubberneck when we see an accident, drawn to the disaster by curiosity (the German word is *Schadenfreude*, the guilty pleasure of watching others suffer). Undoubtedly, train wrecks attract attention; this is, however, not art but happenstance. Someone's bad luck, like nudity, can be magnetic, but it has nothing to do with an actor's artistic choices. Our attention to shock and nudity is fleet-ing, banal, motivated by petty inquiry (like watching a movie star's meltdown), and caused by easy arousal rather than inspiring art-istry. Finally, what passes for good looks is superficial, irrelevant and based on artificial standards of fashionable attractiveness. Acting is not a beauty pageant; it has no connection with the surface glitter of what society deems to be sexy. Such value judgments teeter on pornography, are manufactured by industries to sell products, and have nothing whatever to do with quality acting. Good acting should be sexy, but this is only one of several components that make up its sum total. Galvanizing my attention has little to do with stardom: there are actors who seek attention merely for the sake of it; their acting is an exercise in pronouncing how wonderful or cute they are in order to obtain praise. We all desire praise, but this goal alone produces old tricks, reduces artistic choices and eviscerates the performance's humanity, leaving nothing but superficiality. Stanislavsky's student, Richard Boleslavsky refers to this as "mechanical performances" that "instead of being based on new, specifically discovered [ideas] for that particular play" and evoking new "creative principles," are "produced according to an old commonplace routine. The only standard rule in such kind of a theatre is the motto: 'the public likes it!' ("Creative Theatre," p. 99). Vakhtangov called this kind of actor a "journeyman" one who "grasps with bare hands at feelings and tries to give a definitive form to their expression" (in Cole, p. 144). These actors quickly cry or laugh, as if a show of emotion, cleverness, being "cool," or flaunting sexuality demonstrates the human condition. The opposite is the case: an actor must touch the core of emotions with humility; must be responsible for depth without self-aggrandizement; and must create conviction borne from human relationships and comprehension of the human condition. Only then can an actor reach beneath the surface. The American acting teacher, Stella Adler, put it best when she said that the actor "is expected to create magic. He has to create a character that engages the audience night after night," because audiences come to the theater "for one reason only: to enjoy and fathom the human condition – to be jolted, to have an artistic experience" (*Technique*, p. 7). This engagement must not only occur instantly – the moment the actor enters the stage or appears on the screen – it must also be sustained throughout the performance.

The fundamental tool for every actor is *passion*: you must desire to act for the love of it. Stanislavsky said that the "genuine actor is set on fire by what is happening around him, he is carried away by life, which then becomes the object of his study and his passion" (*An Actor's Work*, p. 115). Along similar lines, the acting teacher Milton Katselas adds that "you have to have the passion within that propels you to burn, to have to be on fire. And politeness is not the answer. And likeability is not the answer" (p. 23), because, as the acting teacher Larry Moss puts it: "You have to find something in every script that ignites your own passion. Don't ever play a part without some personal investment" (p. 102). You must learn to respect the work as an art expressing the human condition. Yet the love of acting must not become narcissistic. Stanislavsky felt that actors can too easily be distracted and seduced by the self-aggrandizing promotion required to succeed in the acting profession. He fought passionately against the influences of "success, applause, vanity, conceit, bohemianism, hamming, self-importance, bragging, gossip, scandal-mongering" and other backstage traps that hinder the art of acting. For Stanislavsky, "Creative, artistic principles, a true love of the art in yourself not yourself in the art, personal awareness, strong beliefs, good habits, and understanding what teamwork implies, a sense of loyalty, these are all powerful antidotes" to the infectious habits plaguing actors (*Actor's Work*, p. 608).

Actors illuminate extraordinary insight into human desires and possibilities, giving the audience a glimpse of who they are and what they might become. Stanislavsky insists that

> The more an actor has seen, observed and understood, the greater his life-experience, his live impressions and memories, the more he feels and thinks, the broader, more varied, and richer his imagination will be, the fuller, the deeper his appreciation of the facts, the more strongly the external and internal life of the role and the play will be created. (*Actor's Work on a Role*, p. 131)

Actors bear a great responsibility because they are proxy for people's hopes and desires, voicing the kinds of thoughts that flicker through an audience that is often unable or unwilling to visit places in their hearts. They might wish they could, but they are perhaps too inhibited or afraid to make the leap. Actors do it for them: immersing people in the actors' imaginative world because they have something to say or to share that illuminates the human condition. Actors must therefore take their art seriously (even when they are being funny; perhaps never more so when they are being funny) because they hold a mirror up to nature and can bend that mirror in ways they choose. Stanislavsky maintains that the actor "is the force that reflects all the mysteries of nature, revealing them to the men who are not endowed with the gift of seeing all those spiritual treasures them-selves" (*On the Art of the Stage*, p. 110). Actors should live their lives fully, opening their hearts and minds to others because they never know whom they might have to portray. The actor-director Joseph Chaikin remarks that "An actor should visit and inspect patients in hospitals, and he should go to night courts, Buddhist services, A. A. meetings, draft boards, ghettos, Bowery flophouses, and public bars of different kinds; otherwise he has only a partial understanding of the dimension of his study" (p. 58). I want to see actors knowledgeable about the world, educated about cultures, broadminded and curious about humanity, and informed about current events. They should have opinions but never close their minds and hearts to anyone or anything; avail them-selves of all kinds of music and art, attend concerts and museums regularly; read newspapers or online news daily in order to be aware of the world around them; read novels, poetry and plays (every play!) voraciously; attend the theater regularly; believe passionately about a cause but never fail to understand the opposing side; believe in justice and fair play; and open themselves to all aspects of humanity.

Acting Training for the Twenty-First Century

Throughout my training and work as a director, actor and acting teacher I have witnessed contretemps between acting methods. These battles, which dominated acting training in the second half of the twentieth century, have lost their relevance. The quality and success of students taught by Lee Strasberg and Stella Adler (among others) trivializes their differences. The stellar track record of actors emerg-ing from the Lee Strasberg Institute, Actors Studio, Stella Adler Conservatory, Neighborhood Playhouse (where Sanford Meisner taught), HB Studio (where Uta Hagen taught), or many other signa-tory acting schools, renders disagreements insignificant. Instead, we should acknowledge the great schools and teachers as providing exhil-arating foundations for actor training and recognize that their tech-niques and approaches are not antithetical. It is no longer feasible or tenable to have an either/or proposition. Actors can, for example, work on Strasberg's affective memory and Adler's physical action *simultaneously*; we can find an objective and work on our voice for the role *at the same time*; and we can embody movements from theories such as Viewpoints while still identifying emotionally with a role (all these terms and exercises will be examined thoroughly in this book). I propose that we need no longer subscribe to the internecine arguments between Method (internal based) and non-Method (external based) approaches to acting; working from within by making the roles personally connected to us and working from outside on our voice and movement in each role are not mutually exclusive ideas. The contributions of the great teachers of acting in the twentieth and twenty-first centuries (Method or otherwise) can be absorbed into the actors' bodies and minds, incorporating a variety of techniques. Put simply, we can work with several methods at once. Throughout this book I will reference many methods, but will avoid the squabbles that have plagued acting training for decades. Instead, I will suggest combinations, focusing on multiple ways of presenting the best possible performance. Despite the insistence of many that certain techniques are diametrically opposed to others, the ideas and exercises described in this book can, I hope, offer students an alternative for the twenty-first century. My background has helped me to conceive of this goal because of the multiple training methods I have been exposed to – and I have never found them to be antithetical.

As a teenager I studied acting at the American Academy of Dramatic Arts during weekends and summers. I attended Carnegie Mellon University studying acting, voice, speech, movement, mime, acrobatics, fencing, commedia, stage combat and dance. I performed in plays ranging from contemporary realism to Shakespeare, from experimental theater to Greek tragedy. I trained with Edith Skinner, who taught me every day for four years and miraculously removed my Brooklyn accent. Bob Parks taught voice, fleshing out my resonance and vocal range. Jewel Walker, student of Étienne Decroux, instructed mime. B. H. Barry taught stage combat, Fran Bennett offered dance-movement workshops, Arnie Zazlov taught *commedia dell' arte* style, and the nonparallel tap dancer Paul Draper helped me to overcome my clumsiness to become a respectable, if hardly great, dancer. Directors Larry Carra, Israel Hicks and John Pasquin, among others, staged plays and coached me on specific roles. During the summer of my sophomore-junior year I studied film with the great cinematographer Haig Manoogian at New York University. I profited greatly from the expertise of all of them.

Yet I graduated from college feeling an emptiness. It seemed odd, because I had much for which to be thankful. Though hardly a professional dancer, I had learned to move well. I was proficient in speech and could produce accents of all sorts. My once-throaty voice had developed richness of tone; I increased my vocal range and sharpened my articulation. Thanks to Skinner and Parks (and to Skinner's assistant, Tim Monich, who coached me privately), my speaking voice pronounced Shakespeare's texts eloquently; I can dissect iambic pentameter and find the emphasis and stress; and while I do not consider myself a singer, I can carry a tune. I studied the Meisner Technique with Morty Lawner and Earle Gister. During my junior year I was taught by Franz Marjenin, Jerzy Grotowski's disciple and the author of a chapter in Grotowski's *Towards a Poor Theatre* (pp. 175–204); I was immersed in Grotowski's physical training for five days a week. I was also trained by the movement teacher, Moshe Feldenkrais, during my senior year, and his month-long workshop had a profound effect on my life. I studied the Alexander Technique, first at The American Center for the Alexander Technique and then privately (with Pamela Anderson) and Feldenkrais' work privately for several years after graduation. Nevertheless, I believed that all these skills could not help me to access my inner life. I felt that while I had learned the skills of movement and voice, flexibility and physicality, I had yet to discover my passion.

I began searching New York for an acting teacher. At the time, I was inspired by the acting I saw on the New York stage, specifically John Cazale and Al Pacino in Heathcote Williams' *The Local Stigmatic*, and John Kani and Winston Ntshona in Athol Fugard's *Sizwe Banzi is Dead*. John Cazale in particular was, in my view, greatly under-appreciated. He created some films of most haunting and profound characters, and was perhaps the greatest actor of my generation, and every student actor and acting teacher should see the documentary *I Knew It Was You: Rediscovering John Cazale* (it is required viewing in my acting classes). Observing Kani and Ntshona taught me the power of acting that can affect social change. I ultimately gained my greatest learning experiences from three people who taught me the foundational exercises that will be described throughout this book: Paul Mann, who taught me the "one action/one objective" exercise; Kim Stanley, who taught me "affective memory"; and Barbara Loden, who presented the ideas of "interstitial scenes." Each was uncompromising and relentless in their demands for excellence, and sometimes brutally honest with me; and while it was occasionally painful to hear them critique my work, I am so much the better (and grateful) for it.

The ideas and exercises offered in this book have evolved into my practice in the acting class. However, I make no claim of inventing the wheel; the work presented here has been expressed and practiced before in various ways. I acknowledge my enormous debt to teachers who have influenced me and demonstrated ways of working; rather than originality, this book is an extension of their ideas, modified and combined to create the most productive results. The technique described here adds variations to tested procedures and exercises. In modifying and combining many well-known exercises from superb instructors, I recognize their spirit ingrained in my work, their brilliance is unassailable, and my gratitude is boundless. Furthermore, from the early twentieth century until this moment *all acting training extends from Stanislavsky.* Let there be no doubt or misunderstanding about this: Grotowski and Strasberg ferociously disagreed on many subjects but they unequivocally concur on this point: Grotowski says that Stanislavsky, "was the first great creator of a method of acting in the theatre, and all those of us who are involved with theatre problems can do no more than give personal answers to the questions he raised" (p. 117); and Strasberg says that the work of Stanislavsky, "is the single most important influence in the modern theatre" (*Stanislavsky: Man and Actor*, p. 212). I have read many books on acting (as the bibliography to this book will attest) and have observed dozens of acting classes in my experience as both an actor and an acting teacher. Without exception, the books and lessons, in one way or another, build on Stanislavsky's principles. They may describe exercises or procedures with different shadings but all are founded on Stanislavsky.

Stanislavsky's contributions were the result of several factors. He was born into a affluent family of textile manufacturers, giving him the opportunity to enjoy a life devoted to the theater without daily financial stress (something few actors experience). He worked in the theater for over 40 years and, most importantly, devoted the time to the study of acting. No one in the history of theater, and specifically in actor training, has given as much time and effort to this one subject, and because of financial security basked in the freedom to concentrate on the subject. Because of Stanislavsky's full-time devotion to the study of acting, and because of his motivation and curiosity, his system covers virtually every aspect of performing: from emotional connection to yoga breathing; from physical actions to psychological motivation; from movement and voice to inner truth and conviction; from sense memory to acrobatics; from affective memory to fencing; and from Western notions of a character's goals (objectives) to the Eastern notions of a character's *prana* (energy, or rays). He ultimately came to the conclusion that only through disciplined devotion to the multiple facets of this art can emerge a truly well-rounded actor. Only when the mind and body work together can an actor achieve quality work; and only when the actor understands and commits to working on herself and the roles she plays can artistry derive and thrive. While Stanislavsky always insisted on actor training that incorporated sonorous vocal development, excellent diction and eloquent movement, through the study of acrobatics, fencing, ballet, gymnastics, stage combat and mime, he maintained his faith in what he called the "experience of emotional identification" with the role. Without this, he said, "there is no life of the spirit and nothing to embody; without emotional involvement, scenic movement loses its purpose of beautiful embodying the life of the spirit; it begins to exist for its own sake and serves not feeling, but only words" (*Selected Works*, p. 141).

Stanislavsky also had the confidence to gather together outstanding pupils and learn from them. His great students – Vakhtangov, Boleslavsky, Chekhov, Meyerhold, Maria Knebel, Leopold Sulerzhitsky, Maria Ouspenskaya and Vera Soloviova – assisted him in developing acting that has dominated training throughout the twentieth and into the twenty-first centuries (see the section Brief Biographies of Key Acting Teachers at the end of the book). It also helps that Russian theater has a long and venerable history, and that being an actor in Russia is viewed, both then and now, as an honorable and noble profession – something that unfortunately does not follow in the United States. Stanislavsky and his pupils established the view that an actor's goal is to create a lived experience through action, emotion, truthful and spontaneous behavior, and the heightening of the senses. The students of Stanislavsky, as well as his disciples in the United States and Europe, advanced his ideas and embellished actor training, creating a vast network of processes and means of rehearsing.

Stanislavsky raised the key questions that all actors, if they are serious about their work, must address: How do we make the most of our art form? How can we nurture the creative state of mind and body that engages an audience? And how do we define quality acting? He came to the conclusion that acting conveys the human spirit. The goal of actors is to bring humanity into focus by watching an actor live and experience rather than represent the human condition; by experience I mean allowing the events to happen spontaneously rather than presenting pre-packaged results. Acting teachers often refer to this as working moment-to-moment – anticipating nothing and alive to all the possibilities around us. Despite the fact that the actor knows the play's conclusion and memorizes the author's dialogue, she is spontaneous, surprised and speaks as if the words had just been discovered. How do actors, then, bring themselves to such a state of creativity that can be conveyed physically to an audience so that their humanity surfaces in all its dimensions? How can actors bring to the stage or movie the soul of a human being, making their performance compelling, artistic and creative? Throughout his long career as a student and teacher of acting, Stanislavsky came to the conclusion that a total commitment of mind and body, a willingness to bring one's personal life to the role, combined with the heightening of the five senses, a willingness to work as an ensemble, and the application of imagination, will, feeling, intelligence, wit, creativity, action and memory was the path to good acting. The study of modern acting technique begins with Stanislavsky, but it does not end with him. It is hoped that future teachers will modify the exercises and ideas presented here, taking the craft to the next level of achievement.

PART I

PREPARING MIND AND BODY

PREPARATION: BREATHING, RELAXATION AND CONCENTRATION

Taking your time to breathe in and out while you look down at the page to read the phrase for yourself allows you to access whatever unconscious thoughts or images it evokes. (Guskin, p. 7)

The training begins with the breath because it offers a psychophysical pathway to the practical attunement of the body and mind. Attentive breathing provides a beginning point toward inhabiting an optimal state of bodymind awareness and readiness in which the "body is all eyes" and one is able to "stand still while not standing still." (Zarrilli, p. 25)

All physical preparation for acting begins with breathing. As acting teachers, Harold Guskin and Phillip Zarrilli could not be further apart philosophically: Guskin coaches movie stars using the American Western system and Zarrilli is a British-based teacher using Eastern techniques of yoga, Japanese Noh, Indian kathakali dance and Beijing opera. Despite their radical differences, both teachers stress breathing – for them, physical, emotional, psychological and sensory work begins with breathing. It is, I contend, the basis of all work in actor training. The movement teacher Moshe Feldenkrais reminds us that "Our breathing reflects every emotional and physical effort and every disturbance" (p. 37). Breathing is pivotal to the mind–body connection, release of stress and the development of our emotional life.

Failure to breathe fully is the root of virtually every fundamental acting problem: tension, breakdown of imagination, lack of concentration, failure to give and take, disconnection from emotions, inability to physicalize, pushing, overacting, histrionics and so on. *When actors stop breathing fully, they stop living fully.* Yet this simple act – breathing – is difficult for actors to execute in performance. They breathe haltingly and shallowly, failing to make use of the vitality, relaxation and concentration obtained by breathing correctly. Actors understand the concept of breathing intellectually – they can comprehend the theory of diaphragm movement – but when told to breathe they often say "I forgot about that." An actor will breathe fully for a time and then fail to breathe deep into the diaphragm; I maintain this resistance is a reflex action.

The reasons why people hold their breath are numerous, but one key factor, I believe, is fear of failure, exposure or rejection. Failing to breathe is primal and hardwired into our DNA. It emerged from our ancestral world, where being hunted was our way of life. Holding one's breath is habitual in stressed animals, an essential response for maneuvering through a dynamic world where dodging predators occurs daily. Creatures being stalked freeze and hold their breath. When "fight or flight" response is no longer an option, freezing occurs, and holding one's breath is part of the physical immobility. Breathing requires movement, and motion can be detected; when we exhale, our air stirs the environment, making the breath detectable. During times of stress, write martial arts and yoga instructors Al Lee and Don Campbell, "Our primal response to fear and anger is either to hold our breath or revert to the quick, shallow breathing associated with the fight-or-flight response." Facing fear and anxiety, "Our natural instinct in 'combat' situations is to tense up our body while our breathing defaults to the short, shallow breathing associated with fight-or-flight" (p. 23). At night, predators use their sense of smell exclusively to ferret out prey; sight is almost useless in the dark, so through evolution the predator's olfactory senses have improved. The predator continues to breathe to keep track of the prey, while the prey does the opposite. Like radar, the predator picks up signals as the prey exhales, and the exhaled air, like sweat, produces odors and stirs the air. According to Nancy Diehl, professor of equine science, this olfactory system detects the movement of airborne molecules, where they are then "collated and processed. Nerves from both the accessory and the main olfactory bulbs project to the limbic system, the part of the brain that deals with emotional perception and response." The more the frightened animal breathes, the easier is it for the predator to track it through the olfactory nerves. Evolution has taught the hunted to restrict breathing when endangered, and the better-equipped prey stops breathing completely. This can be observed and verified in rabbits: when spotted, at first they freeze. A rabbit, motionless and holding its breath, is likely to survive; while a rabbit panting will be revealed and caught. Evolution has weeded out breathers. The result: fear equals holding your breath. When faced with fear – the pressure to perform, fear of failure – actors stop breathing. The goal is to *learn new impulses* by continuing to breathe when under pressure.

Holding one's breath also keeps emotions in check. Have you ever felt like laughing but didn't want to embarrass someone or didn't want the teacher to see you laugh? Like a kettle boiling over, sometimes you burst out laughing despite your best intentions. What occurs is an explosion of air; your body is desperate for oxygen. Withholding emotions is withholding breathing and this tension becomes habitual. It's simple: when you hold your breath you are guarded, defensive and shielding; when you breathe you are sensitive, open and aware. Continuing to breathe in the face of fear requires a relearning process because it is *counter-intuitive*: it goes against the grain of human instincts.

Breathing unlocks the emotional pathways; it frees the actor to experience the moment; and it contributes to relaxation and spontaneity. Actors want to be real, perform truthfully and respond spontaneously. Breathing begins the process because it is the root to emotional and experiential freedom and truthful behavior. We must, then, recognize *the connection between reality and breathing* because (i) you can't fake breathing; (ii) you can't create the same breath twice; and (iii) breathing underpins emotions. First, I can only breathe for myself; I can't breathe for anyone else. On a fundamental level it is *the most honest thing I do onstage or in life*. It is personal, it affects my entire consciousness, and it is thoroughly organic – *it is mine*. I must therefore take *ownership of my breathing*. Given the desire to be real onstage, the *first step is to breathe*. Second, once the air is expelled it is no longer oxygen but carbon dioxide; breathing cannot be repeated – once exhaled it is gone forever. It is, then, *the most spontaneous thing a person will do* because it is purely of the moment. It won't come back. The only breath you can focus on is the one you're engaged with at that moment. It is therefore the fundamental way that actors ground themselves in the present. Anxieties can send us spinning into past failures or anticipating future ones, but breathing awareness keeps us in the here-and-now. By breathing, actors experience moment-to-moment reality. Finally, emotions are supported by breathing. Human beings cannot display emotion unless they breathe: laughter, tears, anguish, anger, compassion – every emotion is inextricably connected to breathing.

The diaphragm, a muscular structure below the lungs, is our "guts," the focus of our emotional life. This is why trained singers have an advantage over actors. Singers depend on breathing, which opens up the performer's instrument, and at the same time allows access to the emotional life and freeing the feelings. Singers cannot afford to hold their breath, so their emotions are immediately accessible. "Breathing," writes acting teacher Robert Cohen, "is the basis of voice, as it is the basis of life. To inspire means to breathe in – as well as to nourish the spirit (from the Latin *spiritus*, meaning breath)." The actor's goal, then, "is simply to breathe naturally while under the pressure of performance – and to provide sufficient lung power to support a voice that may be challenged in acting more than in any other activity" (p. 111). The term "spirit" is *"ruah"* in Hebrew, which also means breath, vitality and *soul*. To move, speak, react, feel, experience and perform actors must therefore consciously create the habit of breathing no matter what fears or anxieties arise.

The underlying theme is this: *put it in the breathing*. Breathing is the principal notion every actor must sustain. Breathing freely and openly will solve many postural, vocal and movement problems. There is more to do than breathe, but without breathing we are without physical, vocal or emotional foundations.

Relaxation

Relaxation is connected to breathing and is essential for everything an actor does. Tension is our greatest enemy. The actor Yoshi Oida insists that "Both body and mind need to be 'awake' and 'ready,' but this does not involve any kind of rigidity or tension" (p. 39). Muscular tension inhibits emotion, movement, voice and every facet of the actor's art. The process of creative development begins with relaxation. "You cannot imagine," Stanislavsky writes, "how damaging muscular tension and physical tightness can be to the creative process" (*Actor's Work*, p. 120). No actor can work while tense. The task is to dissolve tensions and free the actor through the principle of relaxation. The first requirement of acting, Michael Redgrave noted, "is muscular freedom" (p. 59). The atmosphere of an acting class must be relaxed – serious, yes, dedicated, certainly – but free from pressure to perform or impress. Once free, the actor can develop basic conditioning in endurance, flexibility, strength, balance and coordination. When the actor becomes aware of herself kinesthetically, awareness of the world increases. As Moshe Feldenkrais put it, "To learn we need time, attention, and discrimination; to discriminate we must sense. This means that in order to learn we must sharpen our powers of sensing, and if we try to do most things by sheer force we shall achieve precisely the opposite of what we need" (p. 58).

Exercise 1: Breathing Awareness

The aim of this exercise is to increase awareness of your breathing, making breathing effectively into a strong habit until it becomes "second nature," so you don't have to think about it. It also encourages relaxation, the first step in preparing for rehearsal and self-development.

Lie on the floor on your back. First breathe: imagine a coin or a wine bottle cork just below your navel, feeling it rise and fall as you inhale and exhale. Find through this breathing the center of gravity and the central source of your breathing. Imagine feeling the air enter your body like cool, clear water; feel it descend down as far as you can. By down I mean into your hips, toward your feet. It is necessary to take a considerable time to breathe, to feel what it's like to breathe in this position (or any position). At least half an hour a day should be devoted to breathing and relaxation in the supine position. The point is to consciously breathe in order to experience the action.

Second, focus on the point just below the navel. The actor Yoshi Oida writes that, in Japanese classical theatre, "we begin by asking the student to focus their concentration on the 'hara,' the point, about three centimetres below the navel, which is considered to be a major energy center." Following this advice, stay aware of this center as long as you can, still breathing as if you have a wine bottle cork or a coin on the spot. Feel the coin or cork rising and falling. Imagine that you are invisible and the rising and falling is needed to send a signal to someone. As the cork rises and falls, it moves through space; the sense of ease and comfort increases; work at this effortlessly, easily, fluidly. Try to stay focused on this action, sending your energy and awareness into this motion. The "hara" is the beginning of concentration; it is, as Oida remarks, "the first stage in learning about concentration. Once you have understood how to focus your concentration with your body, as well as your mind, then you learn to release it and let it travel freely": p. 41).

While on the floor breathing and focusing on the "hara," take an inventory of your situation: what parts of your body are touching the floor, what parts are not, and what parts are tense. Do not feel there is a right or wrong way to undertake this process; there is merely the reality of where you are. What are you feeling? Release daily stress.

Next, gently and easily rid yourself of tension by first exerting tension in every part of your body and then letting it go as you exhale. Start with the feet, then calves, thighs, buttocks, pelvis, lower back, upper back, spine, arms, head and neck. Feel the release. Let gravity help you by giving way to its pull. Take full, deep breaths, thinking downwardly and outwardly (the air is absorbed through the diaphragm, which is like a pyramid or balloon pointing downward and out toward the feet). Do everything with ease and lightness, gaiety and joy; the expression "there's no gain without pain" is antithetical to acting. There is simply no reason to feel "pain." There should be no force, pushing, straining or working for results. Feldenkrais observes that if a person raises an iron bar they would not feel the difference if a fly landed on it; but if the person held up a feather, she would immediately know that a fly had landed on it. "The same applies to all the senses," he says: "hearing, sight, smell, taste, heat, and cold" (p. 59). The more ease, the greater the function of the senses; the lighter the movement, the greater the expressivity and subtlety. The more we move lightly and easily, the more we can be aware of the smallest detail.

Stretch repeatedly in any direction you wish, then return to the neutral supine position of complete relaxation and breathing. Repeat this several times, stretching in different directions. Think of a cat when it awakes; it stretches. The idea of stretching and releasing should be performed with conscious awareness of the joints; the more the joints open up, the greater the flexibility. Focus on different parts of your body, starting from the feet and working upward. Still lying on the floor, take advantage of gravity by letting your body melt, release and dissolve. Imagine your feet, legs, hips, lower back, upper back, arms, shoulders, head and neck melting and dissolving with the aid of gravity. Place particular emphasis on the jaw, releasing the jaw muscles and letting the whole jaw hang loosely. Other areas, especially the shoulders, hip joints and the bridge of the nose need attention, but *the jaw is primary*: it must be relaxed to allow the spine to relax as well.

The movement instructor Moshe Feldenkrais emphasizes the significance of relaxing the hinge of the jaw:

> It is important to understand how essential part of the body such as the jaw can be in this permanent state of being held up; yet we do not

sense that we are doing anything to hold up our jaw. In order to let our jaw drop freely we actually have to learn to inhibit the muscle involved. If you try to relax the lower jaw until its own weight opens the mouth fully you will find that it is not easy. When you have succeeded you will observe that there are also changes in the expression of the face and in the eyes. It is likely you will discover at the end of this experiment that your jaw is normally shut too tight. (P. 69)

Exercise 2: Relaxation Awareness

The purpose of this exercise is to relax the body further and begin the process of concentration.

Sitting or standing, make a fist and hold it tightly while simultaneously clenching your jaw. Notice how easy it is to tighten your fist. Now make a fist with both hands but let your jaw fall slackly. Your mouth should be open, your tongue relaxed and your jaw responsive to gravity. In other words, your mouth hangs open. Notice now how difficult it is now to tense your fingers and make a clenched fist, as opposed to when you clenched your jaw. This is because most of your tension is related to the jaw muscle. If you relax your jaw, most of your body's tensions will melt away.

As you breathe, relax your jaw. While doing this, concentrate on something you want to accomplish in class, during the day, or in rehearsal. Visualize the task, goal, or something you want to improve on. Encourage imaginative thinking. Change your images and let your thoughts go to a place by the ocean; imagine lying on a beach. Concentrate on the sights, sounds and sensual experience of a beach: breaking waves, the smell of suntan oil, hearing the gulls, sand under your back and so on. Imagine that someone you know and like is lying beside you. This sense of another person next to you is to encourage trust and comfort; images of comradeship bolster credibility and ease stress. Imagine a lake, where you are lying on the grass beside the water. Again, go over all the senses: the smell of freshly cut grass, sun on the eyes, hearing birdsong, and imagine you have brought along a picnic lunch to stimulate taste. Imagine a dog is with you, lying beside you, guarding you from any possible approaching danger.

The warm-up is a way of placing the actor in a physical state of relaxation and imagination, thus fostering a creative mood. Using familiar images of warmth and relaxation starts the imaginative motor running, sharpens concentration and establishes the atmosphere for creativity. To be creative, the actor has to feel that anything is possible, that any behavior is acceptable, and that self-expression has to come from the body, from physical ease and spontaneous activity. According to Stanislavsky,

> An actor's physical qualities, abilities and condition are also of essential importance for his creative mood. These qualities and abilities infuse his physical apparatus of interpretation: voice, mime, diction, speech, movement, attitudes, walk, etc. They must be vivid, colourful, extremely sensitive and responsive, enchanting, and slavishly obedient to the bidding of his inner feeling. The physical subordination gives the actor that creative bodily feeling which fully conforms to his inner state. (*Selected Works*, p. 174)

Images and relaxation start the warm-up as a way of putting actors into this creative-imaginative state where bodies and minds are supple, open and flexible.

Alexander and Feldenkrais Techniques stress movement awareness, and functional integration and relaxation of the mind and body. The Alexander Technique is concerned primarily with the head–neck–shoulder relationship; the back of the neck, in particular, is the central space requiring release of muscular tension. In Alexander, other joints and movements are freed and developed, but the head–neck–shoulder dynamic is the focal point. Think of a "long back of the neck" is a common Alexander phrase. Since we cannot see the backs of our necks unless we use mirrors, it is an area too often neglected. As the backs of our necks collapse, our vocal chords are squeezed together and our spine is restricted. By lengthening the back of the neck, actors open the breathing passages and make a greater diaphragm-image connection.

The connection between our diaphragm and our image of it allows us to bring our imaginative thoughts and ideas into our bodies. The lengthened back of the neck loosens the neck muscles and frees the pathway – the back and forth flow – from our mind to our guts. Particularly useful is the Alexander Technique's re-learning process of sitting and standing. Most if us sit and stand dozens of times a day; this action creates tension by squeezing the back of the neck. We tense up to rise, placing pressure on the back of the neck. Our chin juts forward, crunching the back of the neck, cutting off the vocal chords. The chest stiffens for the effort to rise and we seek to straighten and tense the knees. The vigorous movement of the head leads the process, causing stress and muscular tension. But the exact opposite is required for standing and sitting. By moving in what the Alexander Technique calls "monkey" (moving like a monkey, knees bent, joints loose), the hip and knee joints optimally flex and bend to relieve the larger muscles and thus ameliorate tension and free the voice. Like athletes, the actor must have loose knees, hips and shoulder joints in order to react quickly and impulsively.

The Feldenkrais Technique guides movement training toward a holistic physicality. Actors are made conscious of knees, hips, spine, shoulders, neck joints and jaw through a reorientation of body awareness and lightness of movement. For Feldenkrais, "The more an individual advances his development the greater harmonious organization of the senses and muscles. When activity is freed of tension and superfluous efforts the resulting ease makes for greater sensitivity and better discrimination, which makes for still greater ease in action" (p. 87). The Feldenkrais method rejects symmetry in posture, emphasizing instead the organic and economic application of movement. Symmetry, as Grotowski remarked, is "a concept of gymnasts, not of physical education for the theatre. The theatre requires organic movement" (p. 194). With Feldenkrais, organic movement refreshes the joints, opens gestures, and creates a more flexible body. For him, lightness is bound up inextricably with economy; ease is part of cutting down excessive and extraneous motion.

Feldenkrais is valuable to actors for two key reasons: because he defines the distinction between habit and instinct, and because his system stresses breathing as it is related to relaxation and concentration. Like Stanislavsky, Feldenkrais realized that habits can be misconstrued as instinct; what one does repeatedly becomes "second nature," but it is hardly a rich connection to imagination and fresh discovery. Habit becomes cliché, mistaken for a new response. Freud said as much when he remarked that habit is a kind of "inertia inherent in organic life," an "expression of conservative nature of living substance" because it is restorative – it brings us back to a cocoon of sorts, to our comfort zones that discourage risk-taking and bold imagination (p. 612). Habit mistaken for instinct is really a return to old behaviors cemented by repetition, a way of restoring oneself to a safe place. In a remark that could have come from Freud or Feldenkrais, Stanislavsky warns actors that, when falling into clichés,

> the actor feels more at home than in a new role which is unknown, unexplored territory. Clichés are habits, signs, familiar. But this

familiarity does not have its roots in feeling but only in external mechanical habit. Crammed with clichés you [the actor] felt very much at home in your new role. The most amazing thing of all is that these 'habits' we easily and eagerly took for inspiration. (*Actors Work on a Role*, p. 26)

By being aware of our habits, we can see how we confuse habit with instinct and can free ourselves more easily to acquire new possibilities.

Exercise 3: See-saw Breathing

Feldenkrais's focus on breathing is also essential; he makes clear how rhythms are deeply affected by breathing. One of his key breathing exercises is the "See-saw" (pp. 100-8).

Lie on your back, knees up and bent, feet flat on the floor. Inhale about two-thirds capacity and hold the air. Then rock, in see-saw fashion, the diaphragm from the chest to the stomach, back and forth. This is done lightly and easily, three or four times back and forth (up to the chest and down to the stomach), and then release the air. This exercise increases the diaphragm's capacity to enlarge and fill in an easy manner. Move into various positions – lying on the side or sitting back on the heels – and execute the see-saw again from different positions. Lying on one's side with knees bent increases rib movement, and sitting back on the heels increases capacity of the lower back for greater air flow.

Concentration

Continuing to observe myself and others I understood (i.e. felt) that being creative is above all the *total concentration of the whole mind and body*. It includes not only the eye and the ear but all our five senses. Besides the body and thoughts, it includes intelligence, will, feeling, memory and imagination. During creative work our entire mental and physical nature must be focused on what is happening in the character's mind. (Stanislavsky, *My Life in Art*, p. 258)

In addition to breathing and relaxation, we must be able, as Stanislavsky notes here, to concentrate with greater awareness than the ordinary person.

Exercise 4: Concentration and Personalization

This exercise is designed to increase concentration and segue into personalization. After spending some time on breathing and relaxation, begin to concentrate on an object – focus on it. See its shape, form, color. Where did it come from? How was it made? Who made it? How did it get here? Observe every detail. Touch it. Hold it. Put to your cheek. See like a child. Show it to someone. Make up a story about it in your imagination. When concentrating, consider this Vietnamese proverb: When eating fruit, remember who planted the tree; when drinking clear water, remember who dug the well.

Personalize the object. By personalization I mean making the object personal, weaving one's life experience, imagination and observation into the fabric of the object. Endow the object with something personal, something you've invented, something that moves you. To personalize means to make something or someone mean a great deal to you; personalizing is your unique stamp on a role; it is your "interpretation" that provides your defining artistic presence.

Personalization will be discussed throughout this book: it is the essential feature in the actors' toolkit and must be nourished and cultivated. It is not enough just to see the object; you must bring it into your heart and imagination. For example, if you see a clock on the wall, recall the first clock or watch you ever had; how did this timepiece affect you; what is it about this time of day or night that excites you? If a clock on a wall can move you, you are well on the way toward becoming an actor.

How do you know if something moves you? First, ask yourself if you are moved. Trust your feelings and your intuition – what moves you may not move anyone else, but it is what makes you unique, individual and your own creative person. How do you feel about an object? Take an old shoe, for example. Look at it. Touch it. Place it against your face, your chest, hold it against your stomach. See it from various angles. Think of Van Gogh's painting of an old shoe. Observe how personal he made it, how specific it became to him. The details are everything. I saw Barbara Loden as Mona in Ed Graczyk's play, *Come Back to the Five and Dime, Jimmy Dean, Jimmy Dean*, at the Hudson Guild Theatre in New York in the late 1970s. I hardly remember the play, but I remember her. She entered the stage with a brick façade that was, according to the play, part of a fictional James Dean movie set filmed in her town. She held this object close to her. She endowed it with a personalization that enriched the object, lifted it out of the ordinary and made it extraordinary. This is what is meant by personalization. Peter Brook writes:

> A great actress can make one believe that an ugly plastic water bottle held in her arms in a certain way is a beautiful child. One needs an actor of high quality to bring about the alchemy where one part of the brain sees a bottle, and another part of the brain, without contradiction, without tension, but with joy, sees the baby, the parent holding the child and the sacred nature of their relationship. (*Open Door*, p. 55)

One also needs concentration. We must turn objects, people, places and things into something imaginative, inventive and personal, and in order to do this we need to concentrate on the object with all our senses. Like anything else, relaxation and concentration are not something innate, but must be practiced, cultivated, exercised and trained. Another example of wonderful personalization through concentration was when I saw Peter Brook's production of *The Man Who Mistook His Wife for a Hat* (based on a 1985 book by neurologist Oliver Sacks). In it, Yoshi Oida was shaving, and suddenly he could no longer feel one side of his face. It was simple and startling; he was completely still, staring straight ahead, looking into an imaginary-mimed mirror, yet at that moment I saw through his inner movement – his inner emotional life – the full realization that he has lost contact with his body, his being, his soul. Oida stood motionless for what appeared to be an eternity; yet his inner action – the search for the image he no longer felt – was in constant inner motion. The capacity to create something tangible, real and emotional out of the mundane requires concentrated attention to details, a sense of being alive in the moment you are observing the object, a vivid imagination focused on the object, a keen sensory skill, and a willingness to open oneself, exposing all feelings, thoughts and actions. Do not feel you have to "show" anything; rather, focus your attention solely on the object of your attention.

Exercise 5: Mirror Exercise

The aim of this exercise is to increase concentration and begin to establish a relationship with your fellow actors.

Stand before another actor and follow their motions. Copy everything – gesture, breathing, and intention behind the gesture. Don't take anything for granted. Don't do the exercise mechanically, but rather focus on the soul of your partner and see their spine as if you have X-ray eyes. Work for details and concentrate on each other. The leader in the movements tries to help the other actor to follow. Don't try to "trick" the other actor, but work with her. Incorporate your whole body, not just the face and eyes, but torso, hips, legs and so on. Then switch the leader. Go back and forth several times, switching the leader, and then try to take the lead – work together but try to control the direction of the motion. The mirror exercise is in many ways the way a scene proceeds: each actor tries to take the other actors in a particular direction, but there has to be give-and-take as well.

Change the motion to playing catch. First mime a tennis ball. Follow the direction of the ball together. Concentrate on its arc, motion, direction and speed. Work together: toss the ball so that your partner can catch it. Change the object to a bowling ball; a feather; silk scarf; a set of keys; a fish; a rabbit; a kitten. Throughout the time you are working with your partner try to make the throwing and catching motions believable *together*; follow your partner's hands and arms as she tosses the object toward you. Watch the other's body language; try to read their behavior.

The work on concentration, Stanislavsky says, "demands enormous effort, the will to do it and systematic exercises" (*Actor's Work*, p. 114). To observe and read another person's behavior takes concentration. When we observe others we must be attuned to their actions and question why they did something one way and not another? We study each other with warmth and openness (we're not dissecting a bug); we look closely at the other person's movements and gestures with empathy and understanding. In this way we are dealing with what Stanislavsky called "the most subtle kind of concentration and observation, which are subconscious in origin. Our normal powers of concentration are not sensitive enough fully to search out material in other, living, human souls" (*Actor's Work*, p. 118). We must develop richer and stronger powers of concentration and observation.

Exercise 6: Observation and Imagination

The aim here is to increase your powers of observation and to begin to develop your imagination.

After the mirror exercise and playing catch, stop and look at each other. See your fellow student as if for the first time. How has she changed? Remember what she looked like a year ago, two years ago, three. Has she aged? Is she wiser, more worldly, mature? Turn your back on her and then turn around and look at her again. Did you miss anything? Turn away and walk about the stage, then turn back again to look at her. What did you miss? What was she wearing the first time you saw her? Is she still wearing the same thing? Try and see the beauty in your partner, the humanity, kindness and warmth, sadness and anguish. What makes her laugh? Cry? By all means laugh together – you should never inhibit mutual laughter. If something strikes you as silly or foolish, this is good. Encourage a sense of wonder, a spirit of surprise, and a feeling of childlike amazement at your partner, the room, the world.

Next, work alone and observe the space around you: See in your imagination a landscape, a tree, a rock, the countryside. Place a stream of water running by, moving gently and softly. Reach down and scoop out some water from the stream. Put it to your mouth and drink it. Taste the water. How does it feel? What are you leaning on – grass, rocks, pebbles? Increase your imagination by thinking of your experiences: you see each specific thing yet you feel the entire environment as well. Allow your body to *feel every detail*: what does your spine feel like? What do your feet feel like? Trust yourself! You're not trying to prove anything, but simply working to increase your sense of play and belief. Don't do concentration exercises, or any exercise, to score points, get it right, or show how clever you are. There is nothing to be gained as an actor by getting anything right or seeking approval. Work, instead, at *finding out what moves you*. If you remember clothes you wore, it's not a "point" or a score, but rather it should affect you deeply. If it doesn't affect you, or stimulate your imagination, then look for something else.

Look around the room again, then close your eyes. Try to recount what you saw, what you heard, what you felt. What is the temperature in the room? How is it affecting you physically? Again, if you recall many specific things about the room, you have not scored points, but rather you are exercising your powers of concentration in order to move you emotionally and physically. Concentrate on a spot on the wall. Send your energy to that spot, imagine you have to power to be at one with the object or point.

Exercise 7: Concentration in Motion

The goal now is to increase concentration while in motion.

With everybody walking about the room, locate someone and try to keep her in view without her noticing. Concentrate on her. Imagine you're a spy, or a detective tracing the patterns and behavior of someone. Always work with the idea that you are investing a spirit of beauty and gratitude toward the other person. Concentrate your energy from specific points on your body; in other words, send your energy (what Stanislavsky called *prana* – rays) from your navel, then from your elbow, then from your knee. As you do every concentration exercise, remember to breathe, breathe, breathe, and never try to work on the basis of "getting approval." The work is meant to stimulate creativity and imagination, not paint-by-numbers or scoring points.

Relaxation and concentration are skills to be honed, practiced and refined. Feldenkrais reminds us that

> The more an individual advances his development the greater will be his ease of action, the ease synonymous with harmonious organization of the senses and muscles. When activity is freed of tension and superfluous effort the resulting ease makes for greater sensitivity and better discrimination, which make for still greater ease in action. (p. 87)

Most important, relaxation and concentration are tools to increase and develop the imagination. Without imagination, which is tied indelibly to personal creativity, actors are merely going through the motions, fulfilling a teacher's requirements but never attaining that creative spirit. The key is this: work for your own growth and development, not to please anyone. The development of breathing, relaxation and concentration are the essential building blocks that will support your work in the next chapter, on vocal and physical dynamics.

2

VOCAL AND PHYSICAL DYNAMICS

> We must discover interrelationships, gradations of strength, qualities
> of stress among all the highlighted and unhighlighted words and cre-
> ate a perspective in sound, that will give the sentence life and move-
> ment. (Stanislavsky, *Actor's Work*, p. 436)

Stanislavsky in the quote above stresses physical and vocal training –
as I do also. The actor Michael Redgrave reminds us that the "basis
of all the Stanislavski training was a physical one" (p. 54) and scholar
Rose Whyman contends that "From the beginning of Stanislavsky's
training work for actors there is an emphasis on voice" (p. 140).
Whyman writes that Stanislavsky often spoke of " 'placing the
voice,' which involves the discovery of one's natural pitch in speech
and other aspects of training" (p. 140). Stanislavsky took a great
interest in the training of voice, especially for opera. He was influenced by Sergei Volkonsky's book, *The Expressive Word: An Introduction to the Science of Language* (1913), though, as theater historian
Jean Benedetti informs us, he abandoned Volkonsky's theories later
in his life for being "too rigid and liable to mechanical repetition
without thought or inner justification" (*Stanislavsky: An Introduction*,
p. 50). An actor's voice and body are tools for expressing emotions,
and instruments for developing fully formed artists.

Vocal Dynamics

The following exercise is designed to expand vocal range, which is
important overall, but is especially significant for Shakespeare and

verse. The text used in the exercises is from *Hamlet,* Act I, Scene I, and is often cut from productions. It is expositional, given by Horatio to the Watchmen, Marcellus and Bernardo, who claim to have seen the ghost of the previous king. Horatio is skeptical until he, too, observes the wayward spirit. When the ghost departs, Marcellus asks Horatio why they are on such a strict watch, and why such "daily cast of brazen canon/And foreign mart for implements of war" drape the castle. Horatio attempts to explain the circumstances; but he does so, as the text below shows, in a hypothetical manner. He reports the armed conflict between old Fortinbras and old Hamlet (Hamlet's father), using speculative notions of what *might have happened* had Fortinbras carried the day.

Exercise 8: Vocal Range and Flexibility

The speech's verbal pyrotechnics serve as a strong exercise in breath control, vocal range, articulation and, as I shall explain, primary–secondary–tertiary emphasis. The point of the exercise is to make sense of the text and to allow Marcellus (and the audience) an opportunity to follow the exposition by *vocally stressing the appropriate phrases without losing the secondary thought.* In the speech below, I removed all grammatical punctuation and replaced it with my set of vocal signs. These are designed to emphasize stress, developing what Stanislavsky noted in the quote above: the use of highlighted and unhighlighted words to create a perspective in sound. The only way to accomplish this exercise is to make full use of the voice. I shall leave the very important study of iambic pentameter to other books; here I want to focus on vocal range.

- Underlined phrases mean maximum stress; these denote the main ideas.
- Parentheses indicate secondary clauses; they are strong ideas but could be excluded and the speech would still make sense.
- Square brackets mean tertiary stress; these phrases carry no ideas *per se* but are cosmetic words embellishing the presentation.

> MARCELLUS
> Who is't that can inform me?
> HORATIO
> <u>That can I</u>
> (At least the whisper goes so) <u>Our last king</u>
> (Whose image even but now appear'd to us)
> <u>Was,</u> [as you know] <u>by Fortinbras of Norway</u>
> (Thereto prick'd on by a most emulate pride)
> <u>Dared to the combat</u> [in which] <u>our valiant Hamlet</u>

(For so this side of our know world esteemed him)
Did slay this Fortinbras who (by a seal'd compact
Well ratified by law and heraldry)
Did forfeit (with his life), all [those] his lands
(Which he stood seized of) to the conqueror
[Against the which] a moiety competent
Was gagéd by our king (which had return'd
To the inheritance of Fortinbras
Had he been vanquisher)   (as, by the same covenant
And carriage of the article design'd
His) fell to Hamlet. [Now sir] young Fortinbras
(Of unimproved metal) (hot and full)
Hath (in the skirts of Norway) [here and there]
Shark'd up a list of lawless resolutes
(For food and diet) to some enterprise
(That hath a stomach in't) which is no other
(As it doth well appear unto our state)
But to recover of us (by strong hand
And terms compulsatory) those foresaid lands
So by his father lost [and] this [I take it]
Is the main motive of our preparations
The source of [this] our watch and the chief head
Of this post-haste and romage in the land.

                                        (*Hamlet*, I.i, 79–106)

First, recite the underlined passages only. Notice how they inform the story in the most basic sense. Without any rhetorical flourish the key points are highlighted. Notice, however, how blunt the presentation is without the vocal twists and turns of the other phrases. Next, recite the whole passage, making use of stressed and unstressed (secondary and tertiary) phrases. Try to create variety in your voice, using tone, inflection, pitch, range and emphasis to color the words and give variety to your voice. As always, don't push, and remember to breathe! Emphasis does not mean louder; it means, rather, informing the words with personal meaning and clarity. Third, add inflections, using three means: upward, level and dropped:

- Use dropping or downward inflection *only* when the whole idea is complete.
- Use a level inflection when you still want to carry the thought.
- Use an upward inflection for emphasis.

   One of the biggest difficulties inexperienced actors have with Shakespeare is that they drop inflections at almost every turn. They follow the iambic pentameter slavishly and speak with a downward inflection at the end of every ten beats. Nothing could be more monotonous than hearing this static tempo. This is why I have deleted grammar (something we can never be certain of in any case, since we have no official text from Shakespeare's hand) and inserted instead a new set of grammar designed for the actor. Try this exercise on a David Mamet text, too; he also uses parentheses to convey subtle vocal changes in the subtext. Work to express and articulate the end of every word. Don't drop your inflection or energy just because the sentence ends. The voice is directly related to breath support, which is in turn connected to your energy and commitment.

Physical Dynamics

> Anything is permissible in our art, provided it is done for a clear purpose. And since, in our art, the human body is the primary material, it must be able to imitate thought. (Jacques Lecoq, p. 43)

One's body, as movement teacher Lecoq suggests above, is who one is. The body does not simply occupy space, it inhabits it – it exists in it, around it, and affects it. The movement of the body derives from motivation and dynamics of action driven by self-actualization and social interaction. Without physical expressiveness, the actor's ideas are mere thoughts locked in the mind; without access to physical expressiveness the actor's work remains cerebral, with no physicality to convey it. Bodily expressiveness is required for the outward demonstration of inner motivation; and only when the actor is physically dexterous, supple, open and responsive to stimuli can the inner passions move expressively and spontaneously. Vakhtangov put it best when he said that an actor "should exercise in movement not in order to be able to dance, and not in order to have beautiful gestures on a beautiful stance, but in order to impart to his body (foster in himself) a sense of plasticity." The term "plasticity" comes from the Greek *plastikos*, meaning to mold or give form. It describes what actors do: mold and give form to human expression. The plasticity of a sleeping cat, Vakhtangov maintains, is beautiful motion even in stillness. The actor therefore

> needs to consciously *train* himself to the habit of being graceful in order to unconsciously *reveal* himself as graceful in his ability to wear a suit, in the force of sound, in the ability to physically (through external form) transform himself into the form of a person he is depicting, in his ability to distribute his energy purposefully among his muscles, in his ability to mould himself into anything at all, in gestures, in voice, in the music of speech, in the logic of feelings. (*Diaries*, pp. 122, 123)

Michael Chekhov wrote that "Everything in the method is an avenue: the elaborate body, the concentration, everything leads to the point where the talent feels it is freed." Yet "In our bodies there are so many enemies which stop our creative process, very often in such secret ways that we do not know why we cannot act a certain part." Only when the "body is free, then I am forever free to act" (*The Drama Review*, p. 69). To attain this freedom, the actor, for Chekhov, moves in four ways: with ease, form, beauty and entirety or wholeness (he called these the "four brothers").

Ease means motion that is free from restraint, opening up the joints (especially hips and shoulders) to express freedom and lightness. *Form* is a conscious awareness of the body's structure, how it moves through space, and how it relates to other objects. Size, dynamic and structure are employed. *Beauty* is the feeling of joy and spiritual uplift. *Wholeness* is using the entire body, aware of every aspect of it and its relationship to space. Actors should move about the space, touch objects, see others, and relate to everything as they move in each category. Devoting ten minutes to each of the four is optimal. Chekhov recommended four additional movements: molding, floating (flowing), flying and radiating. These four (modeled after the four basic elements – earth, water, air and fire) create flexibility and body awareness. Each movement (like the four brothers) should be practiced repeatedly: molding space like a sculpture, using the body as if it were wet clay; flowing from one gesture to another, following the image of water; flying means a feeling of lightness in the air, rising up and out; and emitting rays, or radiation, where the actor sends signals to objects or others. Each movement should be an extension of the actor's psyche; as the actor moves, she incorporates one of the movements until it is second nature to her. By moving, using feelings of power and lightness, the actor creates these eight physical expressions in order to develop confidence kinesthetically.

Exercise 9: Chekhov's Movements (Plus)

The following exercise incorporates Michael Chekhov's movements aimed at freeing the body's expression. Move about the studio in a physical warm-up using Chekhov's four movements. These movements help to break with convention and habit; you learn to use your body in new and imaginative ways. Different Chekhov teachers will offer different versions of his exercises; my versions (like everything else in this book) are the ways I find most useful. Like everything else, there is no formula, only imagination and adjustment to individual needs.

Add three sets of physical warm-up activity to Chekhov's work: fast–slow, heavy–light and direct–indirect (these are similar to Laban's to whom I am indebted: direct/indirect, strong/light, sudden/sustained and bound/free). Walk at a neutral speed. Then move fast, but not for the sake of movement – everything must be justified. Why am I moving fast? Am I late? Stop in a neutral, relaxed position, and then move slowly. Again, everything must be justified. After this sequence of fast–slow (each practiced back and forth), examine heavy and light. Again, justify every movement. Caution: heavy tends to encourage slow movement and light instigates speed. This should be resisted: the pace should remain the same, only the body feels light or heavy. This helps with gaining bodily control. Finally, create direct (moving in a straight line) and indirect (moving in circles or figure-of-eight) motion.

After practicing these movements so that they are second nature, combine physical movements: move in different arrangements, such as fast, heavy and direct, or slow, light and indirect. Again, justify this movement. Eventually do not think about the movement but rather the justification and move according to the motivation. Why does someone move this way? Actors touch things, see other people, and heighten senses. Change patterns to a new combination. Incorporate Chekhov's idea of a center – from where the energy radiates – add a central focal point for this The source of the motion can be the navel; then the tail bone; then the left knee.

Chekhov's center was generally located in the sternum, or chest area. Lenard Petit writes that the "chest is where the heart lives, and the world of feelings has always been linked with the heart. In all languages, hearts are broken and mended by love" (p. 25). While I agree, I prefer the center to be located just below the navel – the "hara," as noted in Chapter 1. This is my only departure from Chekhov's excellent physical warm-up and development. I prefer to link the breathing to the emotions; as one moves, breathe and feel the power emerging from the diaphragm, from the basin of the hips and lower back, and from the hara. Chekhov created an exercise of marching, not as a soldier, but rather as a force of nature, with a feeling of inner confidence and power as the actor takes over the space and makes it hers. March across the room as if you are a person of confidence, lightly and easily.

Think of the stage as a safe space to create. Use images to improve the work – Chekhov stressed the feeling of ease rather than relaxation;

think 'up' rather than 'straighten the spine'. The point of the movements, like other Chekhov work, is to stimulate movement that is not necessarily our habitual motion but exploring and creating deeper engagements that are outside our habitual patterns. Rather than the intellect, the intuitive part of us ferrets out new movements and gestures. In *Lessons for the Professional Actor*, Chekhov says "If the gesture for the whole performance has been found ... it awakens the inner life of the actor" (p. 112). The point is not to work mechanically, but intuitively and organically. We create by finding different rhythms, centers, feelings of weight and space that offer the actor new possibilities.

Chekhov offered the notion of images: the actor imagines things that stimulate physical behavior. If, for example, a character says "I'm leaving" the actor must visualize leaving where, going where, and why; the actor has to have mental images of the place, time and path or road where the leaving occurs. It is not enough merely to speak; actors all too often rely on words to do their work. The actor has to have an imagination stimulating multiple images. Practice saying "I'm leaving" and consider where you are going, where you have left, what is in the space that connects to this phrase. If the actor says "I remember an old friend" the actor must conjure up several images of the friend, images that excite the actor physically, even if the playwright's description provides only one or two verbal references. The actor must imagine many more compelling images, so that the words are only one or two of several personal remembrances selected to say. The important thing for the actor is to have images that conjure up physical behavior, and that the images should inspire spontaneity. The image should make us search continuously for a new process, a new idea, a new thought. Marlon Brando noted that "If you watch people's faces when they're talking, they don't know what kind of expressions they're going to have. You can see people search for words, for ideas, reaching for a concept, a feeling, whatever" (p. 112). No matter what the text says, "old friend" cannot exist unless I know who that person is, how we met, why we bonded, why we are apart, how much I miss her and so on, that might not be said but are felt, and an image not fixed but fluid, mobile and subject to change.

Exercise 10: Creating Images

The following suggestions are ways to further stimulate your imagination with specific images. The images offered in a play may not stimulate you; therefore something must be substituted that works personally and effectively. If, for example, you are marching up the steps of a guillotine to be decapitated and the physical act does nothing for you, then you can imagine you are marching toward a cold shower. If a cold shower is terrifying, you can encourage the feeling of trepidation by imagining the march up the steps as if you were headed toward an assault of icy water on your body (imagine a hose dousing you with frigid force). Just the thought of a cold shower can stimulate your creative belief in the situation and evoke a spontaneous physical response. Imagining a cold shower does not violate the playwright's ideas, but rather enhances and illuminates the author's intent by stimulating the actor in a vivid and imaginative way. Try walking in a direction knowing it will take you somewhere uncomfortable. Notice how the images *you choose* affect your tempo-rhythm; make the movements personal; and trust the images. The point is to have specific images that create fluidity and spontaneity, and stimulate imagination toward active behavior.

"You need images to act," Milton Katselas insists, because acting "is emotional, and sometimes bloody. So here you need to find some images and feelings that can knock your socks off" (p. 163).

Physical work is part and parcel of specificity. "Good acting," Declan Donnellan says, "is always specific" (p. 3). Paul Mann shared his audition for Michael Chekhov's acting class with me. He entered the studio with a suitcase of personal props. He asked Chekhov if he could be allowed to set up the props before beginning the monologue. Chekhov nodded yes and Mann began to set the scene. He carefully placed each item according to what he believed to be the specific place it belonged. He held each item, each object – photographs, mementos, glasses, pen, paper, alarm clock and so on – because everything was personal and helped him to believe in the situation; what is often referred to as the "given circumstances." He took his time; he placed items and then changed his mind, moving about the room, setting items down, standing back, checking placement from different angles, and changing his mind again. Sometimes he would tweak an item, turning it a fraction of an inch; he would move the bed into another spot. He walked the space continuously, allowing himself to experience the room to make it his own. His movements through the space were *economical*: there was no wasted motion, no excess, no attempt to "perform." The economy of motion was based on the specificity of each item's meaning for him; he wasn't trying to show how the objects connected to him, but rather trusted his personal belief in them. After placing each item he waited for a moment. The items had emotional value. When he'd finished he turned to Chekhov and said "I'm ready." Chekhov, Mann said, was in tears and said there was no need to audition – he was accepted into the class. Mann was perplexed; he asked Chekhov if he wanted to hear the monologue. Chekhov said it was unnecessary: the manner in which he held each object, connected so personally to it, the way he moved, the way he placed them so specifically, and touched each object with such personalization, convinced him he was an actor.

The actor's *greatest enemy is generality.* Every time I hear an actor say "sort of" or "I kind of feel something," I know immediately that the work will be vague. Details sharpen our focus, fixing an impression and capitalizing on memory and emotion. Acting is different than life in that life is full of details that wash over us, whereas actors must select – indeed, flesh out – details like a musician selects notes and a painter selects colors. I cannot imagine a musician saying "I pick the key of G for the song; it doesn't matter if it is G flat, G sharp, G diminished, G minor, etc.; G is G, so what difference does it make?" Nor can I imagine a painter saying "I'm going to paint the color blue. It doesn't matter what blue – azure, teal, whatever – blue is blue, so what difference does it make?" Musicians will agonize over the right choice of notes; painters will dwell on the selection of just the right color. They will not be satisfied until they select the precise color that provides their unique expression. This is not to be mistaken for overacting: hyperventilating and histrionics have little to do with specific choices.

Specificity means knowing, with confidence, exactly what each thing, relationship and objective means to you, and trusting this belief. Strasberg characterized acting as demanding belief, faith and imagination: "To believe, one must have something to believe in; to have faith, one must have something that encourages faith; to have imagination, once must be able to imagine something specific" (*Dream*, 123). Without specificity actors are adrift; with it, acting is art. Being specific is the actor's creative initiative. The actor Jackson McGarry reported that when he studied with Kim Stanley what he learned was "specificity." Stanley would ask, " 'You're standing in a field. What time of day is it? Where is the sun hitting you?' She went down to the month, the time of day, the nettles on the ground. Was it a dry heat or a humid heat? And if you couldn't get it, she'd do it. This woman would create an environment. A living, pulsating environment in her eyes" (quoted in Krampner, p. 289).

Actors too frequently expect the director to tell them what to feel or what choices to make: "There are a number of actors and actresses who have no creative initiative at all," Stanislavsky said. "They come to rehearsals and expect to be spoon-fed" (*Actor's Work*, pp. 562–3). The reverse must be the case: the actor should have 50 images in place when performing a role, 50 specific ideas informing the work. Why 50? Because it is the actor's hope that five of the 50 will be working at that moment. Actors depend on feelings and images; but details that move us, stimulate our creativity and trigger our emotions are like fickle lovers. We must accept that feelings don't come when we depend on them; they don't surface like magic; and we're not remotes to be clicked on and off at will. We might be moved by one thing during Tuesday's performance, but come Wednesday something else works. Our feelings are subject to change because of mood, digestion, sleep, and the simple fact that we are one day, even one minute, older. We have new breath in our lungs, new thoughts in our mind, and new feelings in our body. Changes in the weather affect us; a cold, rainy day will bring a different set of feelings than a brighter, sunnier day. But if we have 50 reasons why we are doing the role – 50 reasons why Juliet loves Romeo – then we can be confident that at least a handful will emerge. The enjoyable part of acting is that we never know which of the lures we've put in place to trigger our feelings will be successful at that moment. Milton Katselas says:

> I like specific choices that lead to specific behavior, specific emotional responses. I don't like so-called 'specifics' that get into unnecessary character biography: These tend to be academically oriented choices that exist only in the actor's head. Specifics need to exist in the fabric of the work, the behavior, the life on stage. (p. 69)

Clinical analysis is dull and academic – it looks good on paper but is dead in performance. The idea of an actor taking a risk is rooted in the courage of not knowing what you will feel even up to the moment you enter the stage. You have to trust that one of the 50 motivations you set up will move and stimulate your creative spirit.

Swinging Side to Side: Conscious Awareness

The following exercise is designed to increase awareness of our joints through movement, open our torso through our shoulders, and heighten our sensory awareness.

Exercise 11: Swinging Side-to-Side

The following movement is intended to free the shoulder and hip joints. The joints are the most significant form of creative expression; flexibility of the large joints allows actors to connect their will to their bodily expressions. The key to the movement is the separation of the feet and knees as you swing from side to side. Keep the motion going, back and forth; breathe fully and easily; and imagine you're a dancer in a modern company, allowing your shoulders and hips to swing freely.

Figure 2.1   Begin in the position shown, with your right foot close to your left knee

Figure 2.2   Swing your body toward the floor, rotating your shoulders and upper body, and keeping the torso and hips free and open

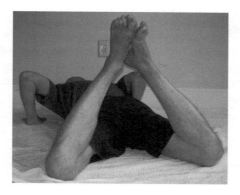

Figure 2.3   Continue toward the floor, face down with knees bent at right angles

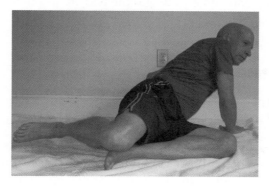

Figure 2.4   Swing your right leg over the left, pivoting your body and moving your hips and shoulders freely and loosely

Figure 2.5   Follow through all the way to the opposite side, preparing to swing the body into a repeat of the movement, but in reverse
(Photographs in Figures 2.1 to 2.5 of and by David Krasner)

At some point, stop right where you are, but not tensely. Keep breathing! Feel free and loose, and breathe. Listen to every sound; see the room; see other people. Use the swinging from side to side to increase your concentration and awareness. As you practice this exercise, work for smoothness and grace; try to make the motion effortless, light, easy. Try to cut down excessive gestures and work economically. The point is to incorporate the motion as a warm-up leading to other movements, allowing your hips and shoulder joints to expand and open easily.

Every movement onstage should have a purpose. Many actors over-gesticulate, walking around onstage, in David Mamet's amusing observation, "like cuttlefish on uppers" (p. 83). Economy of movement refines expression and encourages the body to respond to the will in a graceful manner.

Animal Imagery

> Do not only imitate the tiger. But try to feel what the tiger feels. See the bars of your cage, feel the unrest (Strasberg, *Dream*, 74).

As Strasberg suggests, the imitation of animals is one of the best means of developing the actor's imagination that is translated into the physical. By replicating an animal, preferably a four-legged creature, actors are able to break down physical inhibitions, develop body awareness, and assume shapes not included in socially accustomed behavior. Animal imitation encourages more primitive action and movement, a lessening of the ego and rational self-consciousness, and works for greater spontaneity. It facilitates play, openness and joy, reeducating reflex mechanisms and heightening the senses. It assists in releasing tension and asserts discipline. The aim is precision, imitating the animal as accurately as possible. This imitation also aids the actor's sense of observation and concentration. It helps actors to use their bodies and avoid over-intellectualizing. Peter Brook insists that animals move

> beautifully because they have no tension in their bodies. But they are not totally relaxed either. They are always ready to move at any moment, in order to escape attack, or to pounce on their prey. Animals maintain two physical states at the same time. The body is free and well

balanced, and the mind is focused and aware. Consequently, the animals can react quickly. They can leap in any direction, they can use their strength, or they can employ delicate precision. *This must be the fundamental state of the actor onstage.* (quoted in Oida, p. 39; my emphasis)

Alertness means a release of tension; relaxation and concentration are in unison; and the body is at ease with itself yet ready to leap into action.

Animals think through their bodies; their pelvis, joints and extremities are in sync with the intended movement; the tail is a reflex cord of the brain, moving spontaneously at each impulse. Animal imitation teaches the actor economy of movement; watch a cat waiting to leap, for example. We can see the feline's organic totality as it readies itself for the movement. There is no wasted or extraneous effort and motion. It measures distance, space and dimension; cats rarely if ever fall when jumping (if they do, it's fascinating to watch a cat's embarrassment; it looks around, hoping no one saw the error, and licks its paws in restoration of pride).

Additionally, by imitating animals the actor practices the act of transformation, creating new rhythms and centers of the body associated with another creature. The actor learns to move in a way that is different than her habitual movements. The transformation is on a dual level: both consciously and bodily. Naturally we cannot become the animal, but the actor can be inspired imaginatively by the way people move in ways that correspond to animals. The movement flows, rejects tension and heightens the actor's senses – smell, touch, sight and so on. Movement is more sensuous and organic, joints loosened and utilized. Trust and commitment are bolstered. The important point is not only to imitate and incorporate the movement, but also to make it your own. The actor Morris Carnovsky said:

What makes imitation a *final* act of creation is the admixture of the Self. If I were simply to imitate a monkey, let us say, it might be amusing enough, but it's the final merging of myself with the *idea* of monkey which makes it a creative act. It's all very amusing to see people give vocal representations of Cagney or Barbara Streisand, but they haven't really captured the soul of the person. Acting goes back to the proper use of one's Self within the given circumstances. We return again and again to the formula of Stanislavsky: *Truth in the midst of given circumstances.* This is what the job of the actor is, and the only truth the actor can really hope to command is *his own truth.* (p. 68)

Acting teacher and Stanislavsky scholar Robert Ellermann's description of animal exercises in Kim Stanley's acting classes illuminates an approach to the technique: "Instead of the classic animal improvisation, where it was an individual exercise, Kim would say, 'You're in a jungle. You're in a barnyard.' And she would have fifteen people up there. This would last about forty-five minutes" (quoted in Krampner, 288). The important point here is the relationship that evolves between animals: the search for packs, mates and enemies. The actor learns to physicalize, drop inhibitions, improvise, and feel the freedom of physical expression toward others often obscured by words and language. As actors move, the physical environment changes: move in dry, desert heat; then wet snow; then rain; then spring sunshine and so on. Mating season is announced and the actors search for a mate. Hunting is announced, and the actors move through the room searching for packs to join. Ellermann observed that when the exercise concluded, Kim Stanley "would start at the beginning of the improvisation with each actor and go through almost the whole thing. Everything they did. And she didn't take notes. I don't know of anyone who has that level of concentration" (quoted in Krampner, p. 288).

George C. Scott's performance of Buck Turgidson in the film *Dr. Strangelove* is a model of animal association. He appears to use a gorilla as his image, with gestures, grunts and reactions synonymous with ape-like behavior. Watch his posture closely: his joints move in an ape-like way and his voice snorts. Ned Manderino makes the point that the "ultimate aim of the [animal] exercise is to find something in the behavior of living creatures which you can translate into human terms." As you develop the process, he adds, "you eventually isolate details such as eyes, walk, limbs, or head for desired expression" (p. 72). Rather than try to imitate the animal in entirety, he recommends (following Michael Chekhov's advice) that the actor "begin with one feature of an animal" and build from that physical center (p. 73).

Exercise 12: Animal Imagery

Grotowski offers a worthwhile exercise in animal imagery. Rather than recreate the four-legged animal literally, he encourage the actor to attack "one's subconscious, creating an animal figure whose particular character expresses an aspect of the human condition" (p. 143). Association can be joined with a literal reproduction; the subconscious connection to an aspect of human behavior and the physical, outward manifestation are not mutually exclusive.

Think of an animal you would like to imitate based on Grotowski's idea of association. At first, lie still, on your back. After experiencing relaxation, see the animal in your mind's eye. Be specific, and see the animal through several postures: at rest, hunting, at play, in repose, mating and so on. The inner visual connection is then transferred to the breathing – how does the animal breathe while in that state? "Put it into the breathing" by taking the image and physicalizing it. Relate to other actors *as the animal* (without violence or hostility): find friends and foes; form packs for hunting; and seek a mate or mates. This encourages openness, ensemble activity and uninhibited movement.

Creating Good Habits

To achieve a consistent creative state, which means having a strong sense of mind, body, voice and concentration, actors must have good habits. This means exercising the voice and moving the body daily. But it also means working for consistency. Stanislavsky says that, when he compliments a student on good acting work he asks her to weigh good acting against bad acting: "You acted well, truthfully today," he says, "because all the elements were working properly and you were applying them onstage as in life." He suggests that the actor give herself one point, but *only one*, because tomorrow, he warns, "you won't be in control of the elements. They'll do just what they want, your technique will be weak, so give yourself ten minus points. *Ten*, because bad acting habits are stronger. They eat away like rust." Bad habits teach clichés – the worst things an actor can adopt. "The bad," Stanislavsky insists, "makes a deeper impression than the good. It's easy to be bad, so the bad is stronger, tougher. The good is more difficult, unattainable, and takes more time and trouble to fix" (*Actor's Work*, p. 608–9).

Stanislavsky's point is significant in many ways. Actors get away with bad acting because they make excuses that their acting is "natural" and their behavior is "real." The trite is taken for "truth"; the lack of risk is considered "honest"; and the bar is set so low that motivation derives from the trivial and the actors' energy is virtually nil. They are too often easily satisfied by mediocrity. A cast can be infected by a level of performing that coasts along, unmotivated to rise above the mundane and perfunctory. Instead of focusing on the play and the other actors, we think of our next audition or make excuses that our audiences fail to know what good acting is in any case. Routine takes hold and the merely passable becomes acceptable. We must work against the trivial, creating depth and meaning to every word, image, gesture and emotion. The next chapter moves into personalization through sense and emotion memory, the crucial processes of training in the subtlety and depth of acting.

3

PERSONALIZING: SENSE AND EMOTION MEMORY

Graceful movements and a mellifluous voice cannot disguise the fact that, without personalizing the desires expressed onstage the actor is merely a shell – outer form without inner content. Stanislavsky was unequivocal:

> the actor's own experiences as a living organism, as a human being, can communicate all the elusive nuances, the hidden depths of a role. Only acting of this kind can fully capture an audience and bring them to a point where they not only comprehend but more importantly, experience everything done onstage, and so enrich their own inner lives, leaving a mark that time will not erase. (*Actor's Work*, pp. 20–1)

Two interrelated theories and exercises bolster our connection to ourselves and the role: sense and emotion (or affective) memory. Sense and emotion memory increases the actor's sensory concentration and specificity.

Sense Memory

Sensory work develops the actor's responses and impulses to stimuli. The senses, writes Strasberg, "hold the key to life and experience." Sense memory exercises, he adds, "train the actor to utilize all five senses and to respond as fully and as vividly to imaginary objects on stage as he's capable of doing in real life" (quoted in L. Cohen, p. 14).

Sense memory is the pantomime of an action or activity – sipping a cup of coffee, tying shoe laces and so on – that is simple, yet profoundly affects the actor. The important point to emphasize is detail: every aspect of the action should be considered. Strasberg was adamant about the value of sense memory, and rightly so:

> It is amazing to see what happens when an actor is asked to perform a simple habitual act, such as putting on shoes and stockings, with imaginary shoes and stockings. The actor is completely unaware of the many sensory and muscular experiences which make up this activity. How much more must this be true of the imaginary characters he is called upon to act! (Acting and Actor Training, p. 145)

Daily sense memory practice increases awareness, which in turn improves concentration and observation. Nothing in sensory work is taken for granted; by examining everything, actors open up body and mind, sharpening awareness of the minutiae of everyday activity.

Exercise 13: Sense Memory

Begin with simple activities, using your imagination and trying to recall the sensations. Let them affect you with ease and lightness. If one thing doesn't affect you, try something else.

Close your eyes and visualize a sunset; a rainy day; the color of the room you grew up in; the front door of your house. Recall the smell of a barbeque; a log fire; lemons; onions. Touch a silk scarf; coarse wool cloth; satin; a cat on your lap. Listen to the sounds of surf breaking; rain on a roof; children laughing. Taste pepper; salt; ice cream; a lime. Feel the temperature of humidity and heat; damp cold; cool breeze; warm sun on your face. Recreate the sensations of taking a shower. Be specific. A shower, Strasberg writes, "is experienced separately and differently by different parts of the body. Each area of the body is capable of generating independent responses" (Dream, 139). Go though every detail: getting into the shower, feeling the water temperature, your unsteady balance, soaping, lathering, shampooing your hair, soap in your eyes – and more. Remember to breathe throughout. Take time to discover things, finding new memories and new experiences. You are working "as if" you are really taking a shower. Take the sensory work to a full day:

- Spend a day being opposite-handed (tie your better arm and hand to your waist). Experience the sensory affect on your tactile actions. Using your weaker hand and arm, experience everyday things that you normally take for granted. Brush your teeth, write a list, open a door, touch objects and so on. Notice how your awareness increases.

- Spend a day blindfolded. Notice how the other senses are heightened. Touch an egg, a soft blanket, a rock and other sensory objects while blindfolded.
- Spend a day with ear plugs. As above; the other senses are enriched.
- Spend a day in a botanical garden, trying to identify the scent of each flower. Increase your olfactory awareness. Use your breathing exercises here.

Sensory deprivation of one sort – being unable to see, for example – can lead to the enhancement of other senses, and enhancing your five senses is critical for actors. Our senses are the impetus for expression, action and emotion: we must therefore practice with our sensory apparatus like a musician practices scales. We must have a higher awareness of our senses than ordinary people because our stimuli must be trained to react more keenly and with greater alacrity. A musician fine-tunes her ear; painters have sharper eyes; actors must have all the sense operating at peak levels.

Exercise 14: Eating Soup

This sensory exercise is for advanced work on sense and emotion memory.

Imagine eating soup.

Eating soup, I contend, is crucial. Most of my sensory training was done with an imaginary cup of coffee. This is excellent but I prefer soup. The advantages are that soup can be hot or cold and there is the taste of food involved. Soup is also very comforting, relating to many personal experiences.

Sit in a chair, completely relaxed, and imagine you are eating soup while waiting for someone to come home. Be specific about the soup and the circumstances – what is the situation, the back-story, the events surrounding the conditions you are experiencing? Where are you? Why are you here? How did you arrive here? Recreate every detail – who, what, where, when, why. *There can never be enough details*. Add the following: You have news to tell a person coming home. First, make it good news – you have won a contest, or you are getting married. Then bad news: there has been a tragic loss in the family, or you were not accepted for the school or job you desired. Put yourself in a position of eating the soup (*as if*): what kind of soup? Is it comforting? Are you hungry? Is it a late night snack? Will it help you explain the news better? What is the room temperature, time of day, season? Always work for simple truths, always work from a place of faith and belief, and *never* try to impress the teacher. You needn't "show" anything. This is sensory work designed to stimulate the actor's imagination. You mustn't rush these exercises – take your time! Pay close attention to the effect the sensory work has on your breathing, posture, flexibility, motion, shifts in self-image, and behavior. Notice how you are sitting in the chair. You are free to stand and move about, but only when you feel the need to do this. Let the outcome of the behavior surprise you; the actions you take are unknown to you, which allow you to be present in the moment. Practice living in the unknown, in the sensory world, without a plan to behave a certain way. Let the process develop; put yourself in a safe place where judgments (yours, your peers' or the teacher's) are irrelevant. Find new sensations through new experiences and new images that stimulate you.

Sensory work makes you more alive in the moment, more "present," and exceptionally gifted actors have the ability to be present onstage or onscreen. To have "presence" onstage is to have presence in life, and to do this you have to live your life to the fullest. Sensory exercises help to strengthen nuanced responses and increase "presence." Joseph Chaikin described great acting as "presence," what he calls a "quality that makes you feel as though you're standing right next to the actor, no matter where you are sitting in the theater" (p. 20). Chaikin identifies five actors who have this presence, each influenced by different training: Ekkehard Schall (actor with Brecht's Berliner Ensemble), Ryszard Cieslak (actor with Grotowski's Poor Theatre), Kim Stanley (Lee Strasberg's Method protégée), Ruth White (student of Stanislavsky protégée Maria Ouspenskaya), and Gloria Foster (student of the Goodman Theatre School in Chicago). These actors, Chaikin says, offer a "deep libidinal surrender which the performer reserves for his anonymous audience" (p. 20). Along similar lines, Larry Moss remarks that

> great actors like James Dean and Kim Stanley don't seem to be acting, they seem to be actually living. You know you're in the presence of the best actors when you forget that you're sitting in an audience watching make-believe and instead you are catapulted onto the screen or stage and blasted into the lives of the characters. (p. 4)

Even avant-garde director Robert Wilson, whose work with actors seems programmatic, maintains that, when he saw Kim Stanley in

Lee Strasberg's production of Chekhov's *The Three Sisters*, she seemed, he says, "to get past the lines," rising above the literal text, having "almost forgotten the words" because she is "doing something else," something subtextual (quoted in Shyer, p. 19). The compelling qualities of Kim Stanley (who taught me sense and emotional memory) reside in her abilities (among other things) to surprise and immerse: she isn't acting so much as *being*, living in the here-and-now and creating feelings, thoughts, experiences, actions and relationships through her imagination. These are essential skills, because the better the actor, the more my attention is engaged and my interest galvanized – the actor is able to surprise me repeatedly throughout the performance.

Personalize everything, every sensory activity, every feeling and connection. The term "personalization" has often been described as meaning linking what the character is going through with what the actor is going through. I contend that before we can know what a character is experiencing *actors have to know what they experience*. This cannot be overstated: *we must know who we are and what affects us at any given moment before we can know anything about a character*. The point of sensory work is to make us aware of what we are feeling *at the moment and in our bodies*: not what we felt yesterday or five minutes ago, but what is going on right now – *both physically and emotionally*. Personalizing is not an easy process; it takes time, thought, experimentation, rehearsal, and trial and error. Uta Hagen calls this work "associations." The making of art, she says, "consists of the selection of appropriate life realities to create a new canvas, to make a new living, breathing statement." Forcing ourselves to fit the character without finding links in ourselves will bring about external forms devoid of inner content: "Unless we resist preconceiving the emotional results and actions which are always born out of editorial, fictional, audience responses to the material," she says, "we will be lured into conventional pushing and illustrating, in other words, false theatrics" (*Challenge*, p. 90).

In *The Actor at Work*, Robert Benedetti provides an explanation of the two key elements of Stanislavsky's technique: *magic if* (or *as if*) and *personalization*, both of which are necessary in merging the actor and the role. According to Benedetti, the actor "must feel your character's needs *as if* they were your own needs, select the objectives that can satisfy those needs *as if* they were your own objectives, and then do what the character does to try to win those objectives *as if* they were your own actions." *As if* works only in what he calls the "natural process of transformation;" that is, *personalization*, when "you allow yourself to fully experience what the character experiences with the same urgency and significance as they do *for yourself.*" Benedetti warns that "There is potential danger in personalizing the role, however. If you do not truly reach out into the character's experience but instead merely force the character to fit you, you may end up distorting the character and damaging the play" (*Actor at Work*, p. 89). I agree in so far as it is the job of the actor to walk a mile in the shoes of the character. But we must also remember that a character is merely *words strung together on a page, and nothing more.* There is no such thing as "distorting" a character, since "character" is merely a blueprint to be constructed by the actor in a way she sees fit. And before we can approach a "character" we have to know our instrument – our voice and movement, but also our sensory and emotional capabilities at the moment they occur.

In considering "as if" and "given circumstances" what Stanislavsky said was "*What would I do, as a human being, if I found myself in the same Circumstances as the character I am portraying*" (*Actor's Work*, p. 512 – Stanislavsky's emphasis)? Many people describe "as if" without Stanislavsky's very important phrase "as a human being." This is the crux of Stanislavsky's idea: *You have to understand what it means to be a human being before you can play a human being.* So the first goal of the actor is to be a human being, bringing with it all the necessary details and dimensions. Stanislavsky demanded that the actor be specific in answering the question "What would I do if I found myself in the same circumstances?" with: "Don't try to give me any old answer, in terms of outward form. Be serious and sincere. Involve your feeling and will, let them provide the answer, not just your intelligence. Don't forget the tiniest physical action can create truth and produce feeling in a natural way." He did not rely on feelings *per se*, self-indulgence without form, but rather he encouraged creative choices wrapped in physical actions even in the tiniest detail: "Instead of feelings, which are elusive and unreliable, I turn to easy physical actions, *I look for them in my inner impulses*, I draw the information I need from my own direct, human experience of life" (*Actor's Work*, p. 512 – Stanislavsky's emphasis). To find these impulses we have to search inwardly; before we can get to the role we have to get to ourselves.

Exercise 15: Packing

The aim of this exercise is to incorporate all the previous sensory exercises and contextualize them in a complex situation that uses given circumstances and "as if."

Imagine a situation in which you are packing suitcases or bags, using pantomime. You are going somewhere, and you are leaving somewhere. As always, be as specific as possible. Feel the texture of the clothes you are packing, using all the sense memory; feel the toothbrush, the comb, the hairdryer, all the paraphernalia you need for wherever you are going. Smell and see everything in your imagination; hear every sound the bags make in opening and closing; sense from where you are leaving and where you are going. Packing as a sense memory exercise has great benefits because it should inspire feelings of people and places that have affected your life. Don't rush into these exercises, take time to feel them through. Be sincere and put your mind, body, and soul into the work. Don't work to impress anyone but work to experience what you feel and think at each moment. Stay within the process with your attention on the action of packing; don't worry about results.

The physical action of packing is not merely a movement, but a series of actions that have reactions, gestures and emotional connections to the items being packed. Grotowski acolyte Thomas Richards makes the point that "The mistake of many directors and actors is to fix the movement instead of the whole cycle of little actions (actions, reactions, points of contact) which simply appears in the situations of the movement" (p. 76). The sequence of packing combines action and feeling: we are packing to go somewhere, because of something (some motive), and the process is wholly physical. Yet it is also emotional: the activity has personal resonance. The point of the exercise is to stimulate feelings through sensations and actions. We know our feelings through sensations, through the sensory mechanisms of our organism. If we develop the ability to make sense of our sensations – our five senses – we recognize our feelings and stimulate our emotions. The point of sense memory is a pathway to emotion and emotion memory. Once we have experienced sense memory over a long period of time, practicing and sharpening our sensory apparatus, we have improved our ability to express our emotions more accurately, deeply and truthfully. We are better communicators of the human condition if we immerse ourselves in the sensory process. Our movements, gestures and body language are truer than words; in order to improve our movement, we have to have keener awareness of our sensory impulses. Sense memory leads into emotion memory, and emotion memory (sometimes called affective memory) is, according to Strasberg student, Doug Moston,

> a technique that will allow you to believe what the character believes. It is not a technique that is used to create emotional behavior. This point cannot be overstressed. The characters you play aren't trying to have emotions, they are trying to do something, to accomplish an objective. We are talking about using and trusting a process, not going directly for a result. (p. 110)

Emotion (Affective) Memory

Affective memory derives from Stanislavsky's discovery of the French psychologist Théodule Ribot's two major works, *La Psychologie des Sentiments* (1896) and *Problèmes de Psychologie Affective* (1910). *Affective memory* means selecting a specific and meaningful experience in one's life and remembering the senses –tactile, taste, aural, odor, temperature and visual – present at the time in order to stimulate *actions and feelings* (emphasis on the plural). Strasberg student Ed Kovens insists that affective memory draws on "a *specific* event from the past" (p. 77) in which the actor thinks of a situation in her life that has had a deep impact. But instead of thinking about the emotions surrounding the past event – emotions that have changed over time in any case – the actor concentrates on the senses (sense memory). The actor thinks of the smells, sounds, weather, colors surrounding the event.

Exercise 16: Emotion Memory 1

Before beginning this exercise, be certain you are in a place where you feel safe and secure. Make yourself as comfortable and relaxed as possible – sitting, standing, leaning, or lying on the floor.

Remember a compelling situation in your past. Don't worry whether it was sad or joyous; just feel confident that it affected you deeply. Breathe. Feel secure in yourself; create a feeling of ease; do not feel you ever have to perform. Keep breathing deeply, downwardly and outwardly into the diaphragm. As you recall the situation, try to focus on the senses: what were the smells, sounds, tastes, tactile or visual experiences? Let yourself be surprised: the aim of affective memory is to discover new sensations – new emotions and stimuli – by focusing on what the body sensed during the experience. Allow whatever feelings arise. The point is not to "lock" into a past emotion but to become surprised by the sensations, to experience the memory of sensations – sights, smells and so on – that stir feelings (any feelings) that stimulate you to act. Let the experience travel, move, go places; if you experience a deep feeling, terrific, but don't cling to it like a liferaft. Let it go and discover new feelings. Be surprised by new memories, by sensations you had forgotten that have now arisen. The exercise, moreover, is not restricted to traumas or sadness; laughter is a great resource for affective memory. We often laugh again when we recall a bizarre incident. The laughter changes over time but the desire to laugh remains because we specifically remember the triggers – the sensual experience surrounding the laughter.

Our senses are the pathway to our feelings and they are our unique contributions. No one can feel in the same way as you feel; your senses and emotion memory are your personal possessions. The value of these exercises is that they touch actors' personal lives and make their contributions to the performance individualistic. The process of sense and emotion memory is an attempt to ferret out prime causes and pivotal events from the psychic rubble of our past and the unwieldy conflicts of the present. It is meant to enrich us, make us more alive. In the process of growing up we are taught to repress unruly fantasies and keep anarchic thoughts and histories to ourselves. But acting is a kind of intimacy where human behavior not shown in everyday life is enacted. Acting is a place to express what we have grown accustomed to keeping hidden, in the hope that audiences might better understand our lives and missteps, and help us come to terms with our discarded desires. It is part of the acting experience, where the actors take a direct route to an effectively examined life. Though it can sometimes be a painful experience, and sometimes exhilarating and at other times hilarious, we are in any case charged with playing characters who sometimes exist in multiple circumstances. How can we expect to play characters if we don't understand their pains and frustrations as they relate to our lives? By the same token, we must understand their joy to the fullest extent, because we must also understand our characters' exhilaration. While it is possible to view the whole exercise as self-indulgent – and many detractors of emotion memory consider

it as such – self-examination through sense and emotion memory are
ways to come to terms with experiences that affect us deeply.

Exercise 17: Emotion Memory 2 (Breathing)

After you have remembered the circumstance and have allowed yourself to feel
the experience (whatever the feeling), take your work to the next step: breathing.
 In emotional recall, once you feel comfortable in the situation (no forcing!), the
focus is then on the breathing. Trust that the exercise has affected you; there is no
need to "hold" the moment. Breathing stimulates forward movement; we use the
sensory and creative work but continue to be free in body and mind to accept
new things and the shifts occurring around you. Rather than fixing a moment,
accept the level of belief and adjust the focus on to your breathing. Naturally, the
more you are moved emotionally, the better the consequences; but the point is to
stimulate emotions, and practice shifting them to the breathing. The emotions do
not dwell in the mind but are in the diaphragm – in the body. Breathing becomes
the source of inner activity; once there, you are free to accept any external
stimuli, to be in the moment, and trust that your breathing will support emotions,
movement, voice and action.

In her study of emotion memory, psychologist Margaret Bradley
coined the term "flashbulb memory." Flashbulb memory triggers
what Bradley calls "a special memory mechanism [that] takes 'snap-
shots' of significant, emotionally evocative events, based on evidence
that people seem to remember personal circumstances surrounding
an emotional event (e.g., where one was, how one found out, etc.) vividly (perhaps vertically) and for a long time" (pp. 103–4). When the
actor finds something that triggers the emotions – and not just arbitrary emotion, but something deep, something specific, and always
something that is stimulating – affective memory lures out the feeling and manifests it in action. As I have said elsewhere, "Sense memory and Strasberg's controversial affective memory exercises are
meant to provoke physical action. Affective memory is designed not
merely to provoke emotion but to motivate the actor *to act, to produce active, physical behavior*" (*Method Acting Reconsidered*, p. 19).
This, too, cannot be overstated: emotion memory, affective memory,
or whatever one wants to call it, is designed to create active behavior.
The triggers that move us (notice the word "move") must produce
physical behavior that surfaces onstage or the inner life is no use to

the actor. The essence of our stimuli, Vakhtangov says, "must arise spontaneously on the stage" (quoted in Cole, p. 145).

Waiting for a Bus: Sense and Emotion Memory Incorporating Breathing

> I wait: what does it mean to wait – for a wife, a friend, a child? They are late [coming] home. Has something happened to them? (*Actor's Work*, p. 664)

Emotion recall, as Stanislavsky expresses in the extract above, is an exercise developing a believable sense of a story's given circumstance. Here I use traditional emotion recall work but incorporate a significant component: breathing. I call this the "waiting for a bus" exercise.

Exercise 18: Waiting

Sit in a circle with your fellow actors, facing outward. Your attention is private (you sit facing the wall, not one another; hence, this is a private moment). The circumstances are a bus station and you are waiting for a bus.

There are three situations:

Waiting for an old friend

Be specific: who is the friend? Why are you waiting? What did she once look like? What do you anticipate she looks like now?

Waiting to go to an audition

Audition for what? Do you have a musical instrument with you? How important is this audition? Is it a big break? A chance to revive your career?

Waiting to go to an award ceremony

You won an award – for what? What will you say? Whom will you thank? Will you feign modesty and try to appear humble? Will you accept the award with a speech, or speak impromptu? It is very important that you observe and understand how your imagination and memory work differently but interactively; each can support the other. After each situation is experienced, consider your breathing. How did you breathe in each of the three situations? Once the exercise is sufficiently practiced and you feel fully alive in the circumstance – living in and through the moment – then put work into the breathing. Breathe to the rhythm of the experience and maintain that breathing tempo with ease and lightness. If the breathing rhythm changes, that's fine.

The breathing is designed to increase the actor's "creative circle." Stanislavsky defines "creative circle" as the "degree of concentration on one single thought in which all the nerves through which attention carries on its work are brought into focus." Moreover, the attention must be tied together with "the utmost alertness of mind, so that they [the objects or our creative circle] should all be working in the same direction and the magnet of some thought should attract all the powers of your observation to itself" (*On the Art of the Stage*, p. 145).

We've all experienced emotion memory. You're driving your car and listening to the radio. A song comes on and it's the one that was being played in the background when you experienced your first kiss. The song recreates the passions associated with the moment. Stanislavsky reminds us that "when you [try to] recall an idea or melody you have forgotten," the "more you try, the harder it runs away from you. But if you recall the place, the situation, your overall mood at the time, it comes alive in you again" (*An Actor's Work on a Role*, p. 173). The point is that, as an actor, you must be very detailed and specific about the event; not just the music, but also the weather at the time, whom you were kissing, what s/he looked like, was wearing, smelt of, and so on. This will stimulate you, filling you with a rich need to express yourself physically. The more emotional connections the actor has, the wider her creative palette becomes. Edward Easty explains that, by "having a 'repertoire' of emotional experiences, the actor can call forth, at the proper time, the desire one needs for the character. The broader his 'repertoire,' the greater the resources for creativeness and the greater number of roles he will be able to act" (pp. 45–6). I would add that it is not only about accumulating a personal repertoire of emotional experiences, it is also understanding that *anything can contribute to that repertoire*. It doesn't have to be a "bad" experience, but rather to accept that all one's life is grist for the creative mill. Richard Boleslavsky said the actor "must not think during this work *how* he is going to reproduce a certain feeling – his only concern should be to *find it, to sense it with his entire being, to get used to it and to let nature itself find forms for its expression*" (The Creative Theatre, p. 118). The point of affective memory is to free the actor, not close her down inwardly. Nor is affective memory designed to create "attitude." Attitude is one-note; it doesn't change – it remains static and hence predictable. Think of someone with an attitude; you want to avoid them, not enjoy their creativity – their changing behavior, their ups and downs, their surprises. Evoking a triggering mechanism that inspires action, which in turn inspires multiple emotions, is the reason to exercise affective memory.

Affective memory can sometimes encourage a fetishized self-indulgence; and in the wrong hands it can have adverse consequences. This, as Harold Clurman rightly observes, "was not Stanislavsky's aim nor does it represent the purpose of the Method teachers in America" (p. 187). Affective memory must be put to art's usage; it must be recognized as a wonderful tool among tools; it must function as a way into self-awareness; and then it must be absorbed into the process of rehearsal and performance. Any other usage of affective memory has no place in acting (it is not something employed "for fun" or as a "psychological game"). There are acting teachers who have abused this method; all that can and should be said about such malfeasance is that there are charlatans in every profession – and the misuse of affective memory is probably not the only egregious behavior of acting teachers (I have personally witnessed acting instructors committing far worse misdeeds with other exercises and techniques). Affective memory is a tool for the creation of a better performance; if it fails to improve the performance, increase the connection to the role, or inspire activity, openness and creativity, then change it – find another, more acceptable memory. Furthermore, *affective memory does not cancel out or nullify any other activity.* This cannot be overstated: actors can perform physical activities while at the same time keeping their senses alive and personal experiences active (at the risk of oversimplification, actors can walk and chew gum at the same time!). Still, as Maria Knebel insists, in creating our physical state for any role, ultimately "the actor has no right to limit himself to purely intellectual analysis of the inner world." It is necessary, she says, "to find within oneself, in one's own emotional memory and sensations, the emotions dictated by the author: fear, hate, love, ambition" (*Stanislavski Today*, 52).

Common sense dictates that *connecting emotionally to the role makes the acting better*, and affective memory *is one means of obtaining this connection*. The connection can be both personal and *political*: playing a role that has a specific connection to a political cause can inspire the actor's sense of responsibility and commitment. Robert Ellermann observes that "it was Stanislavsky who first brought the *affective memory* to the attention of the modern actor; who first consciously applied it to modern actor training and performance; and who throughout his life based his understanding of creativity on it" (p. 2). Stanislavsky maintained his support for affective memory from the time he first experimented with it around 1906 to his death in 1938. In a letter dated January 11, 1937, he said "It is untrue and complete nonsense that I have renounced memory of feelings (*chuvstvonanie*). I repeat that it is the main element in our creativity" (quoted in Whyman, p. 76). He believed that without an emotional link created through memory the actor is merely illustrating the role's external features. He said the "aim of the art of emotional identification [experiencing] is to create on the stage *a live life of the human spirit* and *to show this life in artistic scene form*. It can be created only by the actor's truthful, sincere feeling and genuine passion" (*Selected Works*, p. 166). Rose Whyman tells us that Stanislavsky "was certain throughout his career that affective memory is an important key to the expression of emotion in acting" (pp. 102–3), adding that, for him, "the ability to create the *system* is inside us, but we lose what nature has given us when we go on stage and begin to pretend" (p. 108). While Stanislavsky experimented with other techniques and methods, he never abandoned the importance of human experience and emotion as the source of quality acting. He wrote in 1916, at a time when he was developing his first studio to facilitate the actor's work away from commercial pressures, that when the actor "unconsciously choosing his feelings and the events, facts known to him through life experience," then he "unconsciously weaves feeling with the soul and the life of the role" (quoted in Whyman, p. 120).

Affective memory is essential because it helps actors to present the human condition, warts and all. Actors are involved in a social art form: the human condition is social; we perform because we interact with others in a social context. At a fundamental level, functioning in a social context means mastering and containing our impulses; we learn to inhibit behavior and withhold desires. Performing before an audience, which is indeed a "social context," often stimulates repressive habits and socializing norms. In our social life we expend tremendous amounts of energy on maintaining and exercising inhibitions, and ignoring or suppressing thoughts, impulses and desires in order to engage with others in a civilized manner. These acts of suppression are activated both consciously and subconsciously, enabling us to get through our day-to-day life. Our suppressions, Freud would say, are practiced daily and create social habits and conformities that help us to control the potentially explosive nature of our passions. We may, for example, want to call our boss a flagrant hypocrite; drop our pants at an elegant dinner party; or tell our date what we really desire, but we restrict these feelings because to let loose our impulses would invite chaos and opprobrium. Schools, in particular, are designed for conformity, a caldron into which children are pressed at a young and tender age into standardization, and rubber-stamped into a group-think mentality. As a result, we construct barriers, defenses and survival mechanisms for approval, acceptance and community bonding because we need to belong. As our desires and emotions are repressed, we teach ourselves daily to desire and feel less. We accept only what we can reasonably obtain, rationalizing our way through life and learning to conform because society rewards those who show the least passion and follow the herd. Our society, Feldenkrais observes,

> suppresses every nonconformist tendency through penalties of withdrawal of support and simultaneously imbues the individual with values that force him to overcome and discard spontaneous desires. These conditions cause the majority of adults today to live behind a mask, a mask of personality that the individual tries to present to others and to himself. Every aspiration and spontaneous desire is subjected to stringent internal criticism lest they reveal the individual's organic nature. (p. 6)

Through repression and tension we create a form of emotional retreat into an inner citadel; we suppress desire and choke off spontaneity because we are fearful of failure; we diminish our appetites, afraid that exposing them will reveal personal flaws; and we eradicate our foolishness, afraid that others will laugh at our shortcomings. We build defensive walls, minimizing exposure; we want to be as little wounded as possible. By reducing emotions, appetites and desires we diminish the chances of exposing vulnerability and risk. We want to be safe, liked and accepted, conforming to whatever passes for fashionable normalcy and not rejected, or worse – deemed to be "different," unusual, quirky and the subject of laughter. As a consequence, our basic animal instincts are repressed; our childlike responses are largely conditioned out of us; and our visceral experiences and memories are obliterated as we mature. Instead of encouraging raw emotions and instincts associated with our passions, much of our behavior has been consciously suppressed by habits conditioned by parents, teachers, our peers, and the social need to obtain approval. Encouraged by society to conform, deep impulses are blocked and replaced with socially acceptable impulses (in fact, new habits). These impulses, solidified by routine, are taken for instinct and create responses that are tepid – socially appropriate but theatrically dull. Peter Brook put it well when he said:

> One can say that a true artist is always ready to make any number of sacrifices in order to reach a moment of creativity. The mediocre artist prefers not to take risks, which is why he is conventional. Everything that is conventional, everything that is mediocre, is linked to this fear. The conventional actor puts a seal on his work, and sealing is a defensive act. To protect oneself, one 'builds' and one 'seals.' To open oneself, one must knock down the walls. (*Open Door*, p. 27).

The aim of affective memory is to "knock down walls," to reverse suppression and reveal risks, appetites and emotions – to demonstrate vulnerability, rage, pain, hurt, passions, humor, desires and idiosyncrasies – to go to the dark and forbidden places in our lives and to do this energetically, enthusiastically, actively and *in a social context*. Reason and logic may hide us from ourselves and others by imposing excuses and rationalization, but emotions and passions reveal what we need to see about ourselves. The actor must create a deep impression on the audience – what Stanislavsky's student Maria Knebel called a "second level" of emotion. This second level, she says, "is the inner spiritual 'baggage' of the person." While remaining "closely linked with the author's ideational purpose," the second level of emotion

> renders the descriptional characterisation of the image full and all-embracing in relation to life. It is formed from the whole sum total of the character's impressions of life, from all the circumstances of his personal fate and it embraces all shades of his sensations, his perceptions, thoughts and feelings. The presence of a well worked out 'second level' renders all the reactions of the hero to the events of the play more precise, makes them more vivid and significant. (On the Action Analysis of Plays and Roles, p. 37)

The depth of emotion, passion and excitement stirs us imaginatively, providing energy that excites an audience. The term "emotion" contains the word "motion" and is derived from the Latin *emovere*, meaning a stirring, vital physical agitation. Actors perform impressions of human beings at their best and worst, lusting and craving, funny and sad, brave and cowardly, moved by the emotional experience observed through their voices, bodies and behavior. We are nonconformists and our job is to show the inner chaos and irrationality – our *mishegoss*, to borrow a wonderful Yiddish term – that gets repressed by society and our need to conform. Great clowns are great actors because they fearlessly present human folly: their vulnerability is demonstrated, their creativity is couched in human shortcomings, and their ability to make fools of themselves is unabashed. Clowning, Michael Chekhov says, "can be an indispensable adjunct to the actor in perfecting all the other types of performances. The more you practice it, the more courage you can muster as an actor. Your self-confidence will grow with it and a new, gratifying sensation will slowly emerge from within you" (*To the Actor*, p. 143). Actors should emulate clowns; like them, we should not repress our eccentricities and shortcomings but rather let them cascade artfully and interestingly. "Dare to fail," the great theater producer Joseph Papp said, "because you'll never succeed on any level if you're not willing to fail to the worst degree. So make an ass of yourself" (quoted in P. Cohen, p. C6). In life we arrest our passions and create temperate, balanced relationships; onstage we must redirect our impulses by seeking outsized emotions, avoiding the rationalization of our thoughts and rejecting inhibition. Our job is to expose the human spirit through clownishness and seriousness, humor and vulnerability, desire and emotion, aggressive energy and humility, compassion and rage, joy and pain, subtlety and grandiosity, but mostly by bold risk taking and exposing our inner life.

Affective memory is as useful for naturalism as it is for style (plays in verse, plays containing stylized movement and so on). This is not to suggest that every actor can perform every play with equal alacrity; certain plays and roles will contain greater challenges. An actor may do well as Hamlet but fall short as Othello; just because it's Shakespeare doesn't mean that every so-called Shakespearean actor can play *every* Shakespearean role with similar proficiency and beauty. Similarly, an actor's convincing performance in one Chekhov play is no guarantee that she will excel in another. Justified, personalized and physicalized acting is *essential for every actor performing every role*. What the actor justifies will differ, but justification is required. Tom Nelis, an actor with the Saratoga International Theatre Institute (SITI) and one of the leading performers of Anne Bogart's technique called Viewpoints (an acting style developed by Bogart and Mary Overlie, emphasizing shape, form, time and space in motion), makes it clear that without an inner spirit (what he calls psychological realism) emanating from one's personal life, the physical acting required by Viewpoints (see Anne Bogart entry in Brief Biographies, toward the end of the book) and the Suzuki method of actor training (an Asian-based technique influencing Viewpoints) will fail to engage an audience. Nelis says "Psychological realism is necessary for me to do either Suzuki's work or Anne [Bogart]'s work. The beautiful sculptures, the physical narratives that they both create need an enormous amount of specific justification." For Nelis:

> The *physical* exploration that both of them are involved in are radically different than anything I had previously connected with psychological realism, yet without an understanding of psychological realism, I think I would be swimming in their work. I wouldn't be able to make it make sense, so I don't think it would make sense for the audience. (p. 31)

Doubtless, Anne Bogart's Viewpoints are at odds with Strasberg's personalization. But just because they and their techniques cannot achieve a reconciliation doesn't mean that we shouldn't try. My life's focus has been on collecting the work of great teachers and have found the battles between them counterproductive. It's time to call a truce so that the twenty-first-century actor can proceed. Acting is art, and art is creating something that wasn't there previously, or to paraphrase Picasso, art is a lie that tells the truth. From a blank canvas come colors and shapes; from an empty computer screen come a story and a book; from a dormant instrument comes music; and from an actor comes the life of a human spirit.

Vasily Toporkov conveys his impression of the first time he encountered Stanislavsky onstage. Toporkov had been trained as an actor and worked professionally. By the 1920s he felt generally confident about his work and had come to believe in what acting was supposed to be. He had accumulated a set of principles constituting (what he thought were) good acting skills and a philosophy of acting. However, he heard of the Moscow Art Theatre and their new way of working – entirely different than his own. Curious, he went to see the Art Theatre's production of Anton Chekhov's *The Cherry Orchard*. He wanted to verify for himself what occurred there and to consider his involvement in their methods. In the production, Stanislavsky played Gaev, Chekhov's irresponsible albeit charming country gentleman who fritters away his life shooting pool and squandering the family fortune. In the following extract, Toporkov reports seeing Stanislavsky for the first time:

> The tall man [Stanislavsky], as he entered, seemed to bring with him life itself. What I saw seemed a miracle! How could a person, on the stage in front of a thousand people, be so completely occupied with his own cares? It did not occur to me immediately that this was Stanislavski himself. It didn't seem possible that I was seeing on the stage an actor and not an unlucky country gentleman. Stanislavski didn't "astonish" me in any way; he didn't use the usual "big guns" in the actor's arsenal [booming voice, manufactured emotions and so on]. I couldn't determine if, from an actor's point of view, that was good, but I simply couldn't take my eyes off him; it was as if he had bewitched me ... Nothing was done for show, nothing was "theatrical," but everything sank deep into the soul.(p. 35).

This observation is the definition of quality acting. Toporkov *simply couldn't take his eyes off him*. There was no "acting," but rather living complexity and trusting belief in the power of creative choices. For Stanislavsky, everything was simple, but not simplistic; everything was invested in the details of the character's concerns and no interest whatever in impressing the audience. A human being walked onstage; in Stanislavsky's words, "You see real people; you do not see actors" (*Selected Works*, p. 178). Every attention to specificity and simplicity was applied. Stanislavsky said: "There is no strain, so common to actors, no obvious effort to be passionate, no painful striving to produce a lofty emotion, no spasms, no body convulsions in lieu of strength." Rather, actors "arrive at the tears, laughter, or horror naturally, by first passing through a whole range of feelings. In other words, they live the living, they do not simply imitate its end results" (*Selected Works*, pp. 177–8).

To observe affective memory in acting, watch Melissa Leo in the film *Frozen River*. Note the opening scene where she sits in a car and smokes a cigarette, or when she applies mascara in the bathroom before work. She is subtle, simple and compelling; no "acting" here, no strain, no obvious effort to be passionate, no histrionics, just real behavior. She is really putting on mascara: there is no faking, pretending, nor indicating; her emotions are not presented to us as a way of saying "look how good an actress I am." There is no grandstanding, no emotions for their own sake, no sense that we are watching an "actor." In the opening we have yet to learn of the catastrophe that had just happened to her family; but the narrative is already in Leo's embodiment – her breath, feelings, and experience. *Depth is what makes affective memory work.* Whatever she is thinking of – and we do not need to know what it is – is affective. It is only important that Melissa Leo has been affected by images, thoughts and senses. "An actor can only approach the inner intensity by experiencing the entire gamut of his role's emotions," Vakhtangov says, and in order to do this "Every actor must invent something for themselves" (*Vakhtangov Sourcebook*, p. 274). Some image, memory or idea has to stimulate movement, trigger actions and inspire imagination.

I did not learn affective memory overnight and I did not execute it successfully at my first try (or dozens more). Learning affective memory takes time, effort and practice. Kim Stanley taught me affective memory, berating me repeatedly for my reluctance to drop inhibitions and habits in order to unlock emotions and get to the core of my experiences. She never let me off the hook; even as I grew incrementally better at it, she always reminded me that I was far from where I ought to be if I wanted to consider myself an actor. Only after decades of work on this exercise did I finally understand its value and was able to execute it effectively. Kim Stanley could have nodded approvingly while I performed mediocre work; she could have taken the easier route as a teacher and let me "get by." But she never did: she never stopped telling me that I hadn't gone far enough, that there's more depth to me than I'm willing to show, that I was settling for half measures and partial experiences. She encouraged and hounded me because she believed acting was a great art, acceptable only when student actors brought every bit of their lives to the work.

Combining Techniques

In his autobiography, *The Measure of a Man*, Sidney Poitier observed "how lucky I was that I had found my way to two of the greatest teachers of any era, Paul Mann and Lloyd Richards" (p. 142). Richards, director of Lorraine Hansberry's and August Wilson's plays, was a student of Mann's and later a superb teacher in his own right (my teacher at Carnegie Mellon, Earle Gister, was also Mann's student, and I too consider myself lucky to have studied with Mann for six years). Poitier maintains he was fortunate because when he performed in the 1968 film, *The Heat of the Night*, he worked with the

Actors Studio-trained Rod Steiger. Steiger's approach to the role "fascinated" Poitier; his preparation, Poitier said, "was astonishing in its depth. First he explored everything objectively. Then he made *sub*jective everything that he'd found in his *ob*jective exploration." Steiger would then "zero in on his character so completely that for the entire period of making the picture he would speak in the same cadence ... Working or not, he would remain completely immersed in the character of that southern sheriff." Crediting Richards and Mann with providing him with the technique necessary to match Steiger's intensity, Poitier adds: "Throughout the making of that film I sensed that I was on the threshold of discovering what acting really is, which is a way of getting at the core of what *life* really is" (p. 143). I too discovered what acting really is by studying with Mann and Kim Stanley. With their remarkable insights into human behavior and psychology, Mann and Stanley taught me a way of working; their training enabled me to combine affective memory, sense memory, animal exercises and actions. The two ways of working, which really weren't different at all, blended: Mann's style, which is similar to Stella Adler's, and Stanley's, which is a product of Lee Strasberg, worked in synchrony with my Meisner training. The next chapter goes further in blending the three fundamentals of the American Method as taught by Strasberg, Adler and Meisner.

PART II

PASSION AND INSPIRATION

4

SECRETS AND SOURCES

Find your own secret – find what makes you warm and calm and wise – healthy and cheerful. These things are your own secrets, nobody can prompt you. Feel within your own heart and radiate the feeling. Find the sources and sustain them. (Ouspenskaya, 2(3), p. 2)

Lloyd Richards taught me to always have a secret. These secrets give you a rich inner life. Just like you've got secrets right now, and they're a part of who you are. If you think about that secret, it's going to do something to you. As an actor, it may do what you need to be doing at that moment. But even if it doesn't, it gives you an inner life; it makes you a fuller human being. (Alice, p. 72)

An actor achieves the best performance through what the actresses Maria Ouspenskaya and Mary Alice allude to above: secrets. This chapter uses three personal examples to clarify the use of secrets and how they relate to three systems of acting technique: Strasberg's, Meisner's and Adler's. I make no claim to have invented the method of secrets or other ideas; I owe everything to the foundations presented by these three great American acting teachers of the twentieth century. I simply stress their importance as an artistic and practical idea. Secrets for the actor are triggers that coax behavior, drawing from them like a painter draws from the palette. The triggers, I contend, can only surface from three sources: *experience* (personal life); *observation* (either observing other actors or observing people and life in general); and *imagination* (what we can conjure that has never happened).

Experience means the life you have lived, the experiences you have traversed, and the feelings accompanying these. Your experiences and memories ground you in events, provide a back story or history, and give you a sense of personal reference for each role you play. They are not self-indulgences, but rather grist for your creative mill. They offer a sense of personal ownership of a role. I consider experience underlines Lee Strasberg's way of working.

Observation means the things you see, hear and observe that you might not have experienced personally but that you can absorb by watching, listening, reading and empathizing. Bertolt Brecht said that "Observation is a major part of acting. The actor observes his fellow-men with all his nerves and muscles in an act of imitation which is at the same time a process of the mind." By this he means that you not only imitate, but you also interpret: "To achieve a character rather than a caricature, the actor looks at people as though they were playing him their actions, in other words as though they were advising him to give their actions careful consideration" (p. 196). If you play a character who has an illness you have never experienced, you can find a matching situation in your life (personal experience), but you also, and simultaneously, must observe those who *have* experienced the illness. Observation requires research and study; it places demands on the actor to seek out those who have lived what the character is living through; and it necessitates an actor's willingness to analyze the role carefully. This means time to analyze others: their lives, motivations, body language, emotions and actions that parallel the experience of the character. It demands openness of mind and heart, observing without bias or preconceptions. Observation additionally means watching, listening and responding to fellow actors (or an audience in a theatre performance). Your fellow actors, sometimes even more than anything else, can trigger inspiration. The look on a fellow actor's face can often do more to inspire than the text or one's personal background because the look, expression, gesture or voice can trigger feelings spontaneously. As we perform we must observe our fellow actors in detail, engaged by their nuanced gesture and behavior. Observation, I contend, is associated with Sanford Meisner and his way of working.

Imagination inspires us by things that do not exist except in dreams, images, and fantasies. The books you read, the stories you hear, the dreams you have, the music you listen to and the paintings you see in museums and galleries are all founts of passion and excitement. Look, for example, at a fellow actor and see her at the age of 10. You may have only known that actor for a week, but your imagination can stimulate a whole creative and moving picture of the actor's childhood that can inspire you. When was the first time she had a haircut? Picture it in detail; did she cry, laugh, feel proud, amused? None of your imaginative choice need to have actually happened; that *they happen for you* is all that matters. Imagination is the bailiwick of Stella Adler's approach.

The optimal situation is when an actor has all three resources operating simultaneously. Sometimes this fails to occur and the actor has to depend on two or even one of these resources to support the performance. But the desirable goal is *to make all three operative*, combined with an actor's creative state: openness to the existence of here-now-today and the improvisatory immediacy of living in the moment. Following are three examples drawn from my own experience as an actor.

Experience and Jack-in-the-box

I performed in an off-Broadway play, a love story about two people who had unexpectedly lost their spouses and were trying to rebuild their lives after grieving. I played the bereaved lover who had lost his wife and was wooing someone who had lost her husband. In the play I was further along in overcoming the grieving process and was frustrated that the widow was too slow to let go of her memories (the deceased husband would appear as a ghost). In the climactic scene I tried to convince her that the grieving process has to end. At the peak moment, my dialogue was: "Do you think I bounced back from my wife's death like a Jack-in-the-box?" I had tremendous difficulty with the scene. I had never lost a lover by way of death, nor did I find the clichéd scene convincing. The text simply wasn't working; I discovered instead an affective memory that would enable me to flesh out something personal and secretive, something that moved me.

The Jack-in-the-box toy has a very specific history for me. I was terrified of it as a child. I remember the springs (they were silver), the colors of the boxes (reds and blues), and feelings of fear when the clown puppet popped up (they always spring straight up and then fall sideways, swaying menacingly back and forth). The clown that popped up had a devilish smile on his painted face that seemed sarcastically menacing, as if the smile harbored an evil intent. I remember my first encounter with it in nursery school. The other children were playing with something; they had crowded around this new object, obscuring my view. I tried to lean in between the crowd to see what was amusing everybody else. Seeing my frustration (I was smaller than most kids my age), the teacher saw my efforts to get a better look. She pushed aside the other children which allowed me view of the box. She led me right up front. It was a big box (or, given my small size at the time it appeared big) and something or someone sprung it open. I remember the feeling: heart pumping, flushed face and sweating. I couldn't move – my muscles froze in fear – and yet I had a strong impulse to jump backwards and run away. I also remember feeling pride: I wanted to hide my fear. I didn't want anyone to see my cowardliness. I wasn't going to cry. But from then on I would see Jack-in-the-boxes at home and at school, in toy stores or friends' homes, and recoil fearfully. There was Jack himself with that smiling, painted-on clown face. The color red stood out: crimson blood. Only after coaxing by my parents and through personal efforts did I partially overcome my trepidation. The memory, however, is still vivid and I have twinges of panic at the thought of it.

The body has memory. Muscles, sinews and joints remember. Think of a hot stove: if your fingers touch it, they instantly recoil. Only after the recoiling does the pain arrive. This is because if you had to wait until your brain figured out that your fingers were in danger your hand would fry. The same can be said of emotions: we remember them in the recesses of our subconscious, coaxed out only when something consciously triggers them from behind our defenses. We need these defenses to survive, to get through the day, to sustain ourselves in work and in relationships. We repress memories and feelings in the same way that I repressed my fear – I didn't want to show others my cowardly feelings. But the actor must find a way to peel back the defenses, to get at the open, vulnerable wound – the naïve self – because there reside emotions that are effective, deep, rich and spontaneous.

I used the Jack-in-the-box experience as an affective memory. In rehearsing at home I focused on the space I was in when I saw the box – the color, shape, feel, perspective – everything connected to my sensual memory. I relaxed my body, breathed deeply, and concentrated on sense memory. I didn't worry about the emotions but allowed anything to happen. Sometimes intense feelings arose, while at other times the affective memory stimulated only mild feelings. It didn't matter; what mattered was that I recalled the sensory apparatus – the specific sensory details surrounding the event. In affective memory, the actor consciously thinks of sensory details that, in turn, stimulate emotions and actions; the conscious tricks the subconscious out of hiding. I picked up the details, casting my memory back to little things: colors, textures, smells, the weather and so on. I searched my memory for surprises, for things I didn't immediately remember, such as what was I wearing, what were others wearing, what time of day was it, what the temperature was, the tension and anticipation in the air, the unusual rhythms in my behavior or that of others, the sights and smells, or just oddities of behavior. I recalled every example I could remember of Jack-in-the-box encounters and worked to stimulate the sensory details surrounding the events. I was not interested in recreating the exact emotions of my childhood (something that couldn't happen in any case), but rather practiced the sense memory of the event consciously. I exercised my will on my memory and along the way recalled (and there were several instances) how I overcame the fright. I embodied Jack, I called myself Jack, and I tried to become him as a way of overcoming my fear. It had intermittent success; I often reverted, but other times I was brave and less fearful. I exercised dozens of affective memories on the Jack-in-the-box experience; each evoked different feelings. Sometimes I even laughed at my foolishness – my shortcomings and humility. I accepted my vulnerability and as a consequence felt a deep connection to others who experience weakness. The process expanded my horizon, made me look at the moment with greater empathy.

The action affected my whole body because physicalization is indelibly tied to affective memory. The experience affected my breathing, and my whole being was engrossed in Jack-in-the-box. I came to rehearsal after weeks of working on the Jack-in-the-box affective memory and my whole experience had been absorbed into the work. When the time came to say the line I spontaneously became Jack: I physically bent my knees and sprung up so high it lifted me off my feet. Contrary to what many people might think, I did not stop my performance and withdraw inwardly. Rather, I became more alive. "An actor who masters the technique of using the affective memory begins to be more alive in the present," Strasberg confirmed (quoted in Hirsh, p. 141). The affective memory informed my outward action; it triggered the inner spark I needed to transform my performance into something personal and active; and it allowed me to engage in a better way with my fellow actor. My action was to convince the person I loved that breaking free of loss and fear is not easy, that it takes a mighty effort, but it eventually has to be done. Vakhtangov's student B. E. Zakhava notes that an "action is the bait of emotion. If it cannot be captured with your 'bare hands,' so to speak, you must be shrewd and catch it with the help of all sorts of baits, nooses, and traps. But the surest means of possessing an emotion is the action" (in Moore, *Stanislavsky Today*, p. 14). For me, *combining methods* work best. My action and affective memory worked in synchrony. I was not, as the line indicated, so easily disengaged from my dead lover; as with the Jack-in-the-box I had to overcome terror, and I knew what it was like for others to overcome fear. It takes a Herculean effort. The Jack-in-the-box contained the image that inspired me to convince the other character through my physical action.

I remember the look on the actress's face. She was mesmerized. The sound of my voice and my physical action (becoming a Jack-in-the-box) so compelled her that she faced me in a way she had not done so before. From that point forward we had found the key moment of reconciliation. We kissed, the lights dimmed, and the play ended with the next obligatory scene of our matrimonial engagement. The affective memory elevated my acting from the ordinary to something special. I was living through a deeply personal experience. From that point on I couldn't wait to get to the theater every night and create this moment (and anyone who says affective memory is only good for film knows little about acting); I couldn't wait to be surprised by how I would feel. The affective memory was my personal secret (I told no one about it), inspiring not only me as a character, but also as a person. I wanted to get to that point not because of self-indulgence but because I was inspired and I wanted to share this with the audience.

My work on affective memory was not done glibly. Had I physically imitated a Jack-in-the-box at the behest of a director, it would have informed the surface manifestation of what I had worked to accomplish inwardly. If I imitated a Jack-in-the-box without an inner connection, I would have done so dutifully and sincerely, "role playing" Jack-in-the-box instead of creating an action invested in personal memory. If a director had said, "Why don't you jump up like a Jack-in-the-box on that line," I would have followed the director's suggestion and applied a template of "sincerity" to my behavior; in other words,

I would have represented, but not experienced, the role. Stanislavsky said that

> Scenic action is the movement from the soul to the body, from the center to the periphery, from the internal to the external, from the thing an actor feels to its physical form. External action on the stage when not inspired, not justified, not called forth by inner activity, is entertaining only for the eyes and ears; it does not penetrate the heart, it has no significance in the life of a human spirit in a role. (*Creating a Role*, p. 49)

There is a subtle but deeply significant difference between performing the action because it was imposed on me (representing) and doing it because it was inspired by me (experiencing). Movement teacher David Alberts makes clear that "In every instance ... emotion comes first" (p. 16). Performing an action without a personal connection may stir up feelings, but they would hardly be inspiring ones. Vakhtangov noted that inner justification – what motivates the actor and justifies the behavior – *must come before the physical action*. Lawrence Parke, who rightly calls Vakhtangov "the best kept secret" of the Stanislavsky system, says that it was Vakhtangov "who observed that the difference between *action* and the *stimulus that causes* the action" depends on the "actor's ability to be stimulated, incited, by scenic problems" (p. 304). The sequence should always be stimulus first, then the action; what the actor wants to obtain – the objective – must be fully justified by an inner motivation and then, and only then, should the actor begin the action. Stanislavsky was adamant about this; even late in his life, when he was allegedly abandoning affective memory, he said: "Let the physical actions happen but they must be your own, no longer someone else's. You cannot live sincerely actions that are not yours. You have to create your own, similar to the role's, indicated by your consciousness, wants, feelings, logic, sequence, truth and belief" (*An Actor's Work on a Role*, p. 48). Affective memory is aimed at fleshing out deeper feelings and applying them to active behavior. Stanislavsky was unequivocal: "The best thing is when creation occurs spontaneously, intuitively, through inspiration." The technique he created was centered on the actor's ability to coax out the inspiration consciously. This means a drudgery of sorts, what he called the "daily grind" of fleshing out memories and using them to full advantage. "We need this prosaic daily grind as singers need to place the voice and the breath, as musicians need to develop their hands and fingers, as dancers need exercises for their legs. The only difference is that straight actors need this preparatory work to a much higher degree," working on the body, mind, sensory apparatus and emotional recall (*Actor's Work*, p. xxvi).

Affective memory is Stanislavsky's work on the actor's personal experiences that trigger or elicit emotions. Stanislavsky says:

> The point of experiencing emotional memory is not to say we have found that moment in the past which carries a lot of baggage, but to find that feeling which inspires us to act. We must also cherish our store of memories because the actor brings to the role not the first memories that come to mind, but others that have been carefully chosen and are the most dear to him, memories of feelings he has experienced in his own life. (*Actor's Work*, p. 209)

Affective memory means the actor conjures up emotional memories through the recall of physical senses that stimulate past events, which in turn *evoke emotions and physical actions*. Milton Katselas writes:

> The best acting requires personal *investment*, that you are personally *involved*, that somehow you are relating to the events of *this story* and letting them affect you in such a way that you leave the stage knowing that some part of you was left out there in service of this story. (p. 62)

Affective memory is meant to stimulate action and that action must be physicalized, outwardly directed and part of our gesture, motion and vocal expression. Memory is a great source of deeply personal stimulation; but we mustn't cling to the feelings. Robert Lewis cautioned that, for some actors, "You don't want to let the feeling go. But you are using emotion for its own sake, and that is no better than using characterization for its own sake." The key, he says, is "to release yourself from the exercise as you came in and play whatever the situation was, so that the feeling that you had in you went up and down normally the way the emotion does in life, depending on what's happening to you as you play out the moment" (*Educational Theatre Journal*, pp. 485–6). Once the affective memory has been experienced, the actor is free to improvise and adjust with the ebb and flow of the scene and the fellow actor.

Imagination and the Photo

I played Baal off-Broadway in Bertolt Brecht's play of the same name. In the final scene Baal is lying on his deathbed at a remote lumber camp. Baal had lived hedonistically, his excessive drinking and debauchery instigating his downfall. During the play he murdered his lover, Eckert, in a jealous rage. Now, alone on his bed, with nothing but the shirt on his back, he says, "Mama, make Eckert go away!" Until that moment – the final scene of the play – there is no reference to Baal's mother. Baal, until then, never expressed any remorse or guilt for his selfishness, the murder, and certainly never cries out for his mother. We know very little about Baal's past from the text – parents, birthplace, upbringing and so on. This was a very difficult line and moment for me. I didn't know where it came from. I had to make up the given circumstances that justified the text. Furthermore, the line suggests sentimentality through a cry for his mother. Brecht is hardly sentimental, even in this first play, though Brecht's characters do exhibit emotions and empathy (only academics think Brecht's so-called alienation effect is anti-emotion; those who have acted in Brecht's plays know otherwise). I had to connect to this moment emotionally and physically. I struggled, with frustrating weeks of rehearsals going by without believing in the line or the moment.

I usually walked to rehearsals. At the time I lived in the Chelsea section of New York and had a specific path to rehearsals in the East Village. I walked southward toward Greenwich Village and then turned left and went east through Washington Square Park. The walk helped me contemplate the role, preparing for what I wanted to accomplish in rehearsal. The rehearsals took place in October, when New York is just turning cooler and the fall breeze invigorates. One day on my way to rehearsal I stopped at an antique shop. The weather had yet to turn wintry, so many of the shops still displayed their merchandise on the streets. The antique shop had late-nineteenth-century photographs of random people and places scattered in display boxes. They were the size of baseball cards. I thumbed through the old photos and came across a picture of a woman in her late teens, her hair in a bun. She was dressed in a 1890s outfit. Her face caught my attention. I bought the photograph for 25 cents and continued eastward.

I was still early so I stopped in Washington Square Park and sat on a bench. I stared at the photo. The 1890s outfit seemed appropriate for Baal's mother, since Brecht wrote the play in 1918. The woman would have been the correct age based on the play's date. A story emerged, one I created from my imagination. This woman was Baal's mother; she was a prostitute and a washerwoman. She bore Baal out of wedlock and he worked in the brothel as soon as he could walk. She died when Baal was eight, but the other prostitutes kept him on because he was good at washing clothes. They had grown used to him and he was kept cheaply. The photo was all Baal had of her; she was buried in a potter's field without ceremony. I held the photo to my stomach and breathed.

Stanislavsky said that it is the actor's task to use her creative skills to transform the story of the play into *theatrical fact* the actor can believe in; this is what is meant by "justification." The process of turning the story into credible life requires the actor to ask the questions "*who, when, where, why, for what reason, how* – which we asked to stir our imagination, helped us to create a picture of our imaginary, illusory life with greater and greater definition" (*Actor's Work*, p. 83). The picture stirred my imagination. Photos bring us closer to life, showing us things we don't stop to see or ordinarily remember. This idea was not executed to satisfy the director or the audience, but to *stimulate* my imagination and *justify* greater definition for a more vivid and theatrical performance. "The path to justification lies through fantasy," Vakhtangov advises actors, because an actor must "Justify with your feelings, rather than with your brain" (*Vakhtangov Sourcebook*, p. 179). Justifying through photographs is one way to fantasy and imagination. My photo took on a specific life of its own; I carried it with me and put it in my back pocket at all subsequent rehearsals and performances.

I wanted to talk to this woman; to find out who she was, what she did, what were her dreams and disappointments. This was because I had made up a whole story about her and because I wanted some evidence to verify whether my life – my past existence – was true. She was, in my imagination, my mother, and she was, in my reality, someone with whom I had now created a deep bond. I felt an emotional connection to this woman, as if she were really alive and this was the only photo – the only living evidence – I had of her existence. When it came time to perform the scene, something within me wanted her to "make Eckert go away," as the line said. I wanted her to soothe me, hold me and reassure me. I wanted her love and comfort: my action was to reach out to hear her comforting voice. I wanted peace of mind and she was the only way to achieve it.

I reached for her so forcefully that I fell from the bed. I had achieved something immediate, personal, visceral, spontaneous and provocative. I felt my voice overtake the theater as I cried out "Mama." My action was to beg her to take away my guilt and remorse. I wanted her to hug me. There was no one there, but in my imagination there was a relationship. This is a form of affective memory, because there is something of my own mother in this line of thinking. And like the Jack-in-the-box, the photo was "in my back pocket" (this time literally). It was my secret. What Paul Mann and Barbara Loden taught (following in the spirit of Stella Adler) is that imagination is another critical place to trigger emotions and actions. I had created an imaginative story that had nothing to do with my own life (and nothing that Brecht explicitly said in the play). Stanislavsky is very clear on this:

> [the art of] emotional involvement produces a life-like image. It is not an identical animated replica of the role as written by the author. This new living thing has inherited the traits of both the actor who conceived and gave it birth and the role that fecundated it. The new creation is breath of the breath, flesh of the flesh of the role and the actor. (*Selected Works*, p. 174)

This image bore a specificity that surfaced from my imagination. I imagined the story and therefore I *owned* it – it was personal.

The use of photographs can provide a tremendous impetus for imagination. The engagement with the photograph is mine; it is personal by my own choice. My selection empowers me; it makes me feel confident in my inventiveness. It is a secret, something I carried in my back pocket (like I do every day with a real picture of my wife and daughter). I never told the director about this picture; it was unnecessary. Like the Jack-in-the-box, it was something meant to inspire me personally. It was my subtext, my inner monologue. Photographs additionally have what the philosopher Roland Barthes calls a mythological effect relative to politics. Barthes describes how a photograph can trigger "something deep and irrational co-extensive with politics. What is transmitted through the photograph of the candidate are not his plans, but his deep motives, all his family, mental, even erotic circumstances, all this style of life of which he is at once the product, the example and the bait" (*Mythologies*, p. 91). The image creates an enduring impression – think of the 1989 photo of lone man standing before oncoming tanks in China's Tiananmen Square.

For me, the picture created a personal myth, something that lifted me out of a generalized sense of "motherliness" and into a profound notion of justice. I imagined the photo as representing someone who had been treated unjustly.

Photographs isolate and frame people's most intimate moments, illuminating their joys and sorrows affectively. At each rehearsal and performance the image touched my heart. Photos also create a rich source of conflicting, stimulating feelings. They display something that occurred in the past and are endowed with history that becomes blurry over time, provoking provocative questions. Where was the photo taken? What was the person like when the photo was taken? Why am I, or they, wearing these clothes?

Roland Barthes again provides an interesting observation. He writes in *Camera Lucida*:

> One day I received from a photographer a picture of myself which I could not remember being taken, for all my efforts; I inspected the tie, the sweater, to discover in what circumstances I had worn them; to no avail. And yet, *because it was a photograph* I could not deny that I had been *there* (even if I did not know *where*). This distortion between certainty and oblivion gave me a kind of vertigo, something of a 'detective' anguish. (p. 85)

Barthes went "to the photographer's show as to a police investigation, to learn at long last what I no longer knew about myself" (p. 85). The tension between certainty and oblivion is the actor's tipping point: we know what occurred, but our effort to experience the past reveals gaps that stimulate our desire to know (Barthes's detective hunt) and this in turn stimulates the desire for clarity. Barthes' inspection of the tie and sweater are the specific details an actor must look for, even if the observations we try to discover fail to expose certainty. The mystery and anxiety created by *not knowing is as valuable as knowing*: it stimulates an existential void and exposes vulnerability, humility, frailty and the sobering realization that we are flawed creatures: forgetful, unsteady and uncertain of our past history. *Memory plays tricks on us and these tricks are good for the actor*: confusion is not always a bad thing.

Social critic Susan Sontag said that photographs leave out as much as they reveal. Unlike a moving picture, which unfolds a series of pictures that narrate a story, the "ultimate wisdom of the photographic image is to say: 'There is the surface. Now think – or rather feel, intuit – what is beyond it, what the reality must be like if it looks this way.' Photographs, which cannot themselves explain anything, are inexhaustible invitations to deduction, speculation, and fantasy" (p. 23). The invitation to fantasize – to imagine what the picture *does not show* as much as it reveals – stimulates the imagination and applies a supple, visceral, triggering mechanism. We fill in as many blanks with a photograph as we wish, intuiting whatever we want because the picture has so many variables and unknowns. An imaginary picture can sometimes be even better because the gaps we must fill are limitless.

Exercise 19: Photographs

Collect photographs of people, faces, places and things that move you. These photos have personal memory; they can be of people you know, but they can also be strangers. Jot down notes alongside your collection of photographs, reminding you of what each photo means and why you kept it. Accept that at times the photo won't stimulate you, and at other times it will. Let the photo surprise you, stimulating new feelings and thoughts. Always be sure that your imagination is stimulating you physically, not just mentally; moving you to feel and act, not just think. The terms of our work is emotional, not cerebral.

Stanislavsky first raised the idea of photographs when he recommended that the actor "must gather up (collect) photographs, engravings, paintings, sketches of make-up, typical faces, pictures or descriptions in literature. It is this kind of material that, when the imagination runs dry, gives him the nudge and stimulates his affective memory, reminding him of things he had once known but had forgotten" (*An Actor's Work on a Role*, p. 186). Combining affective memory with imagination is one of the surest ways to nourishment, growth, and room to change and evolve in our creative inspiration.

Imagination, unfortunately, is greatly diminished in modern society. The improvisational actor Keith Johnstone writes that imagination has been drained from us in childhood. By the time we're adults our imagination is nil. "Most schools," he says, "encourage children to be unimaginative" (p. 76). An example of this is "paint-by-numbers." As a child I was taught to draw this way. A page was provided that contained outlines. A horse, for example, had an outline and inside it was a number corresponding to the number at the bottom of the page: 1 for brown, 2 for blue, 3 for red and so on. The aim of the art class was to fill in the outline with the corresponding color. Anyone drawing in a different color or going outside the lines was deemed to be "incorrect." Because I drew outside the lines or selected different colors, I was often scolded, labeled uncooperative, a rebel. I received failing grades in art yet my art works were often displayed as examples of children's work at the Brooklyn Museum (I was raised on Eastern Parkway across the street from the Brooklyn Museum and Brooklyn Public Library, two of the three places – theater was the third – where I spent most of my childhood). "You have to be a very stubborn person to remain an artist in this culture," Johnstone rightly observes (p. 77).

Imagination is essential for the actor; but so is reality. The actor must work in both spheres: reality and imagination. The actor, unlike the painter, cannot rely on abstraction, or the musician the sound of an instrument. My feelings are my instrument; my body and voice comprise the conduit through which I express action; and the events that happen occur in the here-and-now. My body is real, my presence is real, and I see and hear what is real before me. There is a great deal in acting that is unreal and I must rely on my imagination to make the fiction inspiring, credible and as close to real as possible. I have to imagine that I am someone I am not; that the actor I work with is my lover when he is not (when playing Baal, Eckert was my lover, but the actor was just another actor); and that the situation I am in is truthful even if I am onstage. Balancing what is real (what is occurring) and what is not (the fiction) is the actor's job, and finding ways to make them work in unison is the creative development of rehearsal and practice.

Using reality and imagination properly is often confusing for young actors. They frequently misconstrue emphasis: what part of acting should they take at face value and what part must be conjured. There is a well-known anecdote about acting that will shed light on reality and imagination. In the movie *The Marathon Man*, Dustin Hoffman is being pursued by a Nazi dentist played by Laurence Olivier. In one scene, Hoffman must appear winded, having run for a long time being chased by killers. In preparation Hoffman ran around the set just before the scene began. After a few takes Olivier asked him why he was running and Hoffman said he wanted to create the reality of shortness of breath. Olivier allegedly said: "Why don't you use your imagination and try acting?" I've heard this tale told many times by acting teachers, with the emphasis on Olivier providing the correct approach. I contend the opposite: Hoffman is correct. The assumption is that Hoffman is avoiding imagination. But how can that be? If anyone has seen Hoffman act it is clear he is imaginative. The point is that there is so much to imagine that no one is capable of imagining everything at once. The actor should properly assign imagination only to areas that cannot be created by reality. Sanford Meisner, who emphasized the "reality of doing," says:

> Let there be no question about what I'm saying here. If you do something, you really do it! Did you walk up the steps to this classroom this morning? You didn't jump up? You didn't skip up, right? You didn't do a ballet pirouette? You really walked up those steps. (*Meisner on Acting*, p. 17)

Hoffman was really running, saving other things for his imagination.

I experienced a similar situation. I was in a play where I was required to eat chocolate candy while seducing someone. I presented a box of candy to the actress and we both picked a chocolate from it. I ate mine, but she didn't; I really picked up food and she faked it. She pretended to chew; I chewed. She acted as if she was swallowing; I swallowed. Each time we performed the scene the food would stick between my teeth (chocolates under stage lights tend to soften quickly and become difficult to chew). In the scene I was wooing the actress but the gooey, melting chocolates weren't cooperating: I had to dig the chocolates out of my mouth. My finger in my mouth became a whole routine: a bit sexy, a lot funny, and always surprising because *it was really happening*. I was actively pursuing my objective in a spontaneous way. The balance was this: imagination was our relationship; reality was food. Melting chocolates in my mouth was something *I didn't have to fake*. While she had to devote attention to the pretense of eating, I was free to react spontaneously to the food, to her, and to the given circumstances of the play. Meisner acolyte Larry Silverberg offers a logical explanation about reality onstage: "Isn't it so much *simpler* and doesn't it make so much more sense when reading a letter on stage to *actually read that letter* rather than pretend to read a piece of paper with squiggly lines on it," he says, adding: "With squiggly lines you must remember to move your eyes in the correct manner to make it look like you *are* actually reading. Why not actually read? Less to think about and much less effort, your eyes will look like they are reading because they are reading and you don't have to work at making the audience believe you" (pp. 5–6).

Imagination is like a box: the bigger the box, the greater your imagination. People with a big imagination have a large box in which they can place images. Declan Donnellan says "The imagination is the capacity to make images" (p. 9), and Adler acolyte Joanna Rotté adds, "Whatever the imagination engenders has a right to exist and does. When Adler asked us to imagine a lemon tree, she believed us capable of growing some kind of lemon tree, whether or not we had actually ever seen one" (p. 60). But imagination has limits. The more the actor really does something, the more she can free herself to imagine other things. There will always be plenty of given circumstances the actor will have to invent. *Create as much reality as you can.* If you have to eat, really eat; if you have to read, really read; if you have to drink, really drink; and if you have to run, really run. Not merely because it creates reality for the actor, but because the actor must prioritize, opening space for images that are part of the fictional story.

Observation, Repetition Exercise and the Letter

As a student of the human condition, an actor must observe everything, and without bias. A student actor, Michael Chekhov insisted, "must train himself to analyze his own motives and to detect the motives of other people. He must keep before himself the problem of determining other people's characters, professions and habits from their appearances" (quoted in Cole, p. 128). The actor must study people objectively, empathetically, and deeply. You never know what role you might be asked to play; entering the rehearsal with prejudice is like running a race with your legs tied.

In an original play about the Warsaw Ghetto, I performed the role of a gang member. We were young Jews who crawled through underground tunnels smuggling contraband: food, weapons, blankets and so on. The play was based on the true story of a survivor who wanted to honor members of his crew. I had one important scene at the end of the first act – my father's funeral (my character was killed off during the intermission and didn't appear in Act 2). According to the script, my father committed suicide because he felt that the shortage of food was killing children. He thought that if he died there would be one less mouth to feed. In the scene, each actor passed by the coffin and spoke to me, his son, praising his nobility, selfless sacrifice, and willingness to give his life so that others might eat.

Given the conditions in the Warsaw Ghetto, food shortage was easy to believe. Still, I found the scene maudlin. I had nothing to say in the scene; all the actors talked to me as I sat alone onstage in front of the coffin. I felt like stone, trying to muster some emotion or action. I knew I could have just sat there and listened, and that would have sufficed. But every word from the other actors praising my father bounced off me with no emotional connection. As a result, I had nothing to give to my fellow actors other than a sympathetic ear; I had no action, emotion or connection. I felt I was letting everyone down. The director, Susan Einhorn, told me I needed to make this moment personal. I tried to connect to the play's circumstances but the scene was (in my opinion) contrived. Because I had prejudged the scene, I couldn't connect to it. As hard as I tried, I was blocked. The play failed me or I failed the play; either way, the scene wasn't working. I'm sure there were people who did indeed commit suicide to help others, but this didn't help me. Intellectually, I understood the given circumstances, but emotionally I was dead.

I experimented. What if every word said in the scene was a lie? What if I knew that my father didn't commit suicide for the reasons the other characters believed, but for an entirely opposite motive: he was *stealing food* and committed suicide *because he was afraid of getting caught*. My father was therefore not the hero everyone in the play said he was. He committed suicide out of shame. At home I wrote out a letter that I pretended my father had written privately to me. The letter confessed everything: his theft, cowardice, shame and humiliation. In it he asked me to keep his secret. I folded my imaginary letter in my back pocket (I tend to like back pockets), and went to rehearsal. I now had this dark secret in my possession. As the other actors approached me one by one, extolling the virtues of my father, I could only sit there and outwardly acknowledge the accuracy of their words. Inwardly I knew it was altogether otherwise. I was torn in two directions. Speak or remain silent? Of course, in the play I had no dialogue, so naturally I wasn't going to speak. And I wasn't going to change the blocking by standing up. I remained exactly where the director had placed me, down center stage in a chair listening dutifully to each actor and nodding in agreement with what they said. I was faithful to the playwright and director – but something inside me had changed. My outer action was to acknowledge their praise; my obstacle was that I knew it was all lies. My breathing was affected by their every word, my body was responding to their every inflection, and I listened to them more intently. My action was to protect my father's memory even though what he did was not what others said about him. I was as silent as I had been in every rehearsal, but there was a difference – my behavior was clear and economical. I wasn't forcing emotion. Stanislavsky said that when the emotions do not come on their own, "don't force it, tantalize it, lure it with mental images." The more specific the actor is regarding these images, the more detailed the moments will be. You must, he said, "really love" the mental images you create, "as well as what is happening to you, inside and out, while you're onstage. Don't rush and don't drag out what you do lest you destroy the linear logic and sequences of your mental image" (*Actor's Work*, p. 542). By watching and listening to the other actors for every detail of their voice and gesture, I picked up the subtle changes in their behavior; and by possessing mental images I felt the conflict within.

The actors in the cast came back to me during intermission and thanked me for giving them so much to work with. But that's beside the point. None of them knew what I had actually done. They didn't need to know. I had found a specific moment onstage that allowed me to relate to them – to listen actively – in a way that was deeply personal and emotional. Active listening means that my inner monologue (my thoughts) are processing the words and gestures of the other actor with purpose. Stanislavsky notes that "All young actors must realize that when we listen to someone in life, this kind of inner monologue goes on. Actors very often think that listening to one's partner on stage means staring at him and not thinking. How many actors rest during the long speeches of other actors and come alive only for their cues" (quoted in Gorchakov, p. 51).

Prior to writing the letter I was trying to conjure up feelings for my dead father; I was squeezing out emotion. My body tensed, hoping that something would stir my emotions. But each time I rehearsed there was nothing but indicating, fakery and fraught emotion emerging from my desire to "act." Stanislavsky's remarks are appropriate; in the light of powerfully emotional scenes, "an actor should always remember not to increase his activity, but rather to cut three-fourths of it. You make a gesture to carry out some action – well then, next time cut it down from seventy-five to ninety percent" (*Creating a Role*, p. 136). By denying what I knew about my father, I had cut ninety percent and simply read the behavior of the other actors and reacted.

In reading the behavior of other actors, I incorporated Sanford Meisner's repetition exercise.

Exercise 20: Repetition

Meisner's repetition exercise is designed to train actors to relate spontaneously to the other actor and develop skills in observation and impulsive reaction. (There are several variations of this exercise, so the way it works for me might not coincide exactly with others.)

Two actors sit facing each other. One comments on what she sees in the other actor. Whoever feels the impulse to speak first might say "You're wearing a red shirt." The other actor says "I'm wearing a red shirt. You're wearing a red shirt" (even if the other actor is not wearing a red shirt). The first actor responds by saying the same thing back: "I'm wearing a red shirt. You're wearing a red shirt." This continues repeatedly, until someone feels the impulse to say something else. The following text is a typical example of two actors performing the repetition exercise:

Actor A: You have on blue jeans.

Actor B: I have on blue jeans. You have on blue jeans.

Actor A: I have on blue jeans. You have on blue jeans.

This dialogue would continue for an undetermined length of time. Eventually Actor A or B would hear and see a total change in the behavior of the other, and the text will change to something like "You're moving your hands." The reply would be "I'm moving my hands. You're moving your hands." This exchange would proceed. Actor A might change again by saying: "You're staring at me" and Actor B, "I'm staring at you. You're staring at me" and the exercise continues to 40 or 50 exchanges.

The point of the exercise is to pay close attention to the other actor and to develop instinct. We often observe the world generally, without attention to detail. Meisner's repetition exercise trains actors to sharpen focus, pick up the minutiae of detail, and learn to accept spontaneous impulses. The exercise encourages spontaneity, honest response and impulsive behavior, not cerebral calculation or cleverness.

There is no time limit on the exercise, and there is no restriction as to how long a phrase can continue. The words become so elastic that their literal meaning is less important than the inner action. The "blue jeans" or the "red shirt" are less important than the *meaning behind the words* – the subtext. Because there is no deviation to the text (you want to say something else but you have to commit to the phrase) the exercise produces frustration – which is perfectly fine. Frustration is an emotional impulse that initially appears to be boredom, but when allowed to continue indefinitely during the course of the exercise, transmutes itself into a catalyst for strong reactions. As the exercise progresses and a phrase is repeated we learn to look for movement in the eyes, bodies that betray feelings, and facial expressions that reveal a great deal about people. Actors learn to measure carefully gesture and voice.

According to Meisner, "your instinct picks up the change in his behavior and the dialogue changes too. I'm talking about instinct" (Longwell, *Meisner on Acting*, pp. 29–30). The words, or phrases, shift when there is an emotional (not cerebral) impulse.

Meisner teacher Williams Esper explains:

> *Thinking* your way into a shift is wrong. It's *in*organic and calculated, like trying to manipulate a conversation. We don't seek to develop our *minds* with Repetition; rather we seek to develop our instincts. Everything that happens in Repetition should be driven by *impulses*. Emotions. You must respond to what you hear from your partner *without analysis*. Anytime you engage your mind during Repetition, you'll mask your true impulses and throw yourself off the exercise. (p. 39)

As I have described elsewhere, the actors "are compelled to deal with observed behaviour rather than dialogue and plot. This helps actors to foster ensemble interplay, or communion, rather than words." Meisner wants actors "to place their focus on subtextual dialogue – the chemistry between the actors and the reality of the situation (human behaviour). If an actor is yelling, that is tangible, something everyone can hear and observe. The other actor reads the behaviour of yelling and reacts to it instinctively. Reading behaviour compels actors to focus on scene partners rather than the artifice of the plot. As a result, actors react spontaneously, play as an ensemble, and read behaviour as it happens organically" (Method Acting, p. 159).

C. C. Courtney, veteran teacher at Meisner's Neighborhood Playhouse, states that the "purpose of the exercise is to learn to read behavior and to respond truthfully" (p. 292). Learning and reading are the operative words: perception is trainable, and like affective memory or imagination, improves with practice.

In the repetition exercise the actor is not so much concerned with the words – eventually the phrases used become meaningless. Instead of words, the actor learns to be attuned to the vocal rhythms and body language of the other actor. The gestures and voice reveal the other actor's subtext – her inner communication. The exercise is designed to stimulate give-and-take and develop commitment to the scene partner. Actors often complain that their scene partner "isn't giving them enough." Milton Katselas responds to this excuse by saying that "This defense doesn't hold up in court. The professional actor can play passionate to a door" (p. 99). The repetition exercise makes an actor commit even if the other actor is a corpse, because even silence is something; if the other actor sits and stares at you, motionless and apparently without feeling, you can still observe the presence of another human being and react to it.

Think of the repetition exercise as a dance. Anyone who has danced with someone knows that there is an instantaneous moment on the dance floor when you assess whether the partner can dance, and how well. You know, by physical contact and movement, whether you have a novice or an expert, or which dance steps your partner does or doesn't know. You can see and feel tension or ease, body language and eye contact, and a range of emotional responses. Actors must be as attuned to their partners in the same way as dancers – must learn their intricacies, nuances and emotional shadings. The way to know this is through observation. But this does not mean that actors "stare" coldly, like scientists in a laboratory. They are *dancing with their partner*, and as dance partners *are simultaneously being observed*. Repetition encourages give-and-take, changes in status, and an increase in generosity. The actors' job is to create synergy, chemistry and sparks between them.

Eventually the observations focus on behavior rather than on surface appearances, so that the phrase might become "You're angry" and the other actor responds "I'm angry. You're angry." I encourage actors to deal with facts first: clothes, hair color and so on, and later to refer to behavior. In other words, read only the things you see with certainty; once you have practiced the exercise for a time you can then make value judgments on the other actor's emotions. I also encourage the actors to stay with one phrase for a while. The point of the exercise is not to make a laundry list of observations, but to use the phrases as sounds, somewhat like gibberish. Actors shift phrases too easily to demonstrate cleverness. The point of the exercise is not to show how smart the participants are, but to develop reactive impulses and respond to them immediately, clearly and actively. The actors must respond truthfully, impulsively and spontaneously, acknowledging what they really see and hear.

Meisner's repetition exercise developed from Stanislavsky's idea of communion. Stanislavsky said that "what you first look for in someone is their soul, their inner world. Look for the living soul in me, my living 'I'" (*Actor's Work*, p. 234). It was a reaction to the "star" system, where actors performed for personal effect rather than as part of the ensemble. Actors working this way behaved like "a piece of merchandise and you [the audience] were the buyer" (*Actor's Work*, p. 241). Rather than creating an effect, Stanislavsky looked for "Emitting and receiving rays, signals. Radiating out, radiating in" (*Actor's Work*, p. 246). The actors sit comfortably in chairs facing each other and think of what they want to emit, to communicate mentally, which is then translated into the body's communication. The development of this communion or communication, Stanislavsky says, comes from the actor having "an iron grip onstage, in the eyes, the ears, in all five sense organs. If you are listening, then listen and hear. If you are smelling, then smell. If you are looking, then look and see, don't let your eyes slide over the object, without latching on to it, just visually licking it. You must, so to speak, sink your teeth in to the object" (*Actor's Work*, p. 251).

This demand for deep concentration and honest observation emerged in part from Stanislavsky's study of Eastern philosophy (brought to him by his student, Leopold Sulerzhitsky). Through Sulerzhitsky, Stanislavsky introduced the concept of *prana* (rays). Phillip Zarrilli defines *prana* from the Sanskrit compound, *prana-vayu*, meaning "the breath(s), wind, vital energy, or life force understood to circulate within" (p. 14), and Al Lee and Don Campbell add that *prana* "is understood to be the universal life force – the energy field that gives life and animation to all things" (p. 69). Stanislavsky encouraged his actors to circulate this energy in a give-and-take atmosphere. This activity reinforces moment-to-moment behavior, cultivates spontaneity, and stimulates ensemble playing.

Another value of Meisner's repetition exercise is the emphasis not only on real listening to stimulate truthful impulses, but also on the reality of the other actor. I acknowledge that the situation on the stage or screen is artificial. Much of what actors do is to create something that isn't real. I'm no more the character I play than anyone else. However much we must create a reality onstage, the fact is that most of what occurs onstage or onscreen is fiction. The actor before me is not my son, daughter, lover or foe; they're actors playing roles. However, one thing is certain: the actor before me *is real* – she is really *here*.

When she smiles, she smiles; when she bows her head, she bows her head. In a world of artifice, reality is crucial. If actors are interested in creating as much reality as possible, then there is hardly anything more real than the other actor onstage. She is *really there*; when she is really sitting or standing, smiling or frowning, yelling or crying, that *reality is unassailable*. My acknowledgement of her reality is as real onstage as it is off; the certainty of talking to a real human being requires no illusion-making. The play's circumstances will dictate the situation and context. But my fellow actor's reality is not something I have to manufacture. I don't have to act, just react. Meisner said that when he invented the repetition exercise, he wanted to create an exercise that avoided intellectualization and instead to "get to where the impulses come from. And I began with the premise that if I repeat what I hear you saying, my head is not working. I'm listening, and there is absolute elimination of the brain" (*Meisner on Acting*, p. 36).

Too often I watch plays and movies where the actors "say" they are lovers or siblings or whatever, but when I look at their performances they appear like complete strangers. You need to establish a truthful *relationship* with your fellow actor. If the story says you are lovers, and you barely recognize the other actor – their behavior, habits, gestures, tone of voice – then how am I to believe you? What does the other actor's smile mean to you? There are dozens of ways each of us smiles. Do you know what each means? When I hear my daughter's voice calling me, I know instantly if she is happy, sad, ill, annoyed, enthusiastic, in danger and so on. I know the voice because I listen to it through the *relationship* I have with her. Actors, then, should have the same deep relationship with other actors onstage. An actor must listen actively, what Uta Hagen called "animated listening," which entails "the interpretation of what is being said to us as it interacts with our battery of psychological and mental actions" (*Challenge*, p. 114). We listen and observe "from our character's point of view and expectations, on the meaning and intent of the verbal actions of the other" (*Challenge*, p. 115). By reading behavior and focusing on the other actor, we are vividly involved in the scene. We listen to the tone of the other person. As Vanessa Redgrave said, "I've worked on myself [to] listen, listen, listen, really listen. You think you're listening, but you really have to work at it" (p. C1).

Every human being has a tone in their voice and gesture. This tone is musical: it is in one's sound and movement, pace and rhythm, intonation and texture, posture and stance; and like music, it reflects emotions. Tone is a human being's instrument outwardly projecting inner feelings. As actors we must be attuned to the tones of others in the same way that a musician is attuned to her fellow musicians. Every performance creates a new tone. The job of the actor is to be sensitive to subtle tone changes. These changes are affected by what we eat, how we sleep, what transpires during the day, the fact that everyone ages, and our emotional comportment. Like a tuning fork, people's tone gives you a lot of information. When a fellow actor relates to you, even if they don't tell you how they feel, you can hear a certain ring in their voice, observe certain postural formation in their body, and glimpse their soul through their eyes. This is "tone," and actors must observe tonal shifts. The human voice and body are like music and all a person has to do is to change attitude, and the tone, like a musical instrument, transposes to a new "key." We can feel the change. Human contact is physical – indeed primal – connected to social bonding and group rituals. Touch also reveals cultural codes, illustrating the different ways societies recognize human interaction. The power of touch can be recognized as temporal and kinesthetic – the length of time for which we make contact and what kind of grip we use communicates distinct emotions. Touch is a sophisticated differential signaling system, and being attuned to it is essential for the actor.

The tone of another person can also be the actor's *trigger mechanism*. If the chosen images used for the trigger fail to evoke something in a performance; if the role has been played repeatedly to the point where it loses inspiration; and if something is bothering us that particular day – then we can observe the tone of our fellow actor and use it as our inspiration. Actors have to accept the fact that sometimes the secret – trigger, decoy, image or inspiration – will fail to inspire. We may have the letter or photo in our back pocket, but some days it just doesn't work for us satisfactorily. Feelings are like fickle lovers; they sometimes elude us when we need them the most. In lieu of this, the other actor can be a surrogate of inspiration. Sometimes just a smile from the other actor is all we need to trigger our creativity and allow us to perform inspiringly. Reading behavior trains our eyes and ears to use the other actor not only as an object of our action, what Declan Donnellan calls the target of our objective, but also provides us with another means of triggering our emotions. The term "chemistry" in acting is often used when roles are being cast: can the actors create chemistry together? The actor might be fine alone, but there is no chemistry with another actor. No matter how good a performer might be, if there is a lack of chemistry with the partner, the performance will fall short. The other person is the source of much of what will affect you onstage; you have to depend on them to absorb your actions and trigger creativity. Donnellan says, "You can never know what you are doing until you first know what you are doing it to. For the actor, all 'doing' has to be done *to* something. The actor can do nothing without the target" (p. 17).

While the repetition exercise is about reading the other's behavior, the idea that we can truly read another's behavior and know what they are thinking is illusionary. Actors observe body language and interpret vocal patterns but they are not mind readers: they cannot know what someone else is thinking. Yet because we are not able to read each other's mind means that we are free to *invent one another*. We are free to evaluate behavior according to what we believe, and our misperceptions are an exciting part of acting. For example, if someone says to me "You're angry," I may or may not be angry, but the fact that I am being evaluated stimulates my reactions and inspires my emotions. We often misread people – many dramatic situations, comic and tragic, hinge on misreading. King Lear entirely misreads his daughters in the opening scene of the play. The two eldest daughters profess love eloquently but actually loathe him, while the youngest speaks plainly. Lear, in the best sense of the repetition exercise, reads behavior carefully yet mistakes eloquence for authenticity. His misreading (the Greeks called this *hamartia*, an archery term meaning missing the mark) sets the play in motion. When Lear banishes his youngest daughter, Cordelia, his friend Kent objects. Lear says "Out of my sight"; and Kent replies, "See better Lear." Likewise Oedipus, who wants to "see" his father's murderer and chooses to read everyone's behavior accordingly (plucking out his eyes is his appropriate response, since he failed to "see"). The repetition exercise encourages actors to see and hear each other intensely even if what we observe is incorrect.

Reading others must be done passionately. In all three examples – Strasberg's affective memory with my experience of Jack-in-the-box; Adler's emphasis on imagination and the use of photographs; and Meisner's repetition exercise encouraging observation of others – I was stimulated and engaged emotionally and physically because I was inspired by *experience, imagination and observation*. I invented triggers and created secrets that not only coaxed my emotions and actions, but made me want to convey this to the other actors. Maria Knebel said:

> The more actively the actor is capable of seeing the living phenomena of reality behind the authorial word, of evoking inside himself a conception of the things that are being talked about, the more powerful will be his impact on the audience. When the actor can see himself what it is he needs to talk about and what he needs to convince his partner of on the stage, he succeeds in grabbing the audience's attention with his visions, his convictions, his beliefs, with his feelings. (On the Action Analysis, p. 44)

Once the inner conviction is secured, we move to the next phase: physicalization.

5

PHYSICALIZATION AND ANALYSIS THROUGH ACTION

Inspiration and triggers must be channeled into action; it is not enough to be inspired; one has to "physicalize" the inspiration, and this is done by discovering the "super-objective." The super-objective, writes Bill Bruehl, "is the one action that characters in a drama pursue from the moment they realize what they want to accomplish until the dramatic action ends" (p. 13). The super-objective is an activity that carries great importance and is something that can be physicalized – done actively through a physical task. Physicalization means creative activities provoking motivated physical behavior. Viola Spolin says an actor "can dissect, analyze, intellectualize, or develop a valuable case history for a part, but if one is unable to assimilate it and communicate it physically, it is useless within the theatre form" (p. 17). This chapter focuses on an exercise designed to flesh out personalization through physicalization; what I call "analysis through action." The following is not the only way to interpret Stanislavsky's "analysis through action" – others will describe this phrase differently – but it is my way of incorporating his intent to combine physicalization and personalization.

"Analysis through action" encourages the link between the senses and physical activity, the active work on internal and external features of creative expression, and places the actor in a situation that encourages urgency, emotional identification and physicalization. Stanislavsky defines this as the "correct actions in the progressive unfolding of the play: inner psychological actions and outer physical actions." According to him, "every physical action has an inner psychological action which gives rise to it. And [for] every psychological inner action there is always a physical action which expresses its psychic nature: the unity of the two is the organic action on the stage" (quoted in Gorchakov, p. 119). Inner life – the actor's personal ideas and passions connected to the role – is not antithetical to physical (outer) expression. To attain this combination of physical and personal, we must create "a scenic feeling of self." We link our experiences and feelings in the context of the scene, which leads to a "scenic feeling," not merely a "feeling." We must fuse our feelings with the given circumstances of the play. Maria Knebel, who has defined "analysis through action" more than anyone, said that, onstage,

> it is important to demonstrate truthfully exactly how a given character in a play acts, and this is possible only through a complete fusion of the psychical and physical self-awareness of a person. A person's physical life exists as psycho-physical self-awareness. Therefore, on the stage the actor cannot restrict himself to abstract psychological reasoning in just the same way that there cannot be physical movement cut off from psychical. Stanislavsky said that there is an inseparable link between scenic movement and the cause, the reason, that gave birth to it: between 'the life of the human body and the life of the human spirit' – full unity. (On the Action Analysis of Plays and Roles, p. 13)

Physicalization is based on the idea of an objective – what a person desires, covets, wants, needs. Referred to as the character's "spine" or "super-objective," it is used to ferret out actors' motives and turn them into actions – into active behavior. To know what moves them, actors have to take an inventory of their emotions. "You must know which stimulates what, what [is the] right bait to get the bite. You have to be the gardener, so to speak, of your own heart, one who knows what grows from which seeds. You must not reject any subject, any stimulus to your Emotion Memory" (*Actor's Work*, pp. 225–6). Actors have to know what excites them, being vigilant as to what inspires and activates their passions; and have to be alert to their imagination and what they invent. They have to ask themselves continually what moves them: actors cannot take anything for granted. *Everything matters*: what is your favorite ice cream, music, color, book, season and so on? What inspires your sense of justice, fair play or politics? What makes you cry, and laugh? Laughter often gets overlooked in the study of acting, but without it actors lack a sense of humor, lose their appreciation of irony, and fail to see how comedy can enlighten them about the human condition. These passions, moreover, *change*; the things that moved me yesterday may no longer move me today. Songs I listened to previously grow tiresome. It is the same with everything; one's feelings change because one's life changes. Keeping abreast of the triggers and inspirations is a vital part of an actor's daily routine.

This begins the actor's work on "objectives" – what human beings desire in their lives. I have heard acting teachers say "the play is not about you," or "you, the actor, are not the central feature of the play." But if the play is not about the person enacting the role, who, then, is it about? Certainly, the playwright guides the events, the director shapes the staging and interpretation of the play, the designer frames the space – but if the actor fails to make it personal and embody the role then it doesn't really matter who plays the role. Any "body" – a puppet, even – could fulfill the character.

To embody the role, we must embody ourselves: what moves us emotionally and physically? The goal or objective cannot be vague: for example, the goal should not be a need to "be smart." Being smart is abstract and relative: "smart" compared to whom? Einstein? To define someone as "kind and generous" is murky, attitudinal and stereotyping. "Generous" compared to whom? Mother Teresa? An objective can be the need to show kindness to someone (a specific target) because her demise is your fault and you wish to repair the damage you inflicted.

Playing an objective comes from life. Objectives are what is at stake in the role. The director James Nicola says that the best stakes "are drawn from life experience with which you identify" (p. 74). They derive from what people "covet." We all covet: success at work, finding romance, achieving fame and fortune, gaining approval of friends and family, winning elections and so on. We covet these things, and these desires move us forward, elicit emotions, make us active, and have stakes inherent in what they mean. Think about your life objectively. What do you covet? Where would you like to be? How are you going about getting there? Isn't this the same as a character's desires? Ask yourself why you do certain things. You must be clear about yourself before you can be clear about a character. If you don't know what you want, how will you know what a character wants? Don't be ashamed if what you want is greedy or selfish – characters are greedy and selfish, too. Find the things that stir you, move you, inspire you – these are tied to your needs. Be precise about what you want, what drives and motivates you to say and do the things you do. Be aware that your needs change. Don't be afraid to want love, companionship, recognition, joy, success, justice – the characters you play desire these things and unless you embody these needs and observe them in others you won't know what to apply to a role. Stanislavsky said "Look back at some stage or other of your life and recall what event was the major one in that segment and then you will immediately understand how it was reflected in your behaviour, in your actions, thoughts and experiences, in your relationships with people" (quoted in Knebel, On the Action Analysis of Plays and Roles, p. 14).

Knowing what people desire is the core of knowing human beings. There are many ways to define someone, but for the most part definitions such as height, weight, age, nationality, gender or ethnicity, while important, are only generalizations. What a person desires is what moves them forward, what defines their actions, and makes their individual choices unique. When students come to acting class, they are motivated to learn. A student wakes up in the morning thinking about what she will do for the class; she prepares mentally, thinking about the assignment and how to make it work. She goes about her daily tasks – brushing her teeth, eating, dressing, her day job and so on – but the inner need is focused on the objective: how to become a successful actor. The objective isn't always consciously in the forefront of our thoughts, yet it guides our activities and moves us forward in life. The objective defines us; it is who we are (even if we aren't always aware of it). If an actor wants to be a success, what are the ways she goes about achieving this goal? It is the same with a character; how does that character achieve what he desires? This is how one begins to link the actor to the role. First and foremost, we have to *know what motivates us*. The actor has to understand what it means to desire, want, dream and so on, *in themselves*. Bill Bruehl says "The purpose of behavior – the purpose of any activity on stage – is to express inner action" (p. 15). Inner actions, however, are not fixed ideas, but flexible ones: they incorporate other actors and events; operate in a fluid state; are able to adjust improvisatorially; and can sometimes take one step back in order to take two steps forward. The inner action or supertask, Stanislavsky said, should be "in the actor's personality, his imagination, his thoughts, his feelings, as firmly as possible" (*Actor's Work*, p. 311). Being creative, he adds, "means approaching the Supertask passionately, directly, intensively, productively, appropriately, and properly" (*Actor's Work on a Role*, p. 23).

Exercise 21: One Action/One Objective I

This exercise is derived from my work with Paul Mann and is designed to help actors practice analyzing their objectives "through action." It is meant to be enacted, improvised and performed before an audience. It should be treated as a piano player treats scales: to be practiced daily so that the actors' sensitivity and ability to execute objectives improves. Keep in mind that the exercise is a process; the following description it is not meant to be a formula for success or a drill in which pre-existing notions of acting are the goal. Nor is it tied to any role in a play; the exercise is my interpretation of Stanislavsky's "analysis through action." The point of the exercise is to execute, spontaneously, a task that has urgency, is personal, is done actively, contains high stakes, requires complete relaxation and concentration, and involves a physical object (no mime). The one action/one objective improvisation should be performed in the spirit of discovery and experimentation, and the actor *breathes fully and completely* throughout the exercise.

Create an improvised situation (given circumstance), in which you must attend to a damaged object or a task that needs to be completed. The activity (the task) consists of repairing the object, which means completing the task. Examples can be: putting on make-up, stringing a guitar, gluing together broken pottery, taping something that is torn, removing a stain from a shirt, putting stuffing back into a doll, or baking a cake. It must be something that is personal, urgent and important; it must be an activity that is physical, not mental (don't write a letter or compose music); you must do it in the theater space; and your objective (the reason why you are doing the task) is tied to the object: *the completion of the task means success, failure means loss.*

The object you have selected to be in need of repair (broken cup, torn shirt and so on) is real, physical and tangible (no mime). The object is endowed with importance to you: it is valuable to you; it has a deep personal connection to you or to somebody you care for. It requires attention or it will remain broken. For example, you need to glue together something that is broken. You enter the stage and you repair it. Really glue it: not half glue it, partially glue it, or accept any incremental repair. *It's all or nothing.* The activity is unfinished until the object is repaired. In the beginning, the object is broken; the middle is the process of repair; the end occurs only when the object is fixed.

There are no shortcuts to the task: if you are gluing something, it should be fixed as if it were new. *Not halfway new, not sort of new, not partially new, not new in general*, but specifically restored *exactly* as it was before it was broken. If you are blow-drying your hair, your hairstyle should be specific and not a random look. For example, you are designing your hair for a wig-making contest; you want your real hair to be the model for the wig designed in a specific contest that your significant other has entered. *You have betrayed your significant other and the only way to make it up to him or her (you hope) is by making your agreed-upon hairstyle exactly the way your lover wants it to be.* Fixing your hair is a specific action, a personal connection, and it is tied to an objective – making amends to your lover. If it doesn't look exactly as your lover wants it to look, you will lose him or her. You have a photo taken by your lover defining the way your hair should appear. You enter the room in order to arrange your hair accordingly. You can only prepare your hair in this room. You can't take the task elsewhere. It has to be fixed *here-now-today*.

Answer the following: How badly do I want this task completed? How important is it? What will I stand to lose if I fail to accomplish it? What will it cost me if I fail? These questions should be answered precisely and your choices should be images and thoughts that move you to believe in the situation. See the image of your lover: the disappointment, the hurt, the feeling of being let down by you. Let the simple image move you; her sad expression might be all you'll need to get your engine going. The objective must be *personal and justified*: you are doing it because it means a great deal to you. Make the task difficult but doable. String a guitar; clean a stain; make a birthday cake; stitch together a doll. Each action should be specific – you cannot cut corners. If you have to recopy something, recopy it *exactly so that one cannot tell the difference between the copy and the original.* Calligraphy is a great activity because the lettering allows no margin for error; it requires exactness of detail – specificity. It's either perfect or not.

Deal with real objects: doors, windows, drinking glasses, pens, paper and so on. If you look out of a window, then have something you see. Don't pretend there is a cab outside waiting for you; if there's no taxi then there's no taxi. (In a play you will certainly have to create things that are not there; but for now avoid mime and deal with reality.) Mime is a great art and can be incorporated later.

The one action/one objective *is in the room, in the theater space, in the here and now, in front of an audience.* The only place you can complete the task is *in the room or on the stage.* You must start from outside the room, enter, attend to the object, complete the task, and exit. You are coming from somewhere (an actual place), and you are going somewhere (an actual place in your imagination). Where you are coming from and where you are going to can be the same; what matters is that you believe in the truth of the situation. Make the space you are working in yours; believe the space is your dorm room, living room, kitchen – whatever you have chosen. Bring in as many props as you need to create believability for yourself; fill the space with things that will help inspire creativity and make you comfortable.

Everything is urgent: you're very late. You stand to lose everything you dream of and believe in if you fail, and all your hopes are tied to the object. You do not come on stage to play a scene but to attend to this one thing that needs your attention. Once it is completed, you must get to where you are supposed to be going. You may take the object with you, or you may leave it in the room, but you cannot fix the object in any other place. If it seems as though your task is nearly impossible to complete successfully in the limited time you have – given the fact that you are five hours late – then, and only then, is the exercise functioning properly. The near impossibility of the task increases your sense of urgency. You must accomplish the task even if it seems like a hopeless cause.

The reason why you are late is because of what you did. You are culpable. It is not because you were stuck in traffic, there was a train wreck, you over-slept and so on. No excuses: you are guilty of being late. Taking responsibility for being late won't let you off the hook. You are complicit in everything you do onstage. Chance and spontaneity will happen onstage, but chance will take care of itself. You must not only know why you are doing everything, you must also take responsibility for everything you do, even the screw-ups. There is something very sobering about admitting complicity. Excuses take us off the hook emotionally; the blame goes elsewhere; we don't have to feel any urgency because, after all, it "wasn't my fault this disaster happened." But as actors we don't want to get off the hook, but instead we *seek ways to put ourselves in situations that demand taking risks*. Taking responsibility empowers the actor, gives her the will to focus on what was done and what needs to be corrected *because she did it*.

Don't overact or push. Trust what you have worked on, trust that the need affects you, trust that what you believe in is operating in your heart. By working on this exercise you gain the most essential feature of acting or any art: *authority*. From the first minute you enter the room or the stage, you must move and speak with authority. You come into the room to do a physical (not mental) task and the success or failure of the action will determine the audience's feelings.

David Mamet writes that, because Method acting allegedly focuses on emotions over action, "the Method actor is excused from that sense of urgency which a desire for an actual performance career might entail, and is offered in its stead: guilt" (p. 109). There are charlatans teaching acting who are more concerned with psychoanalysis and fear-inducing experiences than in teaching acting. But this is not the Method's intent, nor has it ever been mine. The one-action/one objective exercise is all about action, desire and urgency; urgency is essential, allowing the actor to eliminate extraneous movements and wasted energy. The point of the exercise is *not to dwell on guilt, but to rectify it*. The action of fixing a damaged or broken object that will restore the actor's error is immediate, physical and doable; it is not self-indulgent, but outwardly active. The actor is not wallowing in emotion, but trying actively to fix something.

The benefits of this exercise (among others) are preparation, physicalization, entering the stage with purpose, and personalization. We learn from this exercise, in basic non-scripted fashion, how to discover an objective from something that is personal. We come into the room ready for anything: ready to change course if necessary and redirect our energies. We are prepared nonetheless *to do something* and this "something" is immediate, urgent and passionate. We learn to enter the stage with energy and focus. We are essentially saying to the audience "stop what you're doing and pay attention to me." Not because I crave attention; pay attention because I'm about to do something that has real stakes, urgency and investment. From the start of the actor's appearance onstage or onscreen it must be apparent that the audience is being offered something that is worth their while. And what they are about to see is personal and physical: it is an activity that has economy of movement (there is no need to do anything but fix the broken item) and means a lot to the actor.

Actors often perform the improvisation with huge goals: I will lose my lover, or I will lose my job, yet they fail to believe in the situation. As they perform, they lose focus and the urgency dissipates. That is because they are trying to make it truthful with general, grand, oversized expressions that lose credibility as soon as they start working. Work, instead, for little truths and specificity, what Stanislavsky called "small physical actions, small physical truths and moments of belief [that] assume great importance not only in simply passages, but also in very intense, climatic moments when you are experiencing tragedy and drama" (*Actor's Work*, p. 164). This exercise can be very intense; it holds the trap of histrionics and overacting. To avoid this mistake, Stanislavsky says, "you need to take hold of something real, stable, organic, tangible. For that we need some clear, clean, exciting but easily doable physical action that typifies the moment we are experiencing" (*Actor's Work*, p. 165). Trust that what you believe in really works for you. If it doesn't, try something else. If you think something moves you and you do the exercise and you are unmoved, then try something else. Feeling are elusive, fickle, unstable; the point of being an actor *is a constant and vigilant inventory of your emotional life*. Keep digging deeper into your soul; find what excites you; find what is at stake for you. Feelings change because you change; you must accept this and discover new things.

If failing to complete the task means you will lose your lover, then create something detailed and specific about the lover: their smile, for example. Don't try to believe in the giant-sized relationship but follow Stanislavsky's advice: use *simple truths*. It is astonishing how a small detail like a smile can trigger so much in us. If we are relaxed and open, breathing and allowing all of our body and senses to respond, the feelings of a smile will have a powerful impact. At the moment of heightened feelings, the physical object in need of repair increases concentration and helps us to avoid overacting. We endow the object with given circumstances and it feeds us honestly and correctly. If it is something to be repaired, we shall feel the truth of it; if it is falling apart in our hands, we shall respond accordingly; and if it is connected to a simple truth – the smile of a lover, for instance, because she is the owner of the object and you broke it – it will evoke deep feelings and creative imagination.

Don't worry about originality. You needn't derive the most inventive or unusual story. Too many actors begin this exercise by trying to be clever. Leave storytelling to the playwright. Our job as actors is to provide faith in the given circumstances that we invent, justifying the circumstances by making them personal. The exercise is meant to develop your belief in the situation, your execution of an urgent task, and your full commitment to the story you've designed. You must believe in the story because as an actor you must practice believing in many stories. Your belief will compel the audience's belief; your faith in the situation will prompt their curiosity; and your commitment will engage their attention.

Don't use objects that can hurt you, like sharp knives, broken glass and so on. And don't use anything that might endanger you or anyone else. Any improvisation that puts yourself or others in danger must not occur. Also, be alert and careful for tension. Everything you do must be performed with ease and relaxation. Intensity and concentration must not be confused with tension; passion is not squeezed out but experienced with ease. Breathe throughout. You also need not talk during the exercise, but if you do, that's fine. Most people curse; expletives are fine. But you don't have to tell us why you are doing it or what you are doing it for. *The point is not in the story, but in your commitment to the activity.* It is your belief in the story, not the story itself that is useful to the actor. The story is the playwright's job; your responsibility is to believe it. There is no time limit, either, but if the activity goes on for a long time, the instructor may stop it. This is not a bad thing, nor is it a negative reflection on the work.

Don't enter looking for something you lost. You will have to place the object somewhere before you start; consequently, you will always know where it is. No matter how hard you try to act spontaneously, you will always fake it because you know where the item is. As a result, you will lose the element of surprise that is integral to improvisation.

You do not have to rehearse the exercise, but you do have to think it through carefully. The more details you can create, the better it will be. You should be able to answer the following questions *in detail*: Where am I? Why is my activity – the object – so important? Why am I late? Where have I come from, and where am I going to? What are the given circumstances of this scene? How did the object break or become in need of repair? Why did I damage the object? What does the object mean: is it my best friend's "gold watch" and I broke it? Who is my "best friend" and why is she or he so important? Is it a priceless possession of his family, and I spilled something on it? Am I getting dressed for a special occasion, and have torn borrowed clothes, so I have to stitch and iron them? You don't have to have actual priceless objects; but you do have to have belief in that object as something priceless, something of value (an heirloom, a gift from a friend, something that belongs to someone you love and so on). Why is the activity so urgent? Why is fixing, arranging, preparing, rehearsing and so on, so significant to you? Most important, what will happen if you don't get it done? What will you lose if the task goes uncompleted? What will it cost you if you fail? And here reside *the stakes* – the great litmus test: the actor must ask herself: what will happen to me if I fail to accomplish the task?

Don't answer these questions mechanically. It will only lead to emptiness. Ask what is in your heart, what moves you, what excites you. Don't be afraid of the craziest things; bizarre thoughts come from wonderful places in your imagination. You're never going to tell anyone what moves you in any case, so throw caution to the wind. Have fun with the exercise (it's not an act of Calvinist labor).

An example: I am engaged to be married. The wedding ceremony is today. I love this person with heart, mind, body and soul. I plan a life together with this person. I also have a passion for motorcycles. I love riding them, cleaning them, attending to them, even building them from scratch. Unfortunately, my future spouse hates motorcycles; her brother was killed because of a reckless motorcyclist. To marry her I must swear *never to ride or even touch another motorcycle again.* If I do, the wedding is off. I agree. I'm on my way to the wedding rehearsal ceremony when my best man and I see a fantastic Harley-Davidson. It is owned by a mutual friend; it is a fabulous, gleaming, brand-new machine. I've never seen anything like it. We pull our car over and take a look. No harm, I think, in just looking. The friend with the bike starts the engine. It sounds beautiful, humming and churning. I lean into it to get a closer look and suddenly the engine backfires and splashes oil all over my tuxedo. The white shirt is stained with thick, oily grease. I try to get the grease out, but I don't have cleaning material. I get back in the car and rush to the ceremony; I'm already late because I'm trying to get the grease out; now I'm very late. *I have to remove the evidence from my shirt or the wedding will be cancelled.* I get to the place and sneak into the janitor's closet. There are cleaning paraphernalia: soap, bucket, cleansing fluids. I take off my white shirt and try to get the stain and smell out of it. This is my task – to clean the oil-soaked white shirt. Completely out: not partially, not so-so, not 90%. It's all or nothing. Now the task is invested with personal meaning. I have no excuses; I screwed up; I am responsible for selfishness and deceit. I can rectify the situation *only if I can remove the evidence.*

The exercise is now endowed with urgency, justification and physical activity. It is personal: I have made the situation mine and I believe in it fully (if you don't believe in your situation, discard it and find another). It is also invested in physical activity. Cleaning a stain from clothes cannot be executed mentally or abstractly. The success or failure is visible – the shirt is either clean or it is not. There is no middle ground (sort of clean), fudging (partial smell of oil), and way I can cover ("It wasn't my fault, honey – oil spilled from the heavens"). These are unacceptable excuses that will never fly. I did it and that responsibility informs my emotional life and my active behavior. The spontaneity of the exercise will surprise you. If you trust yourself, believe that you are in a private space, and give your feelings free rein, fascinating things will emerge. Your focus on the object increases concentration, sharpens urgency, and makes the action clear. The object will either cooperate or not, and therein lies the improvisation.

Another example: I suspected my lover was cheating on me. My lover is an archeologist and has applied to the best graduate archeology program. The only way for my lover to get into the program is to present a priceless artifact – a cup from ancient times – and lecture on its whereabouts and history. I read my lover's diary – or I thought it was her diary – where I discover betrayal. I broke the cup because I wanted revenge. *I deliberately smashed it.* My lover, knowing what I did, is catching a plane to a faraway place, giving up her quest for graduate school. I find out from my lover, however, that the diary was fictitious, part of my lover's notes surrounding the cup. It had nothing to do with my lover's activities, but was related to the presentation. I broke the cup for *the wrong reason*; I cost my lover a chance to get into the most prestigious graduate school in the country, and I dissolved our relationship – all because of *my mistake.* I must come into the room where the cup is, a room where the graduate school teachers are going to observe the presentation. I must repair it perfectly; I must then get to the airport and stop my lover from leaving. If, in the process of gluing the cup, it starts to look good, I react one way. If it falls apart in the process, I react another way. My feelings will change throughout, but the objective never changes: fix the broken cup.

If the actor fails to complete the task a part of her dies. In this sense the task is life-and-death. Not literally, but in some sense if we don't achieve what we want a part of us dies. If we fail to woo a lover, for example, something in us dies. We lose our dreams of spending time with that person; our sense of what we would do together for ever melts away. People find ways of coping with this; psychologically we learn to live with less, desire less, want less. We rationalize our way out of loss by saying there are other things we can have, other ways of enjoying life, other people to desire. "Plenty of other fish in the sea," we tell ourselves, to ameliorate the hurt. Our rational side dictates ways of mitigating rejection; our survival mechanisms operate to relieve pain and encourage us to forget. But drama, serious or comic, is about people coveting more than the ordinary. Acting is about something extraordinary, demonstrating vulnerability by revealing, in the moment, what we stand to lose. If we try but fail, our vulnerability is visible.

The one action/one objective exercise is meant to distill a whole life into a clear, simple (but not simplistic) action that is physical, doable and enriched by given circumstances, urgency and focus; and it is goal-oriented. From the one action/one objective exercise you will learn what an objective and an action are in a disciplined manner. You will do it for now, for the present, for the immediacy of the activity, and for disciplining yourself to learn how to perform actions.

You will learn to justify activity and the importance of personalizing; and you do it physically. The urgency will affect your emotional and physical state, and you will experience a range of feelings. You will learn to enact objectives in front of an audience, in a spontaneous atmosphere, free from the restraints of a text, play or director. You will learn the craft of coveting that you can then apply to a role, play and production. You will learn spontaneous behavior; there is no guarantee that your task will succeed. The feelings are invested in the object, and the object's state or condition will dictate your emotional response. The object is the obstacle; its broken-ness, or unfinished-ness, is what you must overcome.

One of the biggest difficulties with the exercise (and acting in general) is rationalization: since the task is so late and accomplishing it under these circumstances so trying, many students say "there is no way I can do this successfully." Or "I would never place myself in this kind of situation." But we do place ourselves in compromising situations (we just don't want to admit it). The actor must understand that it is not the success but the trying that matters. Juliet knows the family feud prevents her from having Romeo; if she were rational she would give up for now (she's 13) and wait until she is old enough to marry Romeo without parental consent. Her family wants her to marry Paris; if she were logical she would marry Paris and then at the age of 18 get a good divorce lawyer, separate, and marry Romeo when they are of legal age. But Juliet's coveting – her passion – is irrational, powerful and larger-than-life. The actress must find the passion, the part of herself that drives her toward this one crazy action, this one irrational objective: having Romeo. Before she can play the part the actress has to understand what irrational behavior means to her personally and physically by the process of analysis through action.

Human beings are flawed and it is the job of the actor to demonstrate weaknesses, lusts, wants and shortcomings. People act irrationally, do things against their own best interest, betray those they care about, make embarrassing romantic overtures, and set in motion (consciously or subconsciously) situations they would rather avoid because as human beings they are not always thinking "straight" or behaving logically. People lose their sense of equilibrium, get themselves into situations over their heads, and make bad bets. Dramatic characters – comic or serious – do foolish things; their folly is fodder for the art of theater. This is what makes them funny and sad, crazy and fascinating to watch. The smart thing to do is to walk away from conflict; this is recommended in general to allow people to get through the day. But dramatic characters do not walk away; rather, they hurl headlong into disaster. The one action/one objective exercise is designed to flesh out these crazy experiences, to perform them through physical activity, and try to make amends.

Exercise 22: One Action/One Objective 2

After you have worked on the one action/one objective exercise repeatedly (I did it 100 times before I began to understand it), you are ready to move to the next step. This involves working with a partner. The following is a modification of Meisner's knock on the door exercise.

The exercises requires two people. Actor A performs the one action/one objective as before (in Meisner's work this is called the "independent activity"). Actor B enters the room about 10–15 seconds after the first person. Actor B is still doing the one action/one object, but now instead of an inanimate object the first actor is the "objective." The aim is to get the first actor to leave the space for whatever reason the second actor justifies. The only requirement is that the actors use the repetition exercise (Chapter 4, Exercise 20).

Here's an example: Actor A enters the room to string a guitar. The guitar will be used for an important audition. Actor A is late for the audition; she must use new strings to make the guitar sound strong and powerful; the space is the waiting room for the audition. Actor B enters the room. Actor B is the first actor's father. He doesn't want Actor A, the daughter, to audition. He wants her instead to go to medical school. The objective for Actor B is to get actor A to leave the room and go to the first day of orientation at medical school. In preparation for the exercise, the actors understand the circumstances in the scene and agree on the situation. But rather than talk about the situation in the improvisation, they only use the repetition exercise.

The goal for Actor B is to *persuade* Actor A to go along with him. The objective is to get Actor A to leave willingly with him; the action is the how and the way that Actor A is convinced. Acting is, among other things, a process of changing someone else; if I am Actor B, I want my partner to be persuaded by my entreaties to leave. I want to convince her to do something that she would not ordinarily do. Merely taking someone out of a room physically doesn't require acting, but simple brute strength. I may *wish to carry her out* – in fact the desire to just grab her is vital and good. But I need Actor A to come willingly; so forcing her, however much I may want to do this, will undermine my objective. My obstacle is the fact that Actor A needs to do her one action/one objective (her independent activity) in the room. She will not go with me because she has her given circumstances. I have to persuade her that my needs are greater than hers.

You might ask: how can I persuade her to leave without words? Don't words matter? *Not as much as actions.* How I persuade my partner will tell me everything about the relationship, the give-and-take, and the communion-ensemble between actors. Anyone can say words; just about anyone can memorize texts; but it is the way in which actors develop relationships that makes acting a living, moment-to-moment experience. By asking actors to stay with the repetition exercise, the skills of developing relationships is enhanced and practiced.

The relationship between the actors is vital in stimulating impulses. Each actor gives to and receives stimuli from the other actor, creating reactions that are truthful, spontaneous, immediate and existing in the here-and-now. The behavior results from the response received by the other actor rather than being a pre-planned notion of how to act. The exercise allows the actor to avoid intellectualization. As Meisner put it, the exercise eliminates "all that 'head' work"; it takes away "all the mental manipulations and gets to where the impulses come from" (Longwell, *Meisner on Acting*, p. 36). Larry Silverberg says that the repetition exercise allows the actor to move "towards fully being with another human being;" the aim of repetition is in "becoming fully available to your partner, authentically responsive to each moment" (pp. 42–3). The actions must emerge from relationships; by working with the partner, active listening and behaving, nothing is taken for granted. "An ounce of behavior is worth a pound of words," Meisner often said, because acting is about behavior in relation to other behavior.

In the exercise the actors should discuss with each other the given circumstances. The actor doing the independent activity should tell Actor B what her situation is. This is because the actors should not revert to storytelling. It is easy for Actor A to say "You see what I'm doing, and you should know it is very important!" Or Actor B to say "Come with me now because so-and-so is dying." The other actor can easily reply "But what I want is more important because my story is much more important than yours," but with that no relationship evolves. This behavior leads to rationalization; the actors simply resort to logic, hunker down in defensive postures, and lecture each other. Only through *actions meant to change the other actor* can a living relationship onstage be exciting. By using the repetition exercise, the actor can only report what they see; they can only deal with the reality of the other person's behavior. They cannot resort to story. Story is cerebral, behavior is emotional. Story is fictional; the other person is real. Story is based on rational explanations ("I need you to do this because …"); the repetition exercise encourages organic give-and-take. It is based on what is actually before the actors, not invention.

Another example: Actor A comes into the room and is gluing an expensive vase that she broke. The vase belonged to her sister and the actor thought her sister had betrayed her in some specific fashion. It turns out that the betrayal was untrue, and the destruction of the object was unnecessary. Now she must repair it to look as if it had never been broken. Actor B needs Actor A to be her witness that she didn't cheat. She will be forced to leave school if she is convicted of cheating and the only person who can save her is Actor A. Both actors already know the story; there is no need to repeat it. Repeating the story leads only to lecturing, hectoring and discussion. The scene begins, but rather than using words, behavior, actions and observations are brought into the foreground.

It is important to add that Actor A would, if she didn't have her own pressing need to repair an object, help Actor B. It is too easy for Actor A to ignore and dismiss Actor B. Actor A might grow so annoyed with Actor B's persistence that she wants to push her out of the room, but this is only because that feeling emerges spontaneously from what ensues. The relationship is a loving one, which makes the refusal to help all the more moving and exciting.

David Mamet writes, as Stanislavsky said, "Don't touch it unless you love it" (p. 88). Despite his consistent criticism of Stanislavsky, Mamet returns repeatedly to Stanislavsky's wisdom. Stanislavsky realized that acting can become self-indulgent, and the way to subvert narcissism was to place the focus outward, on to objects and people. The point of the one-action/one-objective exercise is to develop a relationship to things and people, such that you fulfil Mamet's mandate of loving an object or another person. The repetition exercise should, furthermore, not be worn as a badge; it is not a policing activity to be used to condescend to actors who are unfamiliar with it. Instead, it is used as a tool enhancing observation and enriching relationships onstage. We must engage our fellow actors in ways that are loving, caring and engaging, even if they are moral foes in the play. In the next chapter, we shall examine ways of engaging with other actors with greater variety.

6

ACTIONS AND SIX
BASIC ACTIONS

In 1996 I watched Uta Hagen in Nicholas Wright's play, *Mrs Klein*. The story involves a mother-and-daughter conflict. In the climactic scene, Mrs Klein (Hagen), a psychiatrist, and her daughter, Melitta, argue over the work of another psychiatrist, Edward Glover. Melitta has submitted herself as a therapy patient to Klein's rival, Glover. Klein detests Glover; according to her, he sold out to undignified procedures. On discovering her daughter's actions, Klein, according to the stage directions, *"grabs scraps of Melitta's letter out of the wastepaper basket,"* and says, "Eat these. Eat these. I'll stuff them down your throat. Poisoner. Eat. Eat." The stage directions add: *"She hits and attacks Melitta"* (p. 47). In performance, Hagen literally tried to shove the papers down her throat. It was an astonishing moment. Her action was to reject her daughter's words by making her eat them. The action of shoving papers down her throat was rehearsed and choreographed; like stage combat, it was orchestrated to avoid real harm. The important point is not to do harm *but experience the intent.* Hagen despised the rival analyst and viewed her daughter's act as a betrayal. Her action was palpable, physical and thoroughly motivated. Hagen pulled the actress's head back and stuffed the pages into her mouth. Only her assistant, Paula (the third character in the play), stopped her. This is "organic action" – action properly thought out, justified, personalized and physicalized.

Actions are the bread-and-butter of acting. They clarify objectives and move the trajectory of the play forward. According to Strasberg, "Actions, to be of any value, must suggest something that the words themselves do not necessarily imply. Actions are not simply physical or mental, but physical, motivational, and emotional (*Dream*, p. 77). Actions are physical, but this does not mean movement merely for the sake of moving. Even in stillness we can pursue actions. We can be motionless yet still convey intense inner action. Stillness and focus are powerful actions. The following are principles of what I call "six basic actions."

"Action" as described here means the active pursuit of an objective through physical behavior. "Action" is *the physical, emotional, psychological and active pursuit of objectives*. "Action" is not the same as "super-objective," which means the desire or goal that a character seeks. The distinction between "action" and "objective" is a matter of semantics, so it is important that I define what I mean: super-objectives are the characters' *life needs*, the overarching desire for the whole play or film; while objectives are the *goals* of a character in a particular scene. Actions are *the means by which these goals are obtained*; and intentions are the *small tasks associated with each line of text or behavior*. Each of the terms is interrelated and follows what Stanislavsky calls the line of development tied to the "wants":

> This line, and the tasks which create it must not be dead and mechanical. It must be living, vital, truthful. You need *exciting ideas* (*magic 'if,' given circumstances*). They, in turn, require *truth and belief, concentration, wants, etc*. They are all interconnected and create one whole 'creative state' out of the various elements. (*Actor's Work*, p. 587 – Stanislavsky's emphasis)

Actions are the tactics we use to obtain goals. Claus von Clausewitz's *On War* contends that the aim of a politician is ultimately to win (overtake the enemy in toto), and war is one of several means to this end. He writes that the "political objective is the goal, war is the means of reaching it, and means can never be considered in isolation from their purpose." As a result, "war should never be thought of as *something autonomous* but always an *instrument* of policy" (pp. 87–8). Similarly, actions are an instrument aiding the move toward the actor's objective; actions are not an end in themselves, but rather a means to it. The word *action* derives from the Latin *actio*, which means to do or carry out something. The *Oxford English Dictionary* describes action as the "process or condition of acting or doing." Every action has to be supported by the actors' personal investment. Maria Knebel insists that the actor "descends to the level of ordinary commercial acting when he uses only the text, only the words" (*Stanislavski Today*, p. 54), and Stella Adler maintains that "Every physical action has an inner action, and every inner action has a physical action that expresses it psychological nature. The unity between these two must be organic action on the stage" (*On Ibsen*, p. 103). The words of the play are not the first order when defining actions; it's the reverse. As Adler contends, "Inner justification is the thing that belongs to the actor," adding, "Provoke action through justification. Justify it without the words, because the words stink" (*On Ibsen*, p. 301). The words come from the action, and the action from the objective. The objective is what the character wants and the action is what that character does to get it. Doug Moston adds this important coda: "Action is the soul of acting! It is the single most important concept to understand and apply properly. 'Properly' meaning responsibly, economically, and artistically" (p. 2).

Young actors are frequently fixated on character at the expense of the action. An actor will censor actions because she might say "But my character wouldn't do this or that." As a result, performers are often limited to some preconceived (and predictable) notion of character, unable to "do" something because they think they are being "truthful" to the "character." Character becomes an unchangeable description – "the angry young man," "the maternal type," "the domineering boss," and so on – thus encouraging stereotypes. But the opposite is true: actions define character. We are what we do (and not necessarily what we say). Actors will say "I'm playing a nasty person, so I will act nasty." This creates the worst form of generalization that has nothing to do with being a three-dimensional human being. Actions allow characters to be liquid, flexible and spontaneous, rather than rigid and one-note. Strasberg makes this clear when he says that "In making use of 'actions,' three steps are necessary: (1) *action*, what are you doing; (2) *motivation*, why are you doing it; (3) *adjustment*, under what circumstances. The last decides the form in which the action is carried out" (Acting and Actor Training, p. 161). Adjustments mean that actions should come *from relationships*; the actor adjusts according to the scene's give-and-take. Yoshi Oida says the same thing: "remain open to the other actors. Don't fix your attention to any one aspect of the performance. Allow yourself to respond to your fellow performers, and then you will discover how your character reacts" (p. 40). Actions are tied directly to living, breathing human beings – scene partners or the audience – and are something you do to someone because you want something from them. In this way, actions allow the performer to "become," rather than to "be," the character. Actions permit fluidity and spontaneity, since relationships *change organically*.

Actions are also something you follow through. They're not "on" the line, but continue before and after the line and into the next line. You can perform actions while another performer is speaking; you need not stand stone-faced until it is your turn to speak. This is not to suggest that you upstage the other actor (moving while she speaks, say), but rather by active listening. It means avoid rushing; to hasten over things means you are not really doing them, not really listening. Take the time to do the action and to see if your actions are affecting someone else. When you ask someone "What time is it" you have to wait for an answer. Your action is tied to the response, to the consequences of your action. "Stage acting is the fulfillment of tasks," Vakhtangov says (*Vakhtangov Sourcebook*, p. 252), and each task must be justified, motivated, adaptable to changing circumstances, and actively pursued.

Actions, however, are not merely the doing of something. An anarchistic approach to actor training leads to confusion. There are numerous acting books that list "action" verbs. They often appear in some form of glossary. The verbs might be arranged alphabetically or classified under a certain rubric (actions for the "body," actions that are "personal," and so on). At best they are listed according to "good and bad" verbs, separating passive (intransitive) from active (transitive). Actors often select actions *à la carte*. Directors and acting teachers might comment on which "actions" appear to "work." Everything depends on a general feeling of what "works," though frequently what works is hit and miss. Actions are too often selected on the basis of what supports the words of the text and the intellectual construction of the character rather than the human relationships between people. These actions, usually imposed by a teacher or director, are considered to be unalterable because they appear (or seem to appear) in the text. Thus the text, not the actor's imagination or the interrelationships, make the selection. This way of thinking suggests that the actor is merely a spokesperson for the text. Certainly, the actor interprets the author's intent; but the word "interpret" means a personal investment. The glossary *Actions: The Actors' Thesaurus*, edited by Marina Caldarone and Maggie Lloyd Williams, provides a list of action verbs. While the book is useful, it sends a mixed signal: any action verb will suffice. Like ordering in a restaurant, the verbs are selected from a menu and picked according to the taste *du jour.*

Once actions are selected, lingering doubts remain. How are the actions selected? Why were certain actions selected over others? Beginning actors in particular might seek actions enthusiastically, yet often pursue them one-dimensionally, either repeating the same action that seems right according to their intellectual and literary sense of the text, or picking an action comfortably within their range. The problem with the former is that the selection is like a quiz, with the actor selecting as in an academic exercise; and the problem with the latter is the actor's dependence on verbs she has used throughout her life. The choices lack variety. For example, an actor prone "to accuse" will pick this action repeatedly; every time she acts she will accuse her partner. Her verb, to accuse, is organic and convincing but redundant. The actor needs to find an action that excites her and pursue it passionately and energetically. But the single action, derived from habit, is limited. If the actor is asked to find another action, she will hesitate, flounder and apply something that is inorganic and false. Until another action is made habitual through repetition there will be difficulties.

As with bike riding or swimming, when we first ride or swim we're wobbly; it is only through practice and effort that we obtain balance. It is the same with actions: at first we struggle to find their contours, the way we can make them personal, and eventually they become instinctual. However truthful we might be, if what we do to persuade or affect others is the same action continuously our work will be predictable and boring. Using verbs from a grab-bag does not constitute talent or art, either; it is merely formulaic and will fail to help actors increase their range and temperament. I want to consider ways of expanding the actors' range by expanding their repertoire of actions.

An actor must have a range of actions. Shifting behavior adroitly surprises the audience with sudden changes in emphasis and emotion. Watch a good actor and you will see sudden changes, seamless yet always motivated; the new action will surprise yet it will still follow the logical of the objective. Vera Soloviova notes that "the more talent the actor has, the more colors on his palette" (Reality of Doing, p. 222). To portray carnality, vengeance, compassion and so on – all of the behaviors that make up a complex and multifaceted performer's palette – the actor must increase her repertoire of actions. This is important in training actors, because teachers need to increase the range, temperament and spectrum of students' choices. Actors need to do this to attract the interest of audiences, not only at the start, but through the whole course of the play or movie. Employing one or two actions is insufficient no matter how convincing they are. Encouraging a variety of choices is crucial in developing actors. It is essential that the teacher maintains a rigorous focus on the manner in which actions are applied and practiced.

The way to break the habitual pattern of using the same actions is first to accept that an actor must sometimes impose unfamiliar actions in pursuing objectives. I offer six basic actions – to beg (or plead); destroy; seduce; dominate; celebrate; and accuse – as a means of exercising a broad range. In *Female Brando,* Jon Krampner's biography of Kim Stanley, he says that Stanley offered four actions, or "needs": "The need to destroy, the need to seduce, the need to seduce in order to destroy, and the need to celebrate" (p. 290). This list is, unfortunately, incomplete. Stanley was very clear, at least during my two years in her class: there are six actions, she said, distilled for maximum effect. There are many more actions an actor can play, of course; you should not ultimately restrict yourself to these six. However, these are fundamental for several reasons: *they force the actor to stretch; they are bold and theatrical; they are interpersonal; and they are free from text.*

First, the six basic actions encourage actors to change their tactics and perform the actions with a broad brush stroke. It is bolder to celebrate another person than to "enjoy" them; to celebrate implies an expansive, physical activity rather than a timid one. To seduce is bolder and more theatrical than to "charm" or "cajole." The six basic actions foster active, physical behavior and theatricality; there is nothing tentative about them and they therefore encourage actors *to take on bold initiatives.* By practicing these repeatedly the actor's range of actions increases. It is important that actors exercise actions to which they are least accustomed; in this way they can flex their creative muscles in the safety of a classroom.

Second, the six are radically different; moving from one to another encourages actors to try new tactics, thus increasing their palettes and stretching their sensibilities. The way to do this is have the actor present all six actions in an improvisation (more on this shortly). Third, all six demand another person to be the receiver; these actions cannot be performed in a vacuum. You need another actor, an audience, or an imaginary object to focus the action – a target – to borrow a principal term from Declan Donnellan's book, *The Actor and the Target.* Finally, they are untethered from a text. To play these six actions does not require a text. To perform an action "to steal," for example, implies a text: stealing what, from whom? There is a story involved. Certainly, if the play demands that the character steals, then the action "to steal" should be pursued creatively, imaginatively, personally, physically and urgently. However, before we can derive actions from the text we *have to have a text.* These six can be performed immediately and vividly; you don't need a text or a story to work on them, you just need two or more people relating to each other. In this manner, ensemble work is exercised, engagement with other actors is encouraged, the actions affect another person, and the actors understand that the *actions come before the words.* This last point cannot be stressed enough: just because you say something, it doesn't mean that you are pursuing actions. The actions are meant to bolster the actor's confidence in performing actions physically rather than cerebrally (in the head).

Exercise 23: Six Basic Actions

Drill these six actions until they become organic, habitual and spontaneous. The text that follows, beginning with definitions from the *Oxford English Dictionary* (*OED*), defines the actions.

To beg: "to beseech a person to do something." *To plead:* "to make an earnest appeal, entreaty, or supplication" (*OED*). One begs (or pleads) in order to instigate something, or see to it that another person accomplishes something. We plead with others as a way of elevating their status. It is a humbling action, one that requires us to place the other person in a position of power. Actors often resist this action; few of us want to place ourselves in supplication. It is important for actors to use this action as a way of eliciting vulnerability and exercising openness.

To seduce: "to persuade (a vassal, servant, soldier, etc.) for allegiance or service" (*OED*). Seduction doesn't necessarily mean sexuality; politicians and salesman seduce. We seduce people into buying things; we use seduction to gain the upper hand. When we seduce, our voices change: we tend to become mellifluous and resonant. Of course, to seduce also implies sexual enticement and should be used, like the other five actions, focused on the target.

To dominate: "to bear rule over, control, sway; to have a commanding influence on; to master" (*OED*). Dominate is often the flipside of beg; it places one in a position of authority, power and assertion. Status is reversed; the actor comes from a place of strength and power. We seek our objective from positions of authority.

To destroy: "to pull down or undo that which has been built; to demolish, raze to the ground" (*OED*). To destroy is not necessarily harmful. We destroy a part of a person who is self-destructive. For example, we destroy when we see a close friend abusing drugs or alcohol, or when someone is in a bad relationship, and we get involved; we rescue them by destroying the destructive part of them. Or, we destroy a part of ourselves in order to convince someone to do something. We make a bargain: we'll stop doing something if someone will do what we ask.

To celebrate: "to perform publicly and in due form (any religious ceremony, marriage, a funeral, etc.); to hold (a church council); to solemnize" (*OED*). Kim Stanley often said in class that this is the least understood and one of the hardest actions to execute because our culture discourages celebration of others. To celebrate means to love, cherish and adore others; to make them feel that you are glad to be alive and in the same place as they are; and that you honor them. One celebrates another by acknowledging they are glad to know the other person, recognizing the other's strengths, virtues and good qualities. The difficulty with this action is that it requires kindness, an act that can lead to unpredictable consequences. Kindness risks mingling one's needs and desires with the needs and desires of others in a way that self-interest never can. By involving one's own needs, the situation is potentially more promiscuous than sexuality. Society warns us against kindness because it has the potential to be taken advantage of; or, we are often skeptical of kindness and cynical of celebration because they imply an ulterior motive. Yet by closing ourselves off from kindness we shut down an interesting and emotional-laden action, one that involves empathy and compassion.

To accuse: "to charge with a fault; to find fault, blame, or censure" (*OED*). This is often the easiest action, because we live in a culture where blaming others for our faults is commonplace. Still, some actors do shy away from this. Accusing is forceful action; like the others, it has a strong interpersonal dynamic.

Actions to avoid: "to mock," "ignore," or "hector." Human beings perform these actions every day and you should certainly use them when necessary. They tend, however, to disconnect you from your partner and they don't cost you anything; there's hardly any risk or vulnerability involved. If you "mock" someone, it's unlikely she will give you what you want, unless you want her to leave you alone, which isn't a risky or bold choice. To "ignore" also shuts down connections. In Michael Shurtleff's *Audition* (still the best book on auditioning), he too advises against ignoring: "Playwrights are fond of putting 'She ignores him' in stage directions. This is a trap for an actor." Ignoring your partner, he contends, is a "passive choice; it inactivates you"

(p. 169). If you "hector," you become patronizing and self-righteous. Hectoring often leads to shouting at someone, which is a big turn-off for the other actor and for the audience.

One of the best examples of using all six actions is Tilda Swinton's performance in the 2009 film, *Julia*. In the fifth scene (on DVD) she goes to the home of her friend, Nick Costello, to persuade him to join her in a kidnapping scheme. The first moment Swinton sees him she "celebrates." She hugs and kisses him; her action, to celebrate, is physicalized; she is celebrating the friendship in order to make him feel warm and accepting. Underlying the urgency is her need to bring him along with her plan. Everything in her behavior is invested in celebrating him (action) in order to gain her objective. She's not playing action for the sake of an action, but because of her need – her objective – and because of the way the action affects the other actor. Watch how she then shifts from celebrate through the other five actions: seduce next, then destroy, dominate, accuse and beg. Throughout she is improvisatory, spontaneous, reading his behavior, reacting to him, and actively, physically pursuing her actions in order to gain her objective.

Action is not something done in the mind or passively. Action is active, a doing to someone or something. A passive attitude "kills stage action," Stanislavsky reminds us, because it produces "inertia, wallowing in one's own feelings, experiencing for experiencing's sake, technique for technique's sake" (*An Actor's Work on a Role*, p. 137). By finding a focus (person, animal, object, mirror, God) for the action, the action must adjust to suit the target. The best actions create behavior, stir physical activity, and, according to Stanislavsky, "[grip] the actor's feelings immediately as unconscious emotion and [lead] him intuitively to the purpose of the play. Such unconscious, emotional tasks are strong because they are immediate (the Hindus call tasks of this high order superconscious), exciting the creative will, unleashing its forward thrust" (*An Actor's Work on a Role*, p. 139). The actor must not follow slavishly the actions given to her from the play or the director, but rather should discover how to translate what is read on the page or provided by the direction into a personal, individual and entirely meaningful connection. Anyone with speech can say and memorize lines from the play; anyone who can walk can follow blocking; it is the creativity of the actor that turns the words and movement into something personal, provocative, compelling and moving.

Learning New Actions through a New Instinct

> We like to think that instinct is something totally different from knowl-
> edge and understanding. We believe that the bee and the spider and
> the other engineers of the animal kingdom perform by instinct and
> automatically, without any need to learn the things that we do with the
> aid of our brain, consciousness, and will, and only after much elabo-
> rate study. This is only partially correct. Even instinct does not oper-
> ate altogether automatically, and the things that we do deliberately are
> not totally divorced from instinct. (Feldenkrais, p. 71)

The goal of the six basic actions is to make them available for
the actors' use as a way of establishing new habits, knowledge and
understanding. This is what Feldenkrais means when he says that
instinct is connected to learning. We can learn new instincts. "Fake
it till you make it" is a cliché, but it is useful to actors as they learn to
enlarge their palette of actions.

Exercise 24: Mirror/Action Exercise

The point here is to increase your "palette" – your range of actions – so that
you approach your objectives with greater variety. Focus on your weakest link,
practicing the action you find least comfortable.

Begin with the mirror exercise. As described before, the two actors face each
other, one leads a series of movements and the other follows. Then the lead
changes hands. You both commit to the mirror exercise, exchanging leads, until you
have developed a sufficient relationship – an understanding of the other person's
movements and feelings. The relationship develops based on your experience of
the day. If one of you is sad, it should be used; if upbeat, that too should be observed.
Discovering your partner's state of mind is essential and must be established
before moving ahead.

You then work on tossing an imaginary ball to each other. Start with a simple tennis ball. You have to trust each other by following the trajectory of the
object as it is tossed from one to the other. Focus, relaxation and concentration are encouraged as you each follow the other actor's eye, body and hand
movements. The imaginary object then changes: it becomes a medicine ball,
a feather, a bunch of keys, a scarf, a towel and so on. This carries on until you feel
you are both comfortable with each other and with the belief in the imaginary
object.

At this point, cease tossing the imaginary object and instead say "Come to me." You should be about six feet apart, facing each other. You are free to move, but shouldn't touch. The phrase "come to me" means that you are both beckoning. Since you have worked on the mirror exercise and the tossing of the imaginary object, you now assert an objective, a desire to have the other actor come to you. Repeat the phrase "come to me."

After you are comfortable saying the phrase, use one of the six actions. Apply the action but remain with the same phrase "come to me." By doing this the actions are "distilled" – you can practice and value the specifically chosen action without reliance on a text. For example, dominate your partner by using the phrase "come to me" and discover a variety of gestures, inflections and ways to dominate. Exercise this action until it's time to insert another. Find the truth in each action – in other words, perform the action to the best of your ability, and as sincerely as possible. Some of the actions will be more difficult than others; this is OK and the point of the exercise: practicing the actions until they become comfortable.

Practice all six actions over time. I recommend at least ten minutes for each per day, for at least a month. Once you have mastered each, you are free to try any one of the six or more. It is recommended with advanced students that the actions can be inserted in the one action/one objective exercise, repetition exercise, or anything else. *The point is to increase your range of actions in any venue.*

Always vary the use of these six. The class is a laboratory unencumbered with judgment, so practice actions you tend to avoid, building up confidence in their use until the unfamiliar ones become comfortable, spontaneous and familiar.

As you grow in confidence with the six actions, more advanced work begins. This is called "layering" the actions. Layering is the process by which you apply two or more of the six actions. For example, you might accuse, leading to celebrate, and further, to persuade the person to "come to me." This should only be incorporated after a considerable time – at least one year – when you and your fellow actors have developed the six actions (and others) to a level of proficiency demonstrated through comfort and instinct. The work is still based on the improvisation "come to me" with the added dimension of layered or multiple actions. Using two (or even more) actions at once creates depth in the actor's work, while mixing the actions is akin to an artist mixing colors, creating a dynamic palette and multiple arrays of expression.

Applying the actions to texts should occur only *after* considerable attention has been paid to developing the actions without text. The more an actor invests in a variety of actions, the more versatile they become; but the point is not variety for variety's sake alone. The actions must first be organic – the way one learns to swim or ride a bike, for example, so that they are *in the body* and not an intellectual activity.

Finding Beats

Beats or units in a scene are generally breaks where an actor changes her action in order to achieve her objective. They might occur simultaneously with your scene partner, but this is not mandatory. By and large, you should have about four to five beats in one scene (some scenes may have more, some less). Beat or unit changes do not occur on every line. You would want to play your action to the point where you feel it has exhausted its possibilities. The change can occur in the text – sometimes these changes are obvious. But the change should ultimately come from your partner – that is, through reading behavior, where you can see when the action has worn out its welcome and a new action is required.

The actions are distributed through beats, or divisions in a scene or improvisation. But don't rush to set beats. You should go over the scene by yourself and with your partner dozens of times before even thinking about dividing the scene into beats. Many of the beats will surface naturally; you will see where they belong as you grow familiar with the scene. There is a natural tempo-rhythm to a scene, based on the given circumstances, the urgency of the situation, and the relationship to the other character(s), which will inform your decision. Don't merely rely on the text as written, but on the unspoken. Don't lock into a decision, either – let the scene flow in you and in your response to your partner. Only then will the beats come organically, and not be imposed artificially by intellectual choices. Only when actors have developed an organic relationship can the work move into beat consideration within textual analysis. Look for a change in the way the language moves. Does it appear that the character is trying something else to obtain the objective? Look to your partner – does it appear that she has taken a new direction, a new beat, and you might want to catch her change and add a new one yourself. Observe the surface physical actions in the scene as well as the words – actions such as closing a window, getting a drink and so on. These can also suggest a change in action.

Fleshing out the beats and personalizing your choice of actions helps actors to avoid what I call "playing the other actor's action." This happens frequently when an actor, unsure of what to play, or impressed by the other actor's choices, imitates what she sees. It's the mirror exercise gone awry. For example, one actor becomes agitated and starts to raise her voice, then the other actor, seeing her partner becoming overheated, also raises her voice; the same actions square off and the actors have created little more than a shouting match (you can see this often on soap operas, where actors have limited or no rehearsals). Or, their voices grow soft together and they both whisper to each other. When actors play tit-for-tat the scene is devoid of variety and connection to the given circumstances. Each actor is simply mirroring the other in place of their choices, character's objectives, and the situation's given circumstances. When actors consider their beats and their vulnerable positions in the scene, each will work to convey their own personal investment in actions rather than in copying what they see.

Beats should not be set in stone, but neither should it be jettisoned at every whim. Beats are developed through rehearsal. Test them with your partner. The greatest value of beat changes is that they enforce more variety in your performance. They demand a change in your behavior, adding to the variety of ways that you act, react and pursue your objective. Changing actions by delineating them in terms of beats prevents your acting from being one-note and monotonous. Think of it as different colors or musical chords, variation in your pursuit of the objective that adds dimensions to your performance. In all the work, spontaneity derived from improvisation sets the tenor and tone of the work. The next chapter explores improvisation and examines its origins in actor training.

IMPROVISATION AND JAZZ ACTING

Now it is a very difficult thing – and even now a rather uncommon
thing – for an actor who knows exactly what he is going to say to behave
exactly as though he didn't; to let his thoughts (apparently) occur to
him as he goes along, even though they are there in his mind already;
and (apparently) to search for and find the words by which to express
those thoughts, even though these words are at his tongue's very end.
(Gillette, p. 132)

A story about the legendary jazz singer Billie Holiday might be apoc-
ryphal, but none the less illuminates her emphasis on improvisation.
In the 1930s, Holiday begin taping in recording studios when acousti-
cal methods were rudimentary. Lacking computers, sound engineers
adjusted levels manually. Levels were agreed prior to the recording
and manipulated when the recording took place. Holiday rehearsed
a song with the orchestra in one way but once she began recording
she would shift emphasis; phrases previously sung forcefully were
softened, while others rehearsed softly were intensified. She didn't
change the notes or words, simply shifted the emphasis, but her
improvisation set levels off-kilter, and the sound engineer had to stop
and start again. However, when the re-recording began, she changed
the emphasis again. Finally, an exasperated sound engineer emerged
from his glass booth and said "Billie, you rehearse it one way. I set the
levels. Then you sing it another way. You can't do that. You have to
do it the same way every time." Holiday responded ruefully: "Honey,
I don't feel it the same way every time."

This story chimes with William Gillette's comments, quoted above, written in 1915. He raised the idea of "doing something for the first time," even before Stanislavsky. Performers express emotions as if for the first time despite their knowing the text, having rehearsed the scene (or song), and are aware of the play's conclusion. Stanislavsky, too, remarked that "Man is not a machine," and

> he cannot feel a role the same way every time, be stirred by the same stimuli. He feels the role differently every time, and sees the facts that are fixed in the play differently from yesterday. The minute, imperceptible changes in the approach to the facts are often the greatest spurs to new creative activity. Their strength lies in the fact that they are new, unexpected, and fresh. (*Actor's Work on a Role*, p. 133)

Stanislavsky was adamant that fresh discoveries lead to a reappraisal of the given circumstances, prompting in turn a livelier, more immediate, and more organic performance. Actors experience the role as if for the first time because they are always improvising, always alert to new and spontaneous moments, always living in the here-and-now.

Feeling a situation differently every time is a technique emerging from several sources. It is considered to result from the Stanislavsky system and is an integral part of the American Method, signifying a new and spontaneous way of working. Michael Redgrave recognized this change when he noted in 1953 that "In New York some of the best young actors and actresses under Elia Kazan have formed the Actors Studio where they practice physical movement and voice exercises and where a great store is set on improvisation" (p. 54). Meisner's repetition exercise (examined earlier in the book), Lee Strasberg's gibberish (the actor's using gibberish instead of words to convey actions and relationships), and Stella Adler's paraphrasing the text are some of the many useful improvisatory exercises for actors that are designed to evoke spontaneity. Keith Johnstone and Viola Spolin are some of the best known teachers of improvisation. Still, there is another influence that has been overlooked all too frequently.

Improvisation can be described, among other things, as the influence African American actors have had on American acting and performing worldwide. In music, of course, but also in poetry and writing, jazz exerted enormous power. Jack Kerouac, for example, was inspired by the spontaneity of bebop, dubbing his writing methods "blowing" or "sketching." While credit has been forthcoming to actors such as Brando, Dean, Stanley and the next generation

(De Niro, Hoffman, Pacino, Streep, Penn and others), few acting books or teachers credit African American actors and their influence on the art of acting. By using Billie Holiday as an example, I shall examine the phenomenon I call "jazz acting," giving long-overdue recognition to African American performers.

Jazz Acting in "Time"

"Jazz acting" is a method of improvisation that is sensitive to the here-and-now of existence in time. Time is crucial in jazz acting, because time and improvisation are inextricably linked. Improvisation exists in and through time; a good improviser must be aware of the temporal changes in scene partner, situation and feelings. When improvising in this way there is a double demand on conviction. An actor must conjure up the past as it informs the present through sense memory, given circumstances, motivation, personalization and justification; but the actor must at the same time be attuned to the immediate moment, regardless of what the past contains, willing to change everything and reinvent herself spontaneously. Jean Benedetti refers to this as Stanislavsky's "knowing child" – a combination of innocence and awareness that can also describe jazz acting:

> Stanislavsky often referred to the openness, the naivety, of the child. The process of becoming an actor is, in a sense, the process of becoming a child again, doing everything as though for the first time. I need to be as open as a child exploring a new world but, at the same time, I have consciously to experience myself, to realize what is happening in my own mind and body, my organism, so I can use it as an artist. I must be a knowing child. (Benedetti, *Stanislavski and the Actor*, p. 14)

In jazz acting, many emotions and reactions are required. One-dimensional performance cannot include jazz acting. Dance historian Brenda Dixon Gottschild refers to this phenomena as the "Africanist aesthetic," a concept of the "encounter of opposites." Rather than smoothing out contradictory impulses, conflict is embraced, as, for example, the heated passion of a performance with "the aesthetic of the cool, since coolness results from the juxtaposition of detachment with intensity" (p. 13). Jazz acting is multidimensional, spontaneous and surprising, blending many contradictory facets (cold and hot, for example) to create a multilayered experience that defies resolution and closure. In jazz acting, time extends both inwardly and outwardly, because embracing multiple ideas requires a deconstruction of rigidity.

To be a jazz actor you have to be loose, open, contingent and, above all, spontaneous. No matter what you predetermine your actions to be, you mustn't cut off spontaneous behavior. While actors may want to chart out a course through a play or film, they mustn't lose the potential for surprise. If you decide your reactions beforehand and stick to them no matter what, you fail to allow them to emerge organically from the stimuli of the moment, from other actors, or from other unexpected events. Like jazz itself, acting should sustain spontaneity and retain the element of surprise. Vakhtangov's description of spontaneous feeling describes jazz acting superbly: "I do not want the actor to ever perform a particular place of his role the same way, with the same degree of intensity. I want those feelings, and their intensity, to be truthful to today's performance; I want them [feelings] to arise in the actor naturally, on their own accord," and in this way the actor "would improvise the entire performance" (*Vakhtangov Sourcebook*, pp. 211, 212).

Jazz acting demands that every performance be a new, fresh creation born from living through (experiencing) the role, not merely the result of hysteria, pre-packaged ideas, or the mechanical re-creation of yesterday's performance. Yet it also demands rehearsal and practice. Daniel Belgrad writes that jazz jam sessions "offered a forum in which to practice improvisation. The fact that improvisation must be practiced need not be taken as a paradox. Improvising jazz solos does not consist mainly in inventing new licks, but in stringing together learned licks and references in new and appropriate combinations" (p. 180). Jazz improvisation absorbs previous music and refreshes it with a new context; it doesn't reject past melodies but rather reshapes them, sometimes changing them altogether, based on new connections in the ensemble. The great jazz saxophonist John Coltrane's rendition of *My Favorite Things* faithfully remits the basic melodic line of the original song yet, in midstream, takes flight with a jazz riff that leaps and moves into adventurous rhythms and original insights. Coltrane does not violate the song but rather creates a new dynamic with it; without losing touch with the melodic line he instills new meaning by introducing surprising twists and turns – in short, improvising. The song, like a script, provides the framework for the actor. This is the heart of jazz acting: first construct a frame, and then break out of it. In this way the performer enacts a moment of liberation, something beyond the ordinary and commonplace. Coltrane's music – dissonant chords, startling shifts and complex rhythms – always manages to swing hard yet still respects the melody. Using Coltrane as a model for dynamic acting, Susan Batson observes that he transforms *My Favorite Things* "into an organic, vivid, and totally personal creation," and that "Acting has to have the same feverish, risky, seat-of-the-pants, orgasmic life found in a Coltrane solo" (p. 234). Batson is one of the few acting teachers who recognizes jazz improvisation in relation to acting. Inserting new scales as the primary basis of improvisation, Coltrane, Miles Davis and others pioneered changing cycles of dense and sometimes dissonant tones. Improvisation was not just moving away from and around the form, it was a new way for musicians to create a new key or scale without sacrificing the music's rhythmic roots. Like a good anthropologist, Coltrane studies the song *My Favorite Things* and then reinterprets it; he respects its history but also brings it up to date with contemporary rhythm. Jazz acting, likewise, is the ability to layer a performance with past conviction and current immediacy, building on a passionate identification with the material, an emphasis on spontaneity and ensemble, an anthropological study of the role and its context, and moment-to-moment creativity. Jazz themes were a cultural connector of style, a cross-pollination throughout the arts, and Billie Holiday's work can demonstrate the values of jazz acting.

Holiday's influence can be traced not only to singers who have emulated her phrasing and musicality (Frank Sinatra and Sarah Vaughan are prime examples), but also to acting: she is the benchmark of excellence in conviction, believability, improvisation and spontaneity. When we think of great actors of the 1950s – Dean, Brando, Montgomery Clift, for instance – or the novels by Jack Kerouac and Norman Mailer, the poetry of Allen Ginsberg, the art of Jackson Pollock, de Kooning and other abstract expressionists – we observe artists deeply influenced by jazz and its rhythms, freedom and emphasis on ensemble, emotion and spontaneity. Brando and Dean often prepared for scenes by playing bongos, Pollock would often listen to jazz for days before painting, and de Kooning and Franz Klein were also jazz aficionados. Actors have been influenced by jazz, and jazz was a great resource for African American actors in the twentieth century. Notwithstanding the great white jazz artists (Bix Beiderbecke and Gene Krupa, among many others), jazz was nurtured and developed primarily by African Americans. Jazz, with its roots in African American music and culture, can to a certain extent be considered an extension of black history and experience. Three phenomena emanating from jazz affected acting: jazz cool, jazz time and jazz improvisation.

The Three Basics of Jazz Acting

"Jazz cool," which was picked up by the Beat Generation (who in turn influenced the Hippie Generation), signifies historically the black rebuttal of racism's depiction of minstrel tomfoolery. It demonstrates the performers' "cool" attitude or refusal to perform according to certain preconceived expectations. It was a performance mode resisting the continuity of (and stubbornly enduring) nineteenth-century minstrel tradition of white actors dressing up (blacking-up) as black clowns. Minstrelsy represented the overdressed and exaggerated stage (and later film) caricatures of white actors in blackface make-up. From the 1920s through the 1950s, "cool" took root as a fearless stand against racism; if black people were deemed to be simpletons – over-emotional, childlike, and irrational – jazz cool challenged this by demonstrating intelligence, maturity and restraint. The cool musician, writes jazz historiographer Marshall Stern, "refused to play the stereotype role of Negro entertainer, which he rightly associated with Uncle Tomism" (p. 221). Jazz artists characterizing "cool" often turned their backs on the audience, letting their music serve as the link between performer and spectator. By turning their backs, the musician's face was no longer the focus; instead, the music – with all its complexity and subtlety – was communicated. Jazz actors likewise personify rebelliousness and defiance. Brando was famous for turning his back on the audience, experiencing the moment with complete spontaneity and unconcerned about audience approval.

The resistance to flashy showmanship translates into a new sense of rhythm. Jazz is offbeat, downbeat and unpredictable – the individual creativity defying the norm. "Jazz time" is an art form stressing freshness, which translates into the creation of a new tempo and rhythm – a new sense of time. By focusing on an immediate reconfiguration of time, modern jazz actors challenge conventional rhythms by reconfiguring time; the performer is not "on time" but rather "in time," sensitive to the existing moment. Charlie Parker created sounds that seemed to dilate time; it wasn't just the speed of his fingers that made his performances compelling, but also his mental agility, his ability to hear and produce chords with an extraordinary compressed and vivid sense of the moment. Actors need this agility in the moment, responding faster than the ordinary person. The social critic Amiri Baraka observes that jazz musicians "have used the music of the forties with its jagged, exciting rhythms as an initial reference and have restored the hegemony of blues as the most important basic form in Afro-American music" (p. 225). Jazz harnesses energy through controlled yet spontaneous rhythm, giving shape to passions and demons that are lurking beneath pain and frustration.

For jazz actors, time is given a nonconforming rhythm; the actor's tempo is personal rather than regimented; spontaneity occurring with jazz time is engaging and surprising. Peer pressure, culturally induced biases, or what is called the normative effect in which certain behaviors are transmitted across a network of societal conventions, influence conventionality and conformity. Jazz trips the wires affecting these conventions; it coalesces around an ensemble but consistently respects the individual. Jazz improvisation is not, as music critic Albert Murray says, "winging it," or making things up "out of thin air." Rather, the performer "improvises within a very specific context and in terms of very specific idiomatic devices of composition." Improvisation appears at the "moment of truth," the "'break' where you 'do your thing.' The moment of greatest jeopardy is your moment of greatest opportunity." Jazz acting is risky and improvisational "when you establish your identity; it is when you write your signature on the epidermis of actuality. That is how you come to terms with the void" (p. 112).

The actor's rhythm is tied to the ensemble but also to the actor's individuality. African dance is often based on both the ensemble and the individual; the group moves collectively until someone breaks out and performs then returns to the group. Along these lines, the actor has to know her own rhythm and the rhythms surrounding her; our heartbeats change daily, and so too must our sense of rhythm. An actor's sense of time has to be razor sharp, attuned both to her heartbeat and to the rhythms of others (as the cliché goes: timing is everything). It takes great coordination to observe and then respond freely, spontaneously and improvisationally. According to Stanley Crouch, jazz "supplied a new perspective on time, a sense of how freedom and discipline could coexist with the demands of ensemble improvisation, where the moment was bulldogged, tied, and shaped" (p. 191).

Lee Strasberg says that "The actor's task is to create that level of belief on stage, so that the actor is capable of experiencing the imaginary events and objects of the play with the full complement of those automatic physiological responses which accompany a real experience" (*Dream*, p. 132). Billie Holiday echoes this when she says "I can't stand to sing the same song the same way for two nights in succession, let alone two years or ten years. If you can, then it ain't music, it's close-order drill or exercise in yodeling or something, not music" (quoted in O'Meally, p. 105). Robert O'Meally subtitles his book *The Many Faces of Billie Holiday*, because each picture of Holiday represents a different characterization and identity. O'Meally points out that "her art is rich with palpable, dramatic, lived experience" (p. 11). The key feature of her acting – and what every actor should emulate – is conviction and lived experience; Holiday represented conviction in every song she sang and every time she sang it. "She could make you *visualize* a song in a way that was just so clear," said singer Carman McRae. Record producer Milt Gabler observed that "She got *inside* of a song," and music critic Ned Rorem remembers hearing Holiday becoming so wrapped up in her performance that he wondered, "Is this person going to get through this song? She's so involved ... her eyes closed, her head back. It's pure theater" (quoted in O'Meally, p. 43). Holiday's performances were invested in the events of her songs, so much so that when she sang it was as though she was living the experience *for the first time*. Alfred Appel writes that, when Holiday sings George Gershwin's *Summertime*, her "passionate recording makes you believe that they could conceive a child" (p. 151). This sense of making us "believe" something is actually happening is the benchmark for excellence in acting, and few performers carried this conviction with greater strength than Holiday.

Holiday's performance appears to invent a new tempo with each song. Known for her laid-back style – waiting for the last second to come in with the words – she worked both with and against the orchestra. She played with the ensemble but asserted individuality through her unique use of time. She actively used improvisation in her performance by listening to both the rhythm of the orchestra and to her own feelings. Her moment-to-moment sense – the actor's ability to live in the present and react to every detail – characterized her work. Her performance "existed" for the moment – she took responsibility for her feelings and lived them as they unfolded. We can see this influence in the film work of James Dean and Marlon Brando. In the movie

East of Eden, Dean tries to please his father; his objective is to gain his approval. Dean presents his father with money he has earned through his own initiative. When it comes time to show what he has accrued, his father (played by Raymond Massey) refuses it, suspecting the money was gained illegally. Dean is mortified by this rejection; he approaches his father with the money clutched in his fists and tries to put it into his father's jacket pocket. Dean improvises; Massey has no idea Dean would approach him that forcefully and with such emotional intensity. One can confirm this by viewing the way Dean leans into Massey and Massey backs up into the camera, the camera knocked askance because the scene had not been rehearsed that way and the camera operator too was surprised. The director, Elia Kazan, had the sense to keep the film running and capture the improvisatory moment. Kazan also had the sensibility to keep the camera running in *On the Waterfront*, when Eva Marie Saint accidentally drops her glove in the playground and Brando picks it up, puts it on his hand, wears it and uses it for his objective. Brando uses the accident to his advantage. As Stanislavsky says:

> If the actor has his wits about him, if he doesn't get confused or try to ignore the accident but, on the contrary, makes it a part of the play then it becomes a tuning fork for him. It provides one true living note in the midst of convention-bound theatrical lies, it recalls the real truth, it draws the whole line of the play to itself and obliges you to believe and to feel the thing we call "I am being". (*Actor's Work*, p. 338)

For Holiday, Brando, Dean and others, a felt sense of truth and living in the moment came from improvisation.

Living or improvising in the moment can only derive from a sense of faith in the world of the performance and cannot occur when the actor seeks approval. An example of this is a hypothetical story I heard from Lee Strasberg. He describes a speculative situation of what it means to be truthful and to commit to jazz acting (even though he doesn't call it that). The example goes as follows: examine two actors playing the same role. Imagine, if you will, that one actor is playing the role on the East side of town, the other on the West. Imagine the impossible: they are in the same show, directed by the same person, and the other actors are the same – for argument's sake *everything is equal* (same cast, set and so on) except that they are two different actors playing the same role. Now add the fact that the role requires a disability. The text mentions the disability, the characters refer to it, and the plot hinges on it. After both shows finish the audience on the East side of town begins to exit the theater. One audience member says to another: "Did you see the actor's disability? It was so believable. I was so impressed by the actor's work." The audience on the West side of town simultaneously leaves the theater. One audience member says to another: "I never knew the actor was disabled, did you?" There is a subtle difference here. The first actor seeks to impress; she represents the disability rather than experiences it. For Strasberg, there is something inauthentic in the performance that seems to say "see how good I am." The actor's truth, however carefully crafted, is the need for approval. Sam Kogan notes that these actors behave in this way "Because they acted as though they were being watched. Their thoughts were on what the audience thought of them rather than thinking the character's thoughts" (p. 8). As actors we want to be loved and accepted, but we must resist that because it obscures the character and what she is experiencing. The desire for accolades infects the performance, seeping in subtly yet forcefully, creating a block to the truthful core of the performance; it becomes the objective itself. It is akin to Grotowski's concept of *via negativa,* a technique aimed not at "a collection of skills but an eradication of blocks" (p. 17). The idea in Grotowski actor training is to eliminate blocks and get to the core of the human experience. Grotowski wanted actors to wear rags rather than bourgeois uniforms such as shirts, slacks, skirts, jeans, ties and skirts, to remove the accoutrements of respectability and conventional life. For the second actor in Strasberg's example above, there is no such influence because the actor is living through the moment, improvisationally. "Only the living create the living," Stanislavsky said, "and so no dazzling theatrical effects, no stage convention however beautiful, nor the principle of representation itself will create anything live" (*Selected Works,* p. 163).

Billie Holiday as Jazz Actor

Billie Holiday was often compared to singers representing Strasberg's ideas of believability; conviction is the criteria that critics frequently use to separate her performance from others. Musician Bobby Tucker, for example, compares Holiday with her contemporary, Ella Fitzgerald. He remarks that "When Ella sings 'My man he's left me,' you think the guy went down to the street for a loaf of bread. But when Lady sings, you can *see* that guy going down the street. He's got his bags packed and he ain't *never* coming back" (quoted in Blackburn, p. 178). Tucker's exaggeration notwithstanding (Fitzgerald is better than that), his main point accentuates the defining feature of Holiday's artistry. When you listen to Holiday, the depth of her conviction – her believability – is palpable; the line between performing and real life is eradicated. With Holiday, audiences follow the subtext of her feelings because they engage with her consummate presentation of voice, gesture, imagination and immediacy; what you see and hear is the presence of her feelings *at that moment*. There's no fakery or attempt to impress, no effort to represent feelings, but rather a truthful sense that this is what she feels, regardless of whether you like it or not, at this moment. She is *in time, not on time*. In performance she draws a picture suggesting that she is living *in* the story's tale, not *on* it. Frank Shiffman, who ran the Apollo Theatre when Holiday performed, said that "Sometimes you listen to a performer, and every fiber of the performer's body seems to be incorporated in what she is doing. It is not only the voice, you feel what the person is saying or singing comes from the innermost depths of her being – this was one of Billie's characteristics, and this is the thing which endures in the minds of people who remember her" (quoted in Chilton, p. 148). There is hardly a better description of acting than this.

It can be said that great performances are compellingly unpredictable. Holiday's performances have multiple timbres, tones, pitches and rhythms that are ineffable; it is hard to pin her down. There is a restless energy to her singing, as witnessed by the constantly changing tempo and key signatures that mark her work. Pathos is mixed with repulsion; humor combines with violence; and sexuality is potent and bisexual. Surprise, irony, comedy, innuendo and double entendre circulate through her voice and expression. Holiday's performances are shy, serpentine, commanding, calculating, vulnerable, sensual, caustic, ironic ("God Bless the Child That's Got His Own"), tender ("Good Morning, Heartache"), emotional ("Lover Man, Oh Where Can You Be"), compassionate ("Don't Explain"), defiant ("Ain't Nobody's Business"), and seething ("Strange Fruit"). As an actress she conveys multiple meanings depending on the moment, and virtually every delivery is saturated with innuendo and allusion to race, love, individuality and compassion that are, emotionally, at the same time both clear and enigmatic. Holiday trades on our desire for access to forbidden knowledge. John Levy, her bass player, said that "When you listen to her sing, you feel she has lived that experience and she is tell-ing a story about it" (quoted in Blackburn, p. 192). She has "been there and back," an eyewitness reporter, whose joy and suffering guides us through the murky path of living. She allows us to observe her from every angle: as a lover, fighter, down-and-outer or rebounding from love's loss. Musicologist Gary Giddens contends that Holiday's art-istry can be measured in the language of musical technique, "in her use of legato phrasing, ornamentation, melodic variation, chromati-cism"; yet the primary aspect of her singing is "emotional" (p. 91).

Alongside emotion is her minimalism, what I call "economy." Holiday sings economically, without pretense, affectation or exces-sive gesture. O'Meally contends that Holiday jettisons "facile fakery"; hers "was jazz singing of incredible sparseness and economy, of embel-lishment without the glare of grandly electrifying candelabra but with instead the light of a single searing candle" (p. 32). This is precisely what Stanislavsky meant when he insisted that the actor "Get rid of excess gesture and the really characteristic movements will stand out with much greater meaning and strength, like good wine that hasn't been watered down" (*Actors Work*, p. 537). Barney Josephson recalls that, when Holiday "sang 'Strange Fruit,' she never moved. Her hands were down. She didn't even touch the mike. With the little light on her face. The tears never interfered with her voice, but the tears would come and just knock everybody in that house out" (quoted in Clarke, p. 165). Holiday's acting abilities gathered together the complexity of meaning and shaped it into searing emotional intensity through lack of pretense. In the song "Strange Fruit," Billie Holiday gives a rendi-tion that is riveting. She achieves this by having an emotional rela-tionship with the song that comes from a distinctly personal place. The words follow her deep passion about the subject because she has justified the words before she even sings them, and does so without embellishment, without calling attention to her acting.

Stanislavsky said that actors "must set the play to the music of their own feelings and learn to sing that music through the lines they are given to speak. Only when we listen to the melody of the living heart can we fully appreciate the worth and beauty of the text and what it contains" (*Actor's Work*, p. 403). Improvisation opens the heart to the immediacy and rhythms of the moment. At the moment of perform-ance, Ingrid Monson notes, "all the musicians are constantly making decisions regarding what to play and when to play it, all within the framework of a musical groove, which may or may not be organized around a choral structure" (p. 81). In performance, as with jazz, you have to be both disciplined about the work and relaxed about not getting it right; you have to be able to embrace the changes spontaneously yet avoid excessiveness. Never do more, never do less; never overreach, nor underplay. Stanislavsky describes similar acting where there is "no rush, no hysteria, no tension, no forcing the tempo." On the contrary, he says, in good acting there is "concentrated, majestic, quiet calm, a lack of haste" which enables the actor "to do everything thoroughly" (*Actor's Work*, pp. 547–8). Like Zen archery, you hit the bull's eye when you stop thinking about hitting the target. If approval, validation, anticipation or "performing" is what you want, that will become your objective. Stanislavsky observed that the actor must work from the creative "now" without anticipation:

> No other artist can possibly have so clear a conception of the unrepeatable fleeting moment as the actor, for the actor must in that fleeting instant of time grasp the full significance of a remark or of a sudden impulse of his intuition and promptly incorporate it in his part. Never again will he get exactly the same flash of inner illumination, for it is only in that 'now' that he has acquired all the powers that are active in him; his own personality is no longer a hindrance to him, and he has attained what is rightly called inspiration, that is to say, the harmoniously active powers of the mind and the heart, freed from all the influences of everyday life, except those given in his part. (*On the Art of the Stage*, pp. 152–3)

A good improviser, says Keith Johnstone, isn't worried about originality, because the events before her are the living, original moment. An artist, he says, is living in the moment and "accepting his first thoughts" (p. 88). Spontaneity requires a keen sense of awareness that the moment is everything. "No specific choice is more important," Harold Guskin says, "than the true presence of the actor on stage at that moment. The actor, alive on stage, with his humanity – his feelings, his thoughts, his imagination – intact, is the greatest gift he can give the audience" (p. 116).

There is an old adage among performers that actors should never work with animals or children because both are too spontaneous and their improvisation will upstage even the most seasoned veteran. They don't know how to fake it and they can't take direction. They will steal the scene because their spontaneity overshadows an actor trying to hit the mark, reading lines or catching the cue. Rather than being in the moment, actors too often think ahead, trying to listen for the cue, remember the blocking, or play the scene as they did before. The animal or child have no such concerns; they behave impulsively. In the film *The Godfather*, Marlon Brando begins the movie with a kitten on his lap and he ends it in a vegetable garden with his grandchild. I am convinced he did this purposely and defiantly, as if to say to the world "watch me defy the adage, because I am being just as spontaneous and naïve as the cat and child." Brando keeps his concentration on the objective, never stops listening to the other actors while simultaneously stroking the kitten and playing with his grandson. This is because he understands that acting well means combining discipline and spontaneity, focusing on objectives yet open to surprise and most of all deeply relaxed so that his physical expressiveness is never impeded.

Exercise 25: Nursery Rhyme Exercise

This exercise is designed to improve justification of the text in an improvisatory setting.

Take four lines from any nursery rhyme and create a scene based on the text. You must justify each line of the text but the whole creation is performed spontaneously. Why are you saying the words? To whom and for what reason are you speaking? What is the urgency? Where are you coming from, and where are you going to? What is the task, objective, goal? The point of the exercise is to develop justification from four simple lines, transforming them from words on a page to an improvised life.

- Why are you saying the lines? What is at stake? What is urgent?
- Personalize the material. To justify something is to make it personal, whether this personalization comes from your life, observations or imagination.
- You may use as many people from the class as you wish. Tell them their roles, but do not tell them how to react.
- If you're asked to participate with someone else, you are expected to bring all of your technique and work to the stage. You're not merely fodder for another actor; you are an actor, too, and must begin to incorporate a character, circumstance, why you are here and so on.
- Bring in real props; items that mean something to you that have real weight, value, and three-dimensionality. Each image is like a prop too; real things that have happened are specific.
- In life, you recall props and images in all their detail and specificity. So make the same reality for your characters. They deserve the same amount of detail as you have in your life, even if that detail is imaginary. In fact that's exactly what they'll be, because

the events of the character's life didn't "actually" happen. They happen on stage. But in your imagination they happen, and on stage we work from our imagination.

- Wear the appropriate clothes for the scene. Don't come to work, as Stanislavsky says, "with muddy feet. Clean off the dust and dirt outside, leave your galoshes, your petty cares, squabbles and irritations, which complicate your life and distract you from your art, at the stage door" (*Actor's Work*, p. 557).

- The four lines must be distributed in the order in which they are written. But, the rhythm may be broken up. For example, "Mary had a little lamb." You can point to someone who is "Mary." It might be in a courtroom, and you're trying to convince a jury of Mary's innocence. You can say "Mary," as if you are telling the jury who she is. Then you can tell the jury that she "had a little lamb." The "lamb" could be code for a "child." Don't take the words literally if you don't want to; provide subtext. The important thing is that *the words mean something to you*.

- You begin not with the words but with the situation. Where are you coming from? How did you get here? What are the details that brought you here?

This exercise is a warm-up to dramatic texts. It helps to create justification and stakes in something close to gibberish. Remember: Unless there is something at stake for you, this is merely an exercise in illustrating a scenario. Create a story, indeed, but you are also required to have a deeply personal investment in this story. Without personal commitment you are just a replaceable part on an assembly line. The story is not just in your head, it's in your heart and body. If it's in your head, then you might as well just *describe* the story to us. Your task is to embody it and to react to any surprise. Improvisation, Lee Strasberg, says, "leads not only to a process of thought and response, but also helps to discover the logical behavior of the character rather than encouraging the actor 'merely to illustrate' the obvious meaning of the line." He emphasizes the point that actors get confused when "during scenes for which they were praised, they were aware of having thoughts unrelated to the play." This is because the actor's thoughts are hers: they are her unique stamp on the role. The important point is that "it does not matter so much what the actor thinks, but the fact that he is really thinking something that is real to him at that particular moment" (*Dream*, p. 110).

The Mantra

To make the objective organic, the actor must create an inner monologue. An inner monologue, writes Sonia Moore, "is the continuous thinking of the actor as the character he portrays. The way one thinks is an essential part of human individuality. To create a character, the actor must build in his mind the individual logic of his thought" (*Stanislavsky Today*, p. 49). This can be referred to as subtext. Subtext, inner monologue, images or thoughts are what the actor invents to trigger a chain of emotional, psychological and physiological actions. These actions in turn contain immediacy and develop real impact on the mind and body. To facilitate this process, the actor must exercise what I call a "mantra." Mantras involve the objective, the "I want," couched in a phrase reflecting desire. Stanislavsky said that there should be "no soulless, emotionless words in the theatre. Neither should there be unthinking, actionless words. Words must excite all manner of feelings, wants, thoughts, intentions, creative ideas, aural and visual images, and other sensory experiences in the actors and their partners and through them, the audience" (*Actor's Work*, p. 402). Before we can speak the words of the text, we have to put desire into our own words. The mantra needn't be an elaborate statement; it can be an expletive, a prayer, a sound or a grunt. But it must be something the actor believes in.

Exercise 26: Come to Me

Practicing the mantra, start with the phrase "come to me" (see the explanation for this in Chapter 6). You say "come to me" with the intention of actually having your fellow actors come to you – to follow, embrace, do as you say, or whatever you feel when saying "come to me." The phrase is spoken aloud at first, then silently, using only gesture. The important thing to do is to put it into your body, making "come to me" a part of your physical expression. Doing it silently helps you to physicalize the expression.

You and your fellow actors also use the space. Divide the stage in half, with one actor at stage right and the other on the left, then move about freely on your side of the stage, being aware of your physical presence and gaining confidence in your body and voice as you move about. Remain connected to your task and objective, however, always focusing on the physicalization of your needs and wants. The mantra is now incorporated into your body, soul, mind and sinews; it is organic and freely expressed. You are exercising spontaneous wants and creative aims. These, as Stanislavsky noted, stimulate "creative goals, which in their turn begat inner impulses (urges) to action, action resulted in embodiment and that produced a creative act. All these wants, endeavours, and actions resulted in a legitimate creative moment in the life of a role with its central task [main through-line objective] (*Actor's Work on a Role*, pp. 148–9).

Use the mantra in the one action/one objective exercise. Instead of the repetition exercise, substitute the mantra. The actor entering second would say "come to me," and you (committed to the task in hand) would say, "Come to you. Come to me." This exchange would go back and forth. At first you can verbalize it, but eventually can only say it internally, using the repetition exercise alone as the text. Eventually, drop the words and simply have the mantra become part of your physical activity – in you body and vocal behavior. Then return to the repetition exercise, but you will now be doing it with an objective underscoring your actions.

The development of mantras must be encouraged slowly, carefully, and without the need to "get it right." Maria Knebel makes the following observation: "It is necessary *that the actor on the stage should be able to think in the same way as the image created by him thinks.*" To accomplish this, the actor must "fantasize interior monologues to yourself" and "penetrate more and more deeply into the thought process of the image you are creating. These thoughts need to feel intimate, familiar, to the performer" (On the Action Analysis of Plays, p. 42). To find the familiarity and intimacy actors need to improvise, to feel a freedom of activity and action that can only come with a depth of experience of the character's life. The final section of the book, which follows, applies all the ideas presented thus far to the way in which an actor might perform a role.

PART III

PERFORMING THE ROLE

8

LIVING THROUGH AND INTERSTITIAL SCENES

My point of entry for a lot of characters tends to be their shadow. I'm a big believer in the notion that our greatest potential lies in our darkest parts. To a certain extent it's only in facing those parts of ourselves that we can truly grow, and I think that's true of all of the characters I've played. (Quinto, p. 6)

The actor Zachary Quinto quoted above is defining the idea of "living through." Stanislavsky's concept of "experiencing" or "living through" (the Russian word is *perezhivanie*) is one of the most significant and often overlooked parts of his technique. "Living through" for Stanislavsky, Sharon Carnicke says, "creates the role anew at every performance in full view of the audience." Such acting, she adds, "however well planned and well rehearsed, maintains an essentially active and improvisatory nature" (p. 173). "Living through" means the actor's complete embodiment of a role such that the presentation creates a three-dimensional human being shaped imaginatively and inventively, and living in the moment – not in the mind or in the role's preconception, but *actually experienced before an audience.* It is an embrace of both the character's life and his "shadow" – his dark secrets and mysteries.

In the *Dictionary of Theatre Anthropology,* Franco Ruffini's essay "Stanislavsky's System" offers, like Carnicke, a clear explanation of "living through." What Ruffini and Carnicke demonstrate is the difference between what we have come to think of as Stanislavskian "believability" and Stanislavsky's intent. "Living through" is related to believability; however for Stanislavsky, and for me, believability is not the repetition of old habits. Believability can be taken for habit, which is merely something the actor has done repeatedly and now appears organic. Even intense emotions, such as crying on cue, are hardly about truth as a discovery of something new and fresh. Such behavior isn't bad, but in itself has little if anything to do with "living through." If one cries on cue one is not necessarily creating art, merely crying on cue. It's a trick, like doing a back flip. Not bad if you can do it; and like any trick, it's neat to have. Crying, laughing or back flipping on cue are "believable," but in themselves have little to do with the truthful discovery of something original.

Tricks can be emotional and physical, but both fail to enact a fresh, lived experience. To overcome tricks and arrive at the substance of her art, the actor must be "living through." Ruffini says that, for Stanislavsky,

> the character must exist in the role's past and future, that is, even when the role is not temporally present. The character must also exist in acts which are not foreseen by the role, that is, even when the role is not spatially present. Stanislavsky's recommendations in this regard are continuous and unequivocal ... If the actor's body–mind is inorganic, the character's actions, even though conforming to the role's 'given circumstances,' cannot be appropriate reactions to the demands. They can only be mechanical executions of external orders. (p. 152)

The execution of external orders may come from the director's blocking, the script's stage directions, a desire to be "liked" and applauded, the resurfacing of old habits that were once passable, or inserting an attempt to be "real" (trying to act truthfully by imposing a "feeling" on to the performance), but are now eviscerated of any depth or dimension.

"Living through" means, first, if one plays the role of a farmer, for example, one must have a knowledge of farming physically and in perpetuity. One must work on farms, knowing the physical life by instinct and by habit, and come to make the life a part of one's physical behavior. Once physical existence inculcates the life of farming, one's body can react spontaneously and instinctually. One responds as if one is a farmer, without thinking about it – "being" it, enriched by a deep level of emotion that incorporates everything about farming. Equally, if one is a nurse, one must know nursing not just intellectually, but physically and psychologically. One needs to know the psycho-physical life of a nurse in one's body – hence the term "embodying" – through movement, voice, behavior and depth of experience. Second, one must have a creative spirit or ruling idea: a sense of why one is performing the role and what can be brought to it that is original and spontaneous. The framework of the ruling idea derives from the character's circumstances, but ultimately it is the actor's truth, her ruling idea, her actions informed by her guiding principle. The ruling idea must be theatrical; it must incorporate dynamic and unusual choices; and it must take the risk of showing us the depth of the actor, whether it is darkness or compassion. Maria Knebel reminds us,

> Even when the actor is truthful on stage ... if his work is not imbued with a profound idea, he sins cruelly against authentic truth. The living stage experience is necessary, but it is only the rudiments of the actor's work, which must advance further toward embodying the author's intent, toward social generalization, and vividness of theatrical form. (*Stanislavski Today*, p. 55)

Third, one must be imaginative: spontaneity surfaces from the unusualness and creativity borne from imaginatively living in the moment. Richard Boleslavsky explains that an "actor who 'lives his part' uses each time, playing the role, a brand new, fresh feeling." As a result, a "creative actor lends his ear exclusively to his soul, and does not try to *invent* new feelings, but merely invests his own in different forms prompted by his imagination" (Creative Theatre, p. 105). It means working deeply, seriously and spontaneously, bringing mind and body to the circumstances of the play and relationships with the other characters. The actor Daniel Day-Lewis describes the following two attributes of great acting that coincide with "living through": "a great deal of discipline and a wildness of spirit." Discipline and wildness, which seem contradictory but are not, personify the actor's art. With acting, he contends,

> there is always that intangible aspect that goes beyond the practical framework. Brando had that – the freedom that he had was more the instinctive freedom of an animal at times than a human. And De Niro! The world he offered in his performances had a palpable humanity. I was utterly sure that he was that man in *Taxi Driver*. (p. 63)

To live through a role means following through, to exist in the role not just when speaking, but when listening to other actors too. Like an athlete, the actor follows through: a tennis player hits the ball and then doesn't stop playing; rather, she watches the other player as the ball moves towards her and follows through with her swing, ready for the next return. The tennis player doesn't stop being a tennis player after the ball is hit but rather lives through the experience of playing. Actors often say their lines and then go "blank," as if their job were only to say words. An actor, like a tennis player, must follow through the role by inhabiting it. For Stanislavsky, then and only then is the actor *believable* (Stanislavsky often used the Russian phrase *ne veryu*, meaning "I'm unconvinced" when he felt actors failed to "live through"). To be *convincing* requires acting that is thoroughly embodied and inhabited, creating a living portrait of a three-dimensional human being engaged in a reality, within a heightened (dramatic) situation, reacting spontaneously to other actors and events, and willing to expose the consequences (the costs) of the character's losses, failures and shortcomings. Anything resembling exaggerations, pandering to the audience, or what is commonly called "indicating" – pretending to exhibit the feeling or action – must be eradicated.

Largely why "living through" has fallen through the cracks of actor training and is rarely if ever taught, let alone discussed, is because considerable time is required to learn the role. Mel Gordon reports that, for Stanislavsky's Moscow Art Theatre productions, "whole years were taken up with preparations" (p. 5); Jean Benedetti maintains that Stanislavsky required "a minimum of six months" (p. 9) of rehearsal just developing the truth of the character (before one word of text was spoken!); and John Gillett says that "For Stanislavsky, a year's rehearsal was thought appropriate to accommodate a detailed exploration of a play and allow actors time to fully develop truthful and rounded characters" (p. 159). "Living through" develops trust among actors, which is essential for a good ensemble. In "living through," the audience can genuinely feel the relationships among actors, not merely as actor-to-actor but also as character-to-character. If, for example, it is a sibling relationship, time is required to create the honest bond that sibling relationships require. Few theater or film production companies are willing to pay someone for months (indeed, years!) of training just to learn how to be a farmer or a sibling; they seek quick solutions so that they may whip up a hasty production. The actor is therefore forced to achieve credibility through a bag of tricks. Rehearsals don't provide cash, and performances do, so rehearsal periods are curtailed. In lieu of living the role, actors pull tricks from their arsenal. If they have to cry on cue, then they'd better be ready to cry. Their acting is informed by the message: "Look audience, I'm really crying; these are real tears; I cry (or laugh, or get angry, etc.) therefore I'm believable." This is nothing more or less than a back flip, like saying: "Look audience, I did a real back flip – you saw it – I really back flipped." No doubt if you back flip you are believably back flipping (and I don't mean to underestimate back-flipping – it is extremely difficult). No doubt if you are laughing you are really laughing, and doing so on cue is an admirable trick. But let's be candid: it is a trick. And so it goes: the emotion is real, the acting is real; the trick appears organic, hence the acting seems organic. Such work, however, merely skims the surface.

In addition to short rehearsals, actors are impatient. They want quick results and assembly-line processes that assure success. Stanislavsky contends that "Actors always forget that the creative process of experiencing and embodying is not sudden, using one method, but gradual, in several steps and stages" (*Actor's Work on a Role*, p. 175). Experiencing the role means putting it in one's body, mind, thoughts and actions – *which can only take root over time*. Like the creation of a human being, the role is enriched through time: it is born, goes through the pains of growth, develops out of hard work and serious attention, and takes shape as a living human being, filled with complexity and honesty. A character, Stanislavsky says, "is a living organic creation made in the image of a man and not some dead, tired theatrical cliché." As the experiences and passions become part of the life, they can then be, in his words, "stageworthy," where the embodiment of the role is "viable, clearly, visibly in the space that divides actor from audience." Once formed, it can then be refined, or as Stanislavsky put it, "heightened, enacted so as to be clearer" (*Actor's Work on a Role*, pp. 224, 225).

Stanislavsky recoiled from pedestrian actions, the surface examination of a role, what Bella Merlin calls "parochial" choices; instead, he wanted choices creating a "wider significance," evolving "from a literal to a psychological and imaginative plane, which then expands into wider – symbolic – reverberations" (*Stanislavsky*, p. 61). Acting is not a facsimile but rather requires imaginative input and inventive choices. Larry Moss describes Anthony Hopkins' creative process in *The Silence of the Lambs*. Using Stanislavsky's "as if" concept, Hopkins played Hannibal Lector "as if he were a head waiter in a restaurant."

He moved with elegance and formality, even though he was imprisoned. "His carriage was straight, tall, and refined. He acted with his whole body even in close-up." In addition, Moss says, he used "the voice of Hal the computer from *2001: A Space Odyssey*, a disembodied, mechanical voice. These are creative choices, deeply connected to the author's intent and expressed by a gifted actor through his physical instrument" (p. 126). Creative choices make us artists and give depth to performances.

Nor should acting encourage therapeutic analysis. Actors draw from their experiences, create associations with the role, and add imagination. Personalization is required but this doesn't mean they must go into traumatic past experiences or devastating emotional breakdowns in order to create good performances. The actors' past is grist for their creative mill, not self-indulgent psychoanalysis. Stanislavsky demanded a devotion to training and rehearsal that embedded physical habits which in turn became instinct. He understood that acting is narcissistic and will inflate egos by the very nature of the job; this is an unfortunate occupational hazard. He tried to eliminate these habits by having the actor subsume herself into the role – not necessarily the role the playwright imagined, but the "life." "Always play yourself onstage," Stanislavsky said, "but always with different combinations of Tasks, Given Circumstances, which you have nurtured in the crucible of your own emotion memories. They are the best and only material for inner creative work" (*Actor's Work*, p. 210).

Making connections between role and self are the actor's ongoing process: merging the self and the role through trial-and-error, experimenting in rehearsals, improvising ideas and actions, and defining, honing and shaping the actions and desires of the role and the self. Rehearsing is an inculcation process; the mind and body must absorb the habits of the role. Once absorbed, habit becomes instinct. To say, "trust your instinct," is meaningless unless the actor embodies the habits of "living through." Notwithstanding a few primal instincts (desire for food, sleep and so on), instinct is informed by habit – or, to put it another way, *instinct is habit* – and habit is wholly *temporal*. That is, habits can he learned *over time*. What one often thinks is one's "instinct" or "impulse" is in fact merely a habit, a knee-jerk reaction developed through repetition. Habits are learned through repetition (think of Pavlov's dog) and only by "living through" a role can *new habits* (new repetitions) be acquired that can then be called instinctual. So "trust your instinct" is misleading if it fails to embody a whole new set of habits. It should go: new habits create new instincts, or, as Stanislavsky put it (quoting the voice teacher Sergei Volkonsky), "The difficult must be made habitual, the habitual easy, and the easy – beautiful" (*Selected Works*, p. 174). The actor can then perform instinctually in the "given circumstances" of the scene, "trusting" a new set of reactions, vocal tones and gestures informed by new habitual behavior. But this can only occur if the actor "lives through" the role, and to do so takes patience, a willingness to take risks and reinvent oneself, and attention to detail. As Maria Knebel says, "An actor who has performed even only one improvisation acquires invaluable personal experience" (in *Stanislavski Today*, p. 48).

Justification: "Living through" the Interstitial Scene

"Justification" is the means through which the actor incorporates belief in the circumstances of the play. Stella Adler placed great emphasis on justification, saying,

> The justification is not in the lines; it is in you. What you should choose as your justification should agitate you. As a result of the agitation you will experience the action and the emotion. If you choose a justification and experience nothing, you'll have to select something else that will awaken you. Your talent consists of how well you are able to shop for your justification. In your choice lies your talent. (*Technique*, p. 48)

Justification is stimulated by words (mantras), images (pictures), decoys (lures) or other methods fleshing out the central meaning of the role. This is what Stanislavsky called the "creative ideas" which "grant you the right to say [the playwright's] words. And don't just know, but try to see clearly the picture your creative ideas produce" (*Actor's Work*, p. 406). The inspirations an actor selects must occur even before the first lines are spoken. Texts have underlying subtexts and *the subtext must come before the words*. Actors must lead up to the words, not depend on them to do the work.

The actor's goal, Stanislavsky says,

> is to remember, understand, and determine what they should do at such a time so that they can live as if the things described in the play

had happened to them, that is to say to living human beings, and not just characters in a play … [the actor] must always *live his own self and not take his point of departure from his role more than finding in it the given circumstances in which it is played.* (*Creating a Role*, pp. 200–1 – Stanislavsky's emphasis)

Stanislavsky was unequivocal about this. In acting, he said:

Decide what is more interesting, more important to you, what it is you want to believe, that the material world of facts and events exists in the theatre and in the play, or that the feeling which is born in the actor's heart, stirred by a fiction, that is genuine and true.

In the end it doesn't matter where the justification comes from, but rather

always try and justify what you do onstage with your own 'if' and Given Circumstances. Only by creative work of this kind can you satisfy your sense of truth and your belief in the genuineness of your experiencing … [because] Truth is inseparable from belief, and belief from truth. (*Actor's Work*, p. 154)

Discovering the source of justification can be inspiring in itself; making a personal discovery about a role is an exciting venture. Justification stems from an inner truth and belief in the situation, and is connected to the ensemble. The concept of justification was further defined by Vakhtangov, who, according to Mel Gordon, said:

an actor must ask himself the following basic questions: 'Why am I in the theatre?' 'Why am I in this group?' 'Why am I in this play?' 'Why am I playing this part?' In every instance, the actor must have a strong personal motive, or Justification. The answers, however, do not have to be either logical or related to the script. They need only appeal to the performer's rationale or inner need (*Stanislavsky Technique*, p. 82)

The following examples will assist in understanding how justification works on a given play. Each case describes what I call an "interstitial scene." The *Oxford English Dictionary* defines interstitial as "occupying an interval in time or order." Interstitial scenes are scenes not found in the play but are referenced in the script and are related directly to the play's events; they occupy an interval before, between or after the event onstage; and they are impro-vised, acted out and performed with full commitment. For example, Blanche Dubois's experience on the dance floor with her first hus-band in Tennessee Williams' *A Streetcar Named Desire*, or Stanley telling Mitch about Blanche's sullied past in the same play. None of these events appear in the play *per se*, but they deeply inform the actors' behavior.

Another example of an interstitial scene is demonstrated in a 2010 production of August Wilson's *Fences*. The play deals with the rela-tionship between Troy Maxon and his wife, Rose, married for eight-een years. The actors, Denzel Washington and Viola Davis, created a backstory about the couple's courtship that is not in the play but implied and referred to throughout it. Patrick Healy reports that Viola Davis "took the lead, writing out several pages of a conjured origin story about the first date of Rose and Troy, their first night of sex, and the first time that Troy tells Rose that he once killed a man (in self-defense) and spent 15 years in prison as a result." The director Kenny Leon facilitated this improvisation because, accord-ing to him, the performers needed to "seem inseparable in their bones if *Fences* is to truly work." "Chemistry between the actors isn't enough," Leon says, because "You need people who can convey through body language, through pause, even through the pace of their breathing around one another, that Rose and Troy are every-thing to one another" (quoted in Healy, p. 4).

The actors' job is to make the story real to themselves. In the movie *Blue Valentine* (2010), the actors Michelle Williams and Ryan Gosling lived together as a married couple for months to capture the expe-rience of living through a relationship. Rather than pretend to be married they experienced a life together, setting up a home that they shared for months to create for themselves a truthful scenic feeling through many interstitial scenes. As Paul Mann put it:

> I make up specific stories about each person and these become facts for me. The basic material is drawn from the play, but often the play isn't specific enough. It doesn't say what hospital, what office, where it is, what it's like, etc. This is the actor's work. I justify the action for myself. (p. 91)

In the next section I present problems and solutions by using the improvisation of an interstitial scene.

Down by the River

> How much past experience do you need? A small germ can expand and
> expand to produce great emotion. (Ouspenskaya, 2(2)).

I used Maria Ouspenskaya words quoted above as a launching point
when rehearsing Caryl Churchill's *Top Girls*. The play concerns two
sisters, one of whom, Marlene, gives birth to a child, Angie, and the
other, Joyce, unofficially adopts the baby. Both sisters maintain the
pretense that the child, Angie, is Joyce's. Marlene has big plans,
and having a child will only cramp her style. Churchill condemns
capitalism and its Darwinian emphasis on success at the expense
of humanity; according to the play's theme, people must relinquish
their souls to climb the corporate ladder. Marlene is a "top girl," head
of an employment agency. She strives for success at any cost, even
discarding her child. Joyce takes Marlene's out-of-wedlock baby
and raises it as her own. Throughout the play Angie senses the truth
about her biological mother, though she never says so outright.

In the final, climatic scene, Marlene has been induced to come
home and visit Joyce and Angie by a letter from Angie (Angie makes
up a story to entice Marlene). Marlene lives in London but was born
in the working-class neighborhood where Joyce and Angie live. The
scene begins with all three together. Angie exits. Joyce and Marlene,
now alone, bicker about Angie, their mother in a nursing home,
and politics (Marlene is Conservative; Joyce Liberal). In one crisis
moment, when both women express their bitterness and frustration, Marlene says: "You wanted it [Angie], you said you were glad,
I remember the day, you said I'm glad you never got rid of it, I'll look
after it, you said that down by the river. So what are you saying,
sunshine, you don't want her?" (p. 134) I directed the play and the
actresses playing the roles had difficulty with this scene, particularly
this passage. They knew it demanded a great deal of emotion, but
struggled to justify the words and scene. Neither were mothers; the
actress playing Marlene had problems with the fact that she keeps
calling the child "it" and struggled to justify why she gave it up; and
the actress playing Joyce struggled to justify why she agreed to take
Angie as her own.

We created an interstitial scene called "down by the river." The
improvisation we invented does not occur in the play but is referred to
in the lines. I wanted the actresses to know precisely what happened

"down by the river." The only mention of a "river" in the play is quoted above. This is where an interstitial scene presents its greatest value: as a solution to acting problems and a way into justification. Stanislavsky points out that the "dramatist doesn't give us the whole life of a play or a role but only those moments which are presented and performed onstage." As a result, actors "have to supply what the author has not created in his printed text, using our own imagination" (*Actor's Work*, p. 288). With this in mind, we created an interstitial scene.

We examined the given circumstances. How old were they when Marlene became pregnant? Who was the father of the child? The actresses brought into rehearsal pictures – of their parents, boyfriends, schools, rivers, the neighborhood and the house they lived in, and other inspiring photos. Some of the photos were fiction, some from their lives, and some were from people they knew but they imagined them in another context. It was important that the actresses showed each other their pictures: it provided them with perspective and insight into the other's thinking. It helped to bond them, reinforcing their sibling relationship. I asked what they thought about each other: how did they grow up? Did they sleep in the same room (bunk beds?)? Wear identical clothes? Play with the same toys? Each was required to bring to rehearsal a toy that they felt was shared. Did they do homework together? Talk about boys, dating and sex? What were the conversations, trips, walk to the market place and path to school? They listened to music they might have shared while growing up.

Most important, we considered the river, and why a river. The scene takes place in a working-class neighborhood, so we decided that the river was beside a factory where their father worked. The issue of class status, central to Churchill's play, became the guiding focal point and stimulus for their imagination. Many factories of the period used rivers as waste reservoirs, so the water was hardly pristine, though still a place where children played. The actresses talked about their own relationships to their past, what they knew about working-class families and their own parents, and what it meant to play by water. We performed affective memories in relationship to this in order to get the actresses closer to the material. They recalled the sensory facts: weather, colors, foods they ate, odors, images and so on, all associated with rivers.

We then turned to the theater space and marked off a river bank, a bench and a tree. I asked the actresses to talk about the weather on that eventful day. What were they wearing? Did they smell the waste from the factory, or was there a breeze and fresh air around them? How many months pregnant was Marlene? How much was she showing? When did she go to the doctor; how she find out? Why did Joyce want the baby – to show Marlene that she was as good as her, that she could be better than her sister? The actress playing Joyce considered sibling rivalry. She had to be specific. She must not take a generic view of sisterhood because it sounds correct or something that I, the director, suggested; it had to be felt and personal. In other words, she had to take ownership of the choice.

After a considerable time and patient attention to detail, we improvised. The idea was *to enact the day and create what was exchanged – what actually happened*. I wanted the actresses to relive all the events: not talk about them, but experience the situation, aware of the weather, the river, the bench, and insisted that they hear, smell, see and touch everything. I wanted everything to be raw, immediate, sensual, specific and very simple (not simplistic). They were not to push but to let the improvisation happen, going in whatever direction it took them. The only time I stopped them was when they became sophisticated, lecturing about events rather than relating to each other and "living through." I asked them if they had any objects with them when they went to the river – purse, keys, watch, wallet, hair brush, clip – anything that would make the scene believable to them. I told them not to bring things to the improvisation just to satisfy me, as director, but to bring things to satisfy their own imaginations. The sense of truth didn't have to be grandiose, but rather what Stanislavsky called "little truths" stimulating belief and faith.

They improvised several times until the actresses became deeply immersed in the circumstances. Marlene was moved by her feelings of suffocation in this small, provincial place; Joyce seized the opportunity to prove something to her sister. Marlene in particular felt stymied by the town's pedestrian attitudes and working-class traditions; Joyce was moved by maternal desires. The actress playing Marlene began crying, raging and laughing as she confessed her mixed emotions about the child, abortion, relationship to her body, and the unreliable boyfriend who had fathered the child. All this was fiction, of course, but as she built up belief and faith in the circumstances, the fiction was creatively endowed. Joyce, too, was deeply moved and at the spur of the moment agreed to take the baby and raise it as her own. They devised a plan. Marlene came up with the idea of running away, having the child, and then coming back as if it were Joyce's all along. They counted their money, taking out a pencil and paper and adding up what they had and could afford to spend on escaping. They literally took coins and bills from their pockets and purses and counted; spontaneous things occurred. The counting became a wonderful small truth for them, something to build on to bolster their faith and belief. The plan made sense, it moved them. They hugged and cried. They ended laughing, comforting each other, sealing a sisterly bond that carried them through the play.

When the time came for Marlene to say her lines about the river in the scene, the actresses had a common place, a real, mutual point of reference, which allowed both to believe not only in their personal past but in a past they had collectively invented. The interstitial scene was hardly dramatic; much of their conversation was rambling and not stageworthy. But being dramaturgically correct is not the point. The improvisation inspired them and from that point on their work was informed by a real and mutual experience. When Marlene said "I remember the day," the actress playing Joyce seemed to have been shot through with electricity, her whole body jolted by her memory; she did, indeed, remember a real day. And Marlene, using the repetition technique of reading behavior, could see that Joyce remembered. Marlene was inspired to drive home her action and objective. The actresses were transmitting and receiving mental images, using what Stanislavsky called "irradiation, the voice, words, intonations, adaptations: the desire and intention to oblige the object not only to hear and understand but to see with the inner eye *what* the communicating subject is transmitting, and how he is doing it," by constructing an organic process of give-and-take (*Actor's Work*, p. 625). The scene had become a powerful expression of their relationship, creating a chemistry that cannot be obtained merely by reading the play.

Vanya's Dream

I coached an actor playing Uncle Vanya in Anton Chekhov's play with the same title. He was having problems with the first line. In the opening scene of the first act, Vanya wakens from an afternoon nap. His first words are: "Yes ... yes." The actor knew the importance of his first entrance, yet these two words were extremely difficult to justify. "Yes" to *what* and why does he say "yes" *twice*? Chekhov provides fleeting images and clues; events and entities are feelings and images rather than facts and certainties. He never consumes the play with heavy-handed exposition but layers information subtly. The protagonist's name, for example, is "Uncle," which, as Stella Adler astutely observes, is "symbolic. He is not Mister or Daddy. He is Uncle" (*On Ibsen*, p. 245). Uncle symbolizes warmth yet lacks authority (Mister) or intimacy (Daddy). The label makes Vanya an everyman and a nobody simultaneously.

We began work by constructing Vanya's given circumstances, but with caution: analyzing a laundry list of events will fail to inspire. We assembled the facts but always targeting inspiration, imagination, inventiveness and physicality. A character's given circumstances are not a quiz; we're not trying to get the right answers, but to find the inner spark. Vanya lives on a farm in rural Russia. What does this mean? He is forty-seven years old. What does this mean? In 1899, when the play was performed, forty-seven was the cusp of old age. How can the actor make that fact personal? Vanya devoted his whole life to his brother-in-law, the Professor. We know from the play that Vanya and his niece, the Professor's daughter, Sonya, labor on the farm and send money to support the Professor. Vanya translates the Professor's essays on art history into English, French and German. This action is significant: at the time, the Russian intelligentsia wanted to belong to European intellectual and modernist movements in art, music and theatre. But Russia was remote and reactionary; for a Russian professor to gain recognition internationally as an art historian he had to publish in the languages of European modernism: English, French and German. Vanya has therefore not only supported the Professor financially, but he has also been his conduit to recognition in intellectual circles. Without Vanya, the Professor would have failed to attain the success he now enjoys.

At the start of the play, the Professor and his trophy wife (the Professor is in his seventies and his wife, Yelena, is twenty-seven) have arrived at what he describes as his "country estate." The Professor considers he owns an estate; but what he actually owns is a simple farm. In retirement he has quickly been forgotten by the intellectual community because what he wrote, and what Vanya so dutifully translated, is rubbish. He's a "has been" and in Vanya's eyes a fraud who hoodwinked everyone into believing his veritable "divinity." If this is not enough to drive him mad, Vanya is also infatuated with Yelena and can't fathom why she married the Professor.

The actor added up these facts: wasted life; giving up his inheritance on behalf of his sister and her husband, the Professor; running a farm by day; working for the Professor by night, translating his academic and ultimately meaningless essays; and devoting his life to this sanctimonious pedant, who, in the end, is an eminent nobody. Vanya is jealous of the Professor's success with women. We talked about what it meant for the actor to be resentful. What did it feel like to be duped and deceived? After several days working on affective memories and talking it out (my listening, the actor talking), we returned to the lines Vanya first says in the play: "Yes ... yes." What we say to ourselves before our first line is very important. The first beat in the scene is not the first beat, but actually the second. The first beat is what happens before you come onstage. So what happened to Vanya before "Yes ... yes?" Vanya awoke from a nap. If he is napping, is he dreaming? If he is dreaming, what is the dream? The interstitial scene, we decided, is the dream – actually two dreams.

In Act Two, Vanya's monologue recalls a decade before, when he first met Yelena at his sister's house. She was seventeen, he thirty-seven; Vanya wonders why he "didn't fall in love with her then and propose to her? It would have been so easy! And now she would have been my wife" (p. 19). Vanya did not propose. The actress playing Yelena joined us and played out the entire scene – in a way that Vanya wished it to occur. We worked on details: room; clothes; weather; occasion; and where the others were: Vanya's sister, the Professor, Sonya. This was to be Vanya's first dream. The actor developed a sense of what the first "yes" means. It was this dream: "yes" was his affirmation of what *should have been*.

The actors played a new improvisation. They were to act out the way it probably happened – Vanya too shy and self-effacing to ask for Yelena in marriage. Vanya also met the Professor in the dream. Again, we created detail, leaving nothing to chance except the improvisation itself. The words and actions were spontaneous, but the given circumstances were certain. The actor playing Vanya not only developed a history of his relationships to everyone around him. He also incorporated the second "yes" – the circumstances as *they are in the play*.

We created two separate dreams: possibility and reality. Each "yes" had a specific point of reference and each "yes" was informed by given circumstances, both of which stimulated the actor's personal experience in the interstitial scenes. The actor had a reference point, a truthful situation that offered him ownership of his world.

An example of another interstitial scene comes from Stella Adler by way of the acting teacher Milton Justice. Linda is Willy Loman's faithful and beleaguered wife in Arthur Miller's *Death of a Salesman*. Her eldest son, Biff, a promising high school football star, squanders his opportunities. He resents his father, whom he catches in the act of infidelity in a Boston hotel room. For the next 15 years Biff drifts aimlessly. He is arrested for petty larceny and shoplifting (the results of a misplaced desire for consumerism), works on ranches and lives itinerantly. Linda feels his loss deeply. According to Adler, every day Linda walks to the mailbox. This walk is never mentioned in the script, but it is an interstitial scene that can induce the actor's trigger. Adler advises the actress playing the role that she go to the mailbox daily, seeking a letter from her son. The idea of her walking to the mailbox is the actress's emotional connection. In every detail of the walk there is expectation, a sense that today will bring a message. When nothing arrives, she sets her sights on the next day. She walks to the mailbox and back to her front door every day for 15 years with this thought in mind: tomorrow he will write. Such an image can be powerfully moving to the actress, sustaining her commitment to the role performance after performance.

Exercise 27: Interstitial Scene

Actors should work on an interstitial scene because it establishes their *ownership of the role*. It helps to create triggers, exciting inspirations for the actor, and these triggers must occur in each role: "If the actor doesn't invest his own nature as a human being in the role, then what he creates will be dead" (*Actor's Work*, p. 309). Common sense dictates that it must always be performed with an awareness of the author, director and fellow actors, faithful to the play's circumstances, and artistically reflecting taste and sensibility. Do not run amok with interstitial scenes, but create improvisations that coax out triggers, inspire faith in your belief in the circumstances, and create fully formed human beings with tangible pasts and memorable histories. Still, all the work on the play will remain shallow and academic if you do not absorb what Vakhtangov calls "faith" – faith in the play, in your life in the role, and your belief in the circumstances. "The very fascinating thing about the stage," he says, "is that everything there is a lie, and this lie becomes truth for me" (*Vakhtangov Sourcebook*, p. 117). And as you discover the character's past and truths, you must also discover the character's lies.

9

LYING AND DENIAL

What, then, is a great actor? A man who, having learnt the words set down for him by the author, fools you thoroughly, whether in tragedy or comedy. (Diderot, p. 33)

Lying and poetry are arts – arts, as Plato saw, not unconnected with each other – and they require the most careful study. (Wilde, p. 218)

Audrey: I do not know what poetical is. Is it honest in deed and word? Is it a true thing?
Touchstone: No, truly; for the truest poetry is the most feigning.
(Shakespeare, *As You Like It*, III.iii)

Do actors lie? Philosophers such as Diderot, authors such as Wilde, and even Shakespeare, as noted above, considered this question. In *The Republic*, the philosopher Plato banished actors from his ideal city because he believed they created appearances rather than reality. For Plato, actors masquerade as imitators, knowing "nothing worth mentioning of the things he imitates" (p. 827). The creator of a character "fashions" herself as an expert, yet creates only an illusion. An actor playing a doctor, for example, doesn't practice medicine, yet the actor will be taken by the spectator as someone speaking the truth about medicine. For Plato, the actors' duplicity, if executed succinctly, endangers our perceptions and undermines truth. Indeed, the better the acting, the greater the deception. Acting is deception, exploits our weakness for appearances over reality, and, as Plato says, "falls nothing short of witchcraft, and so do jugglery and many other such contrivances" (p. 827).

The foundation of the Stanislavsky system, and indeed most schools of acting, would appear to contradict Plato. Actors, it would seem, express real emotions, emphasize sincerity, and though they might not have a medical degree, they claim to understand the circumstances surrounding a doctor's work. But what happens when an actor portrays a liar? To put it another way: do characters lie? Certainly they do, because we *all* – at some point or in some capacity – exaggerate, pretend, stretch the truth, act self-assuredly when we know we're on shaky ground, make promises we know we cannot keep, or flat-out pronounce what we know is false. We lie on a "small" scale and justify it as "harmless" – necessary to sustain a larger truth or protect the innocent. We lie to children for their well-being; we lie to our bosses and lovers; and most of all we lie to ourselves. We make mistakes and claim we didn't mean it; embellish stories to gain attention or to make the tale more colorful; and convey to ourselves and others positive reinforcements when we actually believe failure is imminent. Even animals lie, using camouflage to snare their prey or hide from a predator. We lie because other people want to hear lies about themselves to gain complements or assurance that we agree with them. We lie because it gives us an advantage over others. Lying is a *social tactic* used to get what we want. Lies are *active actions designed to obtain objectives.*

Are the actions and emotions underlying the lie, then, false? Or the opposite: are the emotions true, even if the facts are false, because of the need to facilitate lies in order to obtain our goals? It takes a lot of energy to carry off lies, because we have to overcome any moral objection; it demands an elaborate disguise; it exercises our best skills of persuasion; and it creates a dual consciousness in us – surface appearance and inner awareness, both of which need to be manipulated in a finely-tuned balancing act. Deception requires the acquired skill of knowing the other person: a lie relies on the ability to fool someone else into thinking that we really mean what we say. Shakespeare's characters are some of the greatest liars in literature. Iago in *Othello*, or the two older daughters in *King Lear* (to note just a couple of examples) perpetuate some of the most elaborate schemes and deceptions in drama. They say one thing and mean another. Who, then, says there's no subtext in Shakespeare when his characters perpetuate deception and manipulation through lies and denial?

Plato is correct: lying is the art of acting, and lying successfully is one of its highest achievements.

If this is the highest achievement, how, then, do we measure the quality of lying? How do we measure a liar's talent? There is only one litmus test: *one will never know*. Great lying means being so convincing that the lie is never exposed. "The lie must become or seem to be truth on the stage in order to be convincing," Stanislavsky says (quoted in Jean Benedetti, *Stanislavski*, p. 34). To lie successfully one has to accept that there will be no accolade, applause or acknowledgement; the completely successful lie must always remain hidden. In Chapter 4 I described an example of lying in which I created a letter in my back pocket that contradicted everything I said in the play. I never revealed the letter to anyone, and never deviated from the play's text. I created an internal conflict between the objective and the action. My goal in the scene was *to act as if I agreed with everything that was being said and to convince everyone that their perception of truth was correct*. I was lying, but in order to be successful at it I had to put on a mask. The mask was my external action. Internally, I believed the opposite; I was lying in the play in order to protect the memory of my father. My objective was personal, but my action of denial had no seeming relationship to the objective; only lying – denial – connected objective and action. My action was to mask the truth and my objective was to agree with a false picture of my father: the better my mask (my denial), the better my performance.

Denial requires work on two levels: one must have the reality inside that one denies having outside. I had to believe in the letter; I had to personalize it, justify it and give it the specific circumstance to make it truthful. When did I find it? How did it arrive? Where did my father put it just before his suicide? Did he leave it in a place where I would find it easily, yet hidden from others? What kinds of words did my father use – words that would affect me? The letter had to be personal. Only after I had incorporated the letter into my memory *could I then deny it to others*. Denial forces the actor to work truthfully internally while working actively externally. Denial therefore creates an interesting dynamic: a lot going on internally while externally there is economical and focused action.

Every actor should *find a moment in their performance where they are lying*. This lie is part of the actors' secret. Once pinpointed, the actor must mask its appearances with the utmost conviction. In this way, the actor employs the most venerable of her tools: the mask.

Masks have a long history in the theater, and the reason for this is self-evident: theater is a playful falsehood dressed up to appear real. The mask is the ultimate "costume": the facial expression which disguises the underlying thoughts. The outer appearance gives the world (or the other characters) what it wants to see, masking inner contradictions, conflicts and complexity. The poet Paul Laurence Dunbar, for example, defined the living experience of African Americans forced to wear a mask of docility in the face of racism (and forced to improvise) when he wrote in a 1895 poem: "We wear the mask that grins and lies/It hides our cheeks and shades our eyes" (p. 281).

Lying is not child's play; children rarely if ever succeed at lying. Only through practice do we sharpen our skills. The ruse is developed through a conscious awareness of self and others, perception and communication, and what Diderot called the paradox of acting. Conveying a truthful imitation of reality, Diderot says, requires keen observation and cool detachment, an art that is built up over time and fine-tuned by practice and rehearsal. The actor, Diderot contends, "watches appearances; the man of sensibility is his model; he thinks over him, and discovers by after-reflection what it will be to add or cut away. And so from mere argument he goes to action" (p. 37). The actor, then, must find the perfect balance between artifice and truth; she observes human behavior meticulously, not only to convey it truthfully but also to know what is accepted as truthful among the people surrounding her.

Acting is an art that moves along a razor's edge of authenticity and artifice. The art resides on the tipping point of spontaneity and control, improvisation and drill, following through with the action (what Stanislavsky often referred to as "the through line of action") and deviation from expectation through improvisation. And when the artifice becomes integrated into the character – when the lie and the truth blend evenly and balance like a juggling act – the actor creates a keen doppelganger. The actor must use irony, humor, deception and mask (the social pretense, the deceptive appearance) to gain an objective, undermine the smugness of our norms, and put a searchlight on what it means to be human in all its contradictions. In "Mask or Faces?" William Archer wrote that the real paradox of acting "resolves itself in the paradox of dual consciousness" (p. 184). The actor walks the fine line of a dual awareness: truth and artifice. The liar walks a similar line. The successful liar, like the actor, has to know what is real and what is false, and make them indistinguishable.

To create this, the actor has to experience a dual consciousness between impulse and form, restraint and abandon, mask and agenda: the better the disguise, the better the liar – and the better the actor. This chapter considers three examples of this dual awareness, and then offers an exercise aimed at developing this skill.

Forrest Whitaker's breakout performance in the 1986 movie, *The Color of Money*, serves as an example of lying. Whitaker is onscreen for precisely four minutes, yet his acting is so compelling that it launched his career. (The performance clip can be viewed by searching for his name and the movie on the internet). One of the many reasons why he is so good in the scene is because nothing he says is true. Absolutely nothing can be verified or confirmed. Whitaker's objective is to hustle Paul Newman by pretending to be a loser at pool. The art of hustling in games or sports is bluffing (an art that every actor should study), requiring an elaborate deception; the hustler must pretend to be bad at the very game at which he excels. The pretense of playing poorly cannot be done randomly; the hustler must lose the game in a convincing manner, suggesting that he is really at the skill-level he presents. The presentation is everything; if the deception is revealed; that is, if the bluffer is discovered to be brilliant at the game, then the ruse is exposed and the hustler will fail to snare his target. The aim of a hustler is to make modest bets with an opponent, deliberately losing in order to lure the opponent into a larger bet, at which point the "true" talent will be revealed. In acting – and this is the crucial point – the "true" skill is appearing to be the character; like the hustler, the actor works in *deception as truth*.

In *The Color of Money*, Whitaker begins by shooting pool badly while simultaneously talking about being the subject of a psychological experiment. This is part of his disguise; he may or may not be the subject of these experiments, but the objective is to give Newman the impression that Whitaker's character is mentally unbalanced and hence a loser. Whitaker's character may, in fact, *be unstable and involved in the experimental project*; but this is neither here nor there. This is the surface manifestation of the action, the *mask*; the internal objective is to win money. After the betting is raised substantially, Whitaker wins repeatedly. As he walks away from the pool hall he asks Newman if he should "lose some weight." The truth of this is, again, *neither here nor there*. His weight is unimportant, the deception is all. What is significant is that the question "appears" to be true. Whitaker is a bit overweight, so the question has an element of truth.

But much more important is the deception, which is the *action*: to throw Newman off balance, make him doubt, deflect his concentration, and ask irrelevant questions that eventually knock his timing off. Newman's character is asked to think about the other character's weight, not pool; deciphering the relevance of the question, not the angles of the balls; and wondering what is going on with the opponent, not his strategy for the game. The litmus test of good hustling is that no one will ever know it's a lie. So we think that Whitaker is genuinely asking the question "Should I lose some weight?" As soon as we know he is lying, he is no longer hustling; if we think that he is making a joke about his weight then the mask is removed. We have to believe that the question is real – and to some it extent *it might be*. This is the essence of acting: we never know if it's a lie. It appears true, it seems true, and it looks like the truth, but is it the truth? Whitaker grasps the irony of this dual consciousness, this concept of truth and artifice rolled into one.

Deception is *rooted in some aspect of truth*; you cannot deceive successfully without some suggestion of truth. The art of deception is in the tipping point of just enough but not too much. In the *Art of War*, Sun Tzu emphasized the importance of "seeming" and "feigning" when he wrote that "All warfare is based on deception. Hence, when able to attack, we must seem unable; when using our forces, we must seem inactive; when we are near, we must make the enemy believe we are far away; when far away, we must make him believe we are near. Hold out baits to entice the enemy. Feign disorder, and crush him." In the end, Sun Tzu says, "These military devices, leading to victory, must not be divulged beforehand" (p. 9). Feigning depletes all matter of substance once revealed; lying is only fruitful to the liar when everyone else accepts it as true.

Commedia dell'arte actors understand that the mask is what we want the world to see, even if what we are (or think we are) is not what we appear to be. The mask aids the deception; it is the studied look of what the world has come to believe is confidence, poise, intelligence and so on, no matter what the person really feels. The mask is the performance, the image we project to the world. The actor has to appreciate the mask as much as the feeling. The mime Jacques Lecoq said, "To make a mask come to life you have to know it, become friends with it. It must also be made so that it can perform" (p. 103). Denial is a performance mask that tacitly says "look not *in* me, but *at* me." The "neutral mask" presents the clean lines of a blank slate and perfect shield; the neutral mask is the ultimate "poker face." The poker face compels us to look because we know that something lurks beneath the disguise, but discovering it demands the most penetrating gaze. A poker face is unrevealing, stonewalling and unwavering. It creates a magnetic attraction because we know something is beneath it. Likewise the neutral mask, which presents economy and simplicity; the neutral mask and the poker face are "denial" personified, surface phenomena requiring great artistic skill to deflect the knowing gaze.

Poker-face masking is evident throughout Lee Strasberg's portrayal of Hyman Roth in *The Godfather, Part II*. His performance is deceptively simple. He is trying to enlarge his criminal empire by cozying up to Michael Corleone (played by Al Pacino) and pretending to be on his side of the mob conflict. Strasberg, the so-called "godfather" of emotionalism in acting, is remarkably unemotional in the film: no tearful scenes, histrionics or executing all the alleged faults associated with his Method acting. He appears, in fact, without hair-trigger emotion: instead, his character is avuncular, warm, reassuring and mild mannered – an unthreatening, trustworthy, "regular" guy. He dons the neutral mask for the performance; his action to deceive is cloaked in poker-faced warmth and simplicity. The reason that we don't observe how carefully Strasberg selects details and plots his malevolence is because he is working to obscure this labor from us (and from Michael Corleone). He is disguising his objective because he is playing denial. For many he is merely *the mask he adorns*: a friendly uncle-like partner to Michael Corleone and, in the words of one of his biggest detractors, Richard Hornby, little more than "thousands of other Hollywood character actors" (p. 23). Strasberg is certainly a character actor; but there is another dimension here, one overlooked by Hornby and so many others. Strasberg is *faking*; his character's warmth oozing with paternal affection for Michael Corleone is false. It is worth watching the video of Strasberg and Pacino to observe their father/son-like relationship in *The Godfather* and in *Justice for All* to note a wonderful contrast. In the latter, observe a warmer bond between the two.

In his condemnation of Strasberg, Gordon Rogoff writes that "in life, behavioral actions often tell lies about the truth within, frequently without planning to do so. These are lies that the [Method] System was initially designed to intercept" (p. 268). Rogoff, like many others, misunderstands the point of Method acting, and Strasberg in particular; the actions and the inner life are in a constant state of ironic interaction, two strands of the same DNA, where what one wants and what one shows square off in a creative dance – sometimes coinciding, sometimes diverging. Action and objective become polar opposites, at the same time attracting and repelling. This is the conflict that actors should pursue. The affect of Strasberg's actions is lifelike – in an artificial way.

One of Strasberg's many actions in *The Godfather* is to persuade Michael Corleone through his belly: His character Roth acts friendly, continuously trying to feed Corleone, first with a Florida orange delivered by his henchman, then with sandwiches made by his wife in his modest Florida home, and then with a cake for his birthday in Havana, Cuba. These gestures are endowed with great importance, but they are the ruse disguising the objective. Like Whitaker's question "Do I need to lose some weight?" in *The Color of Money*, Hyman Roth is presenting food in the foreground in order to shield the background. Like Sun Tzu's advice, the offerings are deceptions made to woo Corleone and deflect his true objective: to bring Corleone to his knees. What is significant is that the action is performed without a wink and nod to the audience; Strasberg is not trying to obtain accolades ("see how good a liar I am"), but rather performing the actions so convincingly that we accept them as "harmless" sincerity.

Strasberg's Hyman Roth is playing an elaborate chess game of deception. In a world of deceit there is no margin for error; in the story of Mafia gangsters where no one is trustworthy, Strasberg must mask any visual appearance of deception. He feigns illness to such an extent that one believes that his character is actually ill, even nearing death. He pretends to have little or no interest in the street fight for criminal turf between Frankie "Five Angels" Pentangeli and the "Rosato brothers" (a gang of brothers he is, in fact, supporting). Corleone comes to Roth asking for permission to kill Pentangeli because he believes it was he who ordered the assassination in his bedroom. When Strasberg bites on his sandwich and calls Pentangeli "small potatoes," effectively sanctioning the execution, we believe him, though in fact he suspects Corleone of lying. (Roth is correct: Pacino's Corleone is deceiving Roth, knowing full well that it was not Pentangeli but Roth himself who orchestrated the assassination – the game of deception works both ways). At the reconciliatory meeting between Pentangeli and the Rosato brothers in a bar owned by the Rosatos, Roth arranges a fake murder plot: he makes it look as if

Corleone is trying to kill his lieutenant Pentangeli by having the mur-derer say Corleone's name to Pentangeli while strangling him; and another elaborate fakery follows with the appearance of a so-called policeman. The fake policeman interrupts the attempted murder, cre-ating the appearance of a stroke of luck. Pentangeli is meant to think that Corleone is trying to have him killed, which motivates him to testify against Corleone at a Senate Crime Investigating Committee. This complex game of lies and denial is the foundation of this movie, and the actors convey the lies so convincingly that audiences rarely if ever see through the machinations.

In Havana, Strasberg acts gregariously and generously at his birth-day party, dividing a cake as a symbol of his kingdom; he hands out gambling hotels like King Lear bestowing land on his daughters, but with the difference that Hyman Roth knows full well that Fidel Castro and the rebels will eventually prevail and render the hotels worth-less. He is selling off his criminal empire through deception and denial: on the surface he is practically giving it away, asking for only "modest" payment. Knowing that the hotels will soon be overrun by rebels, Hyman Roth has to get whatever he can for them before it's too late. The point is that Strasberg isn't "acting" deceptively; he is *actually deceiving.*

In the film *Raging Bull*, Robert De Niro portrays the middleweight prize fighter Jake La Motta. He accuses his brother Joey, played by Joe Pesci, of having an affair with his wife. In their confrontation, De Niro is eating a sandwich while fixing a broken television and, moti-vated by frustration and weight gain, turns to his brother and asks him point blank whether he is "fucking my wife" (the scene can be found on the internet by searching for the film and Pesci's name). The bluntness of the question and Pesci's denial leaves one to believe that De Niro, portraying the self-destructive, psychopathic Jake La Motta, is deranged. Pesci's denial is convincing because, through-out the film, we have come to know De Niro's character as an anti-social maniac with a hair-trigger temper, and Pesci convinces us that his character is innocent by the steadiness of his gaze (his neutral mask). The verdict falls in favor of Pesci because we see De Niro as the sadomasochistic prize fighter jealous at every turn and Pesci as the loyal brother and manager suffering from an abusive, out of con-trol sibling. Pesci's character isn't sleeping with La Motta's wife; how could he be when we observe Pesci's denial with such poker-faced conviction? After viewing the movie many times, not least because of the performances, I am convinced that he *is* having an affair. But you would never it know from the acting, because, like Whitaker and Strasberg, Pesci never tips his hand. His performance is an example of denial: the tension between authenticity and deception creates an enigma; Pesci barely moves, but his inner life is riveting. He must convince his brother of his innocence by denying the accusation; and we have every reason to doubt De Niro's La Motta, given his paranoia. But watch closely – the art of denial, as with Whitaker and Strasberg, is as good as it gets here.

Denial allows the actor to create an illusion. Plato was right that we are illusionists, with the best of us creating the illusion so well that the sense of truth and artifice is indistinguishable. In every role an actor should find a way to incorporate denial. The goal is to examine the text's given circumstances and ask: is there anything I say or do in this play that is untrue or deceptive? Don't assume that everything a character says, or what others say about the character, is gospel. Is there manipulation and strategy in the words and actions? If our objectives are so urgent and strong – if what we covet is affecting us powerfully – wouldn't we lie in order to obtain them?

Entrances

An entrance is like a force of nature coming into the space; audiences need to be engaged immediately. Uta Hagen said about entrances that, in each set of given circumstances, "you have set yourself the task of a continuance of your life, which has brought you from the past into the present with a future at stake, as opposed to the task of 'entering' or simply getting on stage." While waiting in the wings, "you have responded to an imagined immediately preceding event by a real doing which allows you to continue your assumed life on stage" (*Respect*, p. 99). An entrance must be love-at-first-sight; the audience must be riveted from the moment you enter. The way to make an entrance is to make it personal, to create a full and complex world around the entrance. Stanislavsky insists that one enters "With some kind of concern, an inner goal, with curiosity, not empty." He adds:

> You made an entrance like an actor but I want a human being. In life there are other impulses to action. Find them, on stage ... The usual theatrical entrance, on the other hand, prevents this and produces

something quite different: external, showy histrionics. Your entrance was theatrical, 'in general,' there was no logic or sequence in your actions ... How can you not know on stage where you have come from and why! You must know that in detail. Entrances from 'outer space' never work in the theatre. (*Actor's Work on a Role*, pp. 49, 50)

Exercise 28: Entrance with a Lie

In the following exercise, an entrance with a lie, enter the room from the doorway and wait in the room. You are waiting to face one of the following scenarios:

1. Funeral parlor: You have lost someone close. You want to say goodbye, but you also must appear strong for the rest of those coming into the room (family, friends and so on). Someone else is, in fact, having a very difficult time with this. Everyone is about to enter the place where the casket is; you are alone and only have a moment before they arrive. How will you prepare to greet everyone?
2. Romantic liaison: You had been in a motel room with someone other than your significant other. While you wait, think of what you will say to your significant other. Are you denying marriage or having a relationship? How much does your significant other know about your personal relationships?
3. Someone else's success: Having viewed your best friend's successful recital (you coached him/her), you enter a room. Or, you are in a green room where your friend has just won an award. You feel you deserve the award, the compliments, the accolades. Try to compliment the friend convincingly, knowing that you are the reason for her success yet she will receive all the credit. What exactly did you do to support your friend's success? Are you jealous? How will you mask the jealousy?

The three entrances concern sex, death and success, three critical experiences. And each entrance deals with a lie, cover, mask, or something that is going on internally and externally. You have to have what Stanislavsky calls two tempo-rhythms: an inner rhythm (what you feel about the situation), and an outer rhythm (what you must convey to others). Jean Benedetti remarks that there are occasions "when we have to appear outwardly calm and in control although we are in turmoil on the inside" (*Stanislavski and the Actor*, p. 85). These exercises are intended to stimulate the contradictory tempo-rhythms in heightened dramatic situations.

In each entrance, be specific: the work is in the detail. Don't indicate anything. Breathe and experience the improvisation. Work internally, from your imagination and personal experience. Have specific objects in the room. Heighten your awareness of sight, smell, taste, clothing, hearing and so on. Why are you here? What time of day is it? What is the weather like? What do you wish to say to someone if they are to come into the room after you? What are the given circumstances? How would you behave if you were in this situation? What were you doing before you entered? All this must be answered by following your notion of the role's "ruling idea" – a subject taken up in the next chapter.

10

THE ROLE:
PSYCHOLOGICAL
GESTURE, HOMEWORK
AND REHEARSAL

A role is ready only when the actor has made the words of the character
his own words. (Vakhtangov, *Diaries*, p. 121)

As Vakhtangov suggests here, there are words on a page and there
is the actor's life. The incongruity of the two is often daunting. How
can I fit my life into this character? Or, more important: How can I
breathe life into the role? First, by reading the play repeatedly. The
words on the page are road maps guiding the actor from a lifeless
literary object to a human experience. Until the actor takes ownership of the words through justifying, personalizing and physicalizing, the play remains literature. The expression "breathing life into
the role" is exactly that. The first step is to read the play and breathe
it – literally breathe as you read. The breathing helps the actor focus
on the inner life, stimulate the imagination, and take responsibility
for her creative contribution: "The actor must communicate on the
highest level. He must be the master of both words and ideas" (Adler,
Technique, p. 7).

Second, we have to find the "hook" or "ruling idea," the key feature
of the role that inspires you. The ruling idea is the unifying theme
that underlies a performance. The actor must have a vision, concept
and inner compelling drive informing the execution of the role. The
ruling idea can come from several sources, and each original idea
doesn't need to cancel out the others. Franc Chamberlain, compar-
ing Stanislavsky and Michael Chekhov, writes that "In a scene where
a character's child is ill, the Stanislavskian actor will behave as if

this were their own child. This adapts the character to the actor's life and patterns of feelings and behaviour." On the other hand, the Chekhovian actor, he says, "will focus on the character and observe how the character responds to the child and behave in that way. In this case the actor is adapting to the character" (p. 15). I think these are excellent suggestions for the actor *to do both* – work from personal experience *and* adapt to the character's given circumstances. The play's circumstances naturally are not mine. This is why we have imagination. If, for example, as an actor, I was born rich but in the play I am poor, of course I must look upon my child as underprivileged and the illness will go unheeded because of my poverty. I naturally have to use my imagination to observe my child within the context of the play's given circumstances. But I still treat the child *as if it is my own*, connecting viscerally and spontaneously with *my emotions*. The only way to make a character live is to personalize the role, endowed with *the actor's feelings, thoughts and experiences*. This is, then, my "ruling idea."

We must ask: What is the ruling idea of the role and what do I, the actor, want to say about it? We interpret the role through our beliefs, emotions, actions and convictions. We serve the author and director, and must work in unison with their visions; but we also serve ourselves and the audience. What do we want to say to an audience with this role? With each possibility we test ideas; we consider ramifications and consequences; we look to imaginative ways of bringing life to the role; and we always take these tools and breathe them. We literally think and feel and breathe with this in mind.

Third, we look for characters' objectives – what do they want? What are they seeking to accomplish? What are the obstacles preventing the characters from obtaining their goals? Larry Moss explains that the objective "is so emotionally powerful to your character that it will make you try to obliterate any obstacle in your path" (p. 21). Our goal, then, is to incorporate the characters' desires into our desires. By incorporating the characters' desires into the actors' personal lives, the actors meld with the characters. Think of DNA: the role's context must merge with an actor's experience like two strands. One strand is the actor's personal life, and the other is the role. The strands of DNA spiral around each other, intersecting and traveling in the same direction, both seeking the same line, or goal, and each leaning on the other for support. The two strands merge seamlessly, making it hard to distinguish one from the other.

The objective is the *basic desire of the character in the overall arc of the role*. From then on the actor looks for a through line (or spine) of behavior that serves this objective. It is, in Stanislavsky's words, "the quintessence of the play. The through line of action is the leitmotif which runs through the entire work." This objective, he adds, is "the inborn vital purpose and aspiration rooted in our being, in our mysterious 'I'" (*Creating a Role*, p. 79). By "I" Stanislavsky is referring to the "I am being," the act of merging or transforming into the character by absorbing all the character's given circumstances as a part of the actor's life: "I have put myself in the centre of a situation I have invented, that I feel really inside it, that I really exist at its very heart, in a world of imaginary objects, and that I am beginning to act as me, with full responsibility for myself" (*Actor's Work*, p. 70). The objective and the "I am being" must be framed in terms of what Bella Merlin calls "the ruling idea of the script" (*Stanislavsky Toolkit*, p. 220).

However, *before we understand what a character wants, we have to understand what we want*. Until the actor understands who she is and how her desires are physicalized – acted out in a physical manner – she is merely fitting into a script's framework without knowing how to make an inner connection to the role. "Acting is the art of Self," Charles Marowitz writes, "the supreme revealment of Self. On stage, it is Self which feeds the actor and Self which is fed upon" (*Stanislavsky and the Method*, p. 42). We first have to know what moves us before we can apply this knowledge to a play; we first have to exercise our Self before we can embody a role. The "hook," "ruling idea" and "objective" are not cerebral considerations; they are not an academic exercise in getting something correct for a test or to please a teacher. They are creative and flexible acts, bodily expressions that define the features of your performance. This book has been about you as a creative artist, someone who looks deeply into him- or herself and finds desires, dreams, imagination, passions and actions. You are responsible for the presentation of the human condition in all its facets; now that you have explored them, you are ready to examine a role.

The play's given circumstances are a blueprint for the actor. Characters are not, however, merely the invention of the playwright or the pawn of the director; they are also invested in the play's social context. Cultural conditions are a motivational factor; the actor should look to world events for inspiration. The actor secures the performance by studying the play's events in the context of history, economics and cultural backdrop. Stella Adler says that the "play-wright gives you the play, the idea, the style, the conflict, the character, etc. The background life of the character will be made up of the social cultural, political, historical, and geographical situation in which the author places him." The actor studies these contexts "within the framework of the character's own time and situation" (The Reality of Doing, p. 222). For actors to accomplish this, they must study the times, observe paintings, read newspapers and magazines of the period, examine architecture, understand the surrounding events, and listen to music corresponding to the time and place of the play. In this way the actors become what Paul Mann calls "actor-anthropologist[s]" (p. 87).

Like a detective, the actor's job in analyzing a script is to ferret out clues: objectives, relationships and specificity of the character's life as described in the text; but the actor is not an interchangeable spoke on a wheel. The actor's choices are individual – you cannot make a choice for one actor and expect it to work for another. The interpretation of the role demands nuance, creativity and revelations of self. Individual choices are our unique contributions. Stella Adler says emphatically that "*in your choice is your talent*. Acting is everything but the cold words" (*Technique*, p. 26). Unless an actor has a personal connection to the material, circumstances and other actors, and makes choices along these lines, the role will fail to inspire. And without inspiration the performance will never rise above the pedestrian. Characters in fiction are not people; the actor *makes them people by virtue of embodying them*.

The actor studies a script similar to the way a carpenter studies an architectural blueprint: the outline of the building is on paper but the living organism is unrealized until the builder turns the design into a concrete entity. Hamlet doesn't experience emotion; the actor playing Hamlet does. The play (or a character in the play) may say that Hamlet is getting angry, but this is *a statement, not a feeling*. The script of a play or film may say that the character is sad or happy or whatever, but these are literary descriptions devoid of flesh and blood – a mental concept unrealized as a living organism. The actor's emotions and choices are the character's emotions and choices because the actor's are the only concrete feelings occurring. Words certainly guide emotion and action; if, for example, another character asks "Why are you so happy?" the actor must investigate why that was said and what in the actor's behavior prompts the other character to make the remark. But in and of themselves words are nothing more than suggestive landmarks. Actors cannot change the words, but once we understand that words have a multitude of meanings, the possibilities are limitless. My thoughts are the character's thoughts, my feelings are as his, my relationships to the other actors are the character's relationships, my choices are the character's, and my passions are his passions. If I play Romeo, it is how I feel about Juliet (and specifically how I feel about the actress playing her) that defines how Romeo feels towards Juliet. It is not "Romeo loves Juliet," but "I love the actress playing Juliet." I can read the text and it is says Romeo loves Juliet; I don't need an actor to figure this out. I go to the theater to see *how* this actor *specifically* loves *this specific Juliet* (and the operative word here is "specific"). If I, the actor, fail to feel anything about her, then *I fail, not the words on the page.* If a different actress takes the role of Juliet, I must feel something different because Juliet is different. She walks differently, talks differently and so on, and I must adjust. The job of the actor is *to develop the relationship with the other actor.* There are more than a billion ways to love Juliet – each person's love is different. The same can be said about every emotion and relationship. *I go to the theater to see human relationships, something I cannot obtain from reading the play.*

In reading the play repeatedly, look for relationships, goals, desires – take nothing for granted, because everything counts. What does the character want and whom does she want it from? Why does she want it, and why now? What is the obstacle to getting it? What are the actions with which she proceeds to obtain it? Don't worry about emotions. Feelings will come when your desires are either thwarted or rewarded. Ask yourself – what excites me about this role? What aspects do I connect with? Do I connect with several elements in the role? Don't rely on one exciting event or relationship – look for many, try to accumulate several exciting things you feel about the role. What is the character's journey – what is the character experiencing throughout the play as well as before and after it?

Vakhtangov contends that

> Unless the actor makes the essence of the play the essence *for himself* and most importantly, believes that the secret of genuine creativity lies in trusting the subconscious mind (which itself reacts from the essence), he is forced to act by means of stock methods he has built up in the past during bad rehearsals. Everything will be boring and familiar to all.

Predictability will arise because "the audience will know in advance how the actor will play this or that episode" (*Diaries*, p. 121).

Accumulating stock methods or practiced physical gestures can appear "truthful," in so far as they have become habitual. But they lead to predictability. Find the inner spark that moves you in the role and then work to convey that spark. Find something new in each role. This is one of the greatest offerings actors can give to the world: they see new things about human behavior every minute of every day. They bring new ideas to each role. Otherwise acting is merely working for the audience's approval, slavishly following the dictates of the director, executing motion mechanically, or just playing the same thing that has performed year in, year out. To apply an external judgment or quality about a character – to represent the role rather than experience it – is to generalize and editorialize. If you don't feel the character's inner life, then why bother? Is it merely a pay check that motivates you? I would suggest that, if money is the objective, get out of acting immediately and do something where profit comes faster (much faster!). Are you playing the role merely to gain attention? There is some degree of exhibitionism apparent in acting; but if this is the sole reason to act, audiences will spot this desire for approval instantly. Actors should perform their roles because they want to convey something about the human condition. The role is the conduit for their expression, and the voice and body's expressiveness is the instrument through which actors convey thoughts and feelings. What is passion if not "inner?" What do people desire? What do they covet? These are the questions we must ask constantly to understand the human condition.

Psychological Gesture and Characterization

Michael Chekhov defined "psychological gesture" in this way: "Take a certain gesture as 'to grasp.' Do it physically. Now only do it inwardly, remaining physically unmoved. As soon as we have developed this gesture, it becomes a certain 'psychology,' and that is what we want" (*The Drama Review*, p. 63). The physical gesture is connected to a psychological desire. Chekhov wanted the work to be in the body, in movement, and in the process, not in the head. Because of his own physiological condition (he suffered a nervous breakdown), he found Stanislavsky's emphasis on emotions too personal and too short on physicality. However, far too much has been made about their differences and not enough about their similarities. Christine Edwards says that Chekhov's method "is really a further means of building a characterization. It differs from Stanislavsky in its emphasis upon outside environment and its effect upon the actor. If used with Stanislavsky's System as a base, Chekhov's technique can greatly enrich the actor's palette of emotions" (p. 257). Once we have obtained inner connections to a role, we can start to find the physical actions and expressions.

Chekhov worked to create physical changes in actors' bodies by means of atmosphere, quality of motion and acknowledgment of the body in space. The mind is an extension of space, he contends, and not encased in the brain; we live and exist in the world around us and our thoughts exist in the world. The character you play is different than you, having a different body, thoughts and rhythm. As a result, Chekhov developed skills to transform himself into characters behaving differently. For Chekhov, the creation of a character was a way into the role's symbolic archetype; it wasn't necessarily pathological or psychological, but rather the necessary uncovering of the unconscious using a physical language that he shared with the choreographer and dance educationalist Rudolf Laban. The physical states coax the unconscious mind, offering a means toward self-awareness more profound (in Chekhov's view) than the groping for the subconscious through psychology alone. Armed with this conviction, Chekhov embarked on his Jungian journey into his creativity (in contrast to Stanislavsky's more Pavlov-oriented approach).

Exercise 29: Stepping into Character

One of his exercises for characterization is "stepping into character." Stand with your eyes shut, relax, and visualize the character's imaginary spine. See the character's spine as if the character had lined up directly in front of you. It is important to take your time with this, seeing every muscle and joint as if the character was standing there with their back to you. Choices should be tried and discarded if you feel they are uninspiring. Stand easily, with your knees loose and joints flexible, eyes closed, and visualize the character's spine. Franc Chamberlain "suggests taking on the body parts, perhaps starting with the hands, or the feet, or the nose. Eventually we take on the whole of the character's body, which is different from ours in significant ways" (pp. 77–8). Visualize a body part, open your eyes and "step forward," taking on the body part of the character. Primarily you embody the character's center: every person emanates energy from a certain part of their body. An imaginary center, Chamberlain says, "can be visualized anywhere in the body" (p. 79). Different centers stimulate different energy: groin center will create a different energy – a different walk, attitude and physicality – than a center emanating from the chin. It is important in working this way that, as Lenard Pettit says, "The image must *hold* you. You appear stiff when you hold the image" (p. 165). In other words, the image should be in motion, fluid and not rigid. It should be incorporated into your breathing so that it becomes part of a flowing and loose process. The body of an actor, Chekhov says, "must absorb psychological qualities, must be filled and permeated with them so that they will convert it gradually into a sensitive membrane, a kind of receiver and conveyor of the subtlest images, feelings, emotions, and will impulses" (*To the Actor*, p. 2). Once you feel comfortable with your choice of energy center, the character's power will radiate from this. This exercise enables you, via your imagination, to physicalize the body of the character, fostering characterization. Chekhov stressed artistic forms that are selective and refined – artistic awareness (for Chekhov, likewise Stanislavsky, not everything is stageworthy) – which offers a sense of empowerment. Once you step forward, move about the stage, with your energy guiding you from the center.

Exercise 30: Psychological Gesture I

Find the character's objective – their wants, desires, needs and so on, and translate it into a gesture. Make the gesture vivid and theatrical; repeat the gesture several times, experimenting with it, refining it, changing it as you see fit. Don't be afraid to make it big, bold and visceral; don't be timid. Continue breathing as you practice the gesture (do it several times) and take stock of your breathing rhythms as you perform it. Then, see it in your mind's eye; in other words, visualize the gesture without actually moving. The gesture should move you emotionally, excite you, stimulate your creativity and passion, and affect your breathing patterns.

Chekhov says that when the actor experiments with a Psychological Gesture, eventually she

> begins to love it, and experience it, and use it, then we shall see that this gesture is like a magnet which attracts so many things of a more complicated kind, through our psychology. They will be our

individual things, not what has been written about the part – that is not important – what is important is to know what the actor feels.

When we do the gesture many times, he adds, "we will see something. It must come of itself. That is the whole secret" (*Lessons for the Professional Actor*, p. 110). Chekhov's aim was to deemphasize analytic (mental) procedure and replace it with synthesis – the whole body, mind, soul, vision, passion and so on. The Psychological Gesture must be executed as typical of the character, performed with strength, definition, total body involvement, and encapsulating the character's desire. Actors must find ways of transforming into character in an aesthetically pleasing way. But Chekhov was very clear that unless the transformation is organic and experienced, relaxed and improvisatory, it is a mere shell without heartbeat; motion without emotional connection. "Everything in the method is an avenue," he said, "the elaborate body, the concentration, everything leads to the point where the talent feels it is freed" (*The Drama Review*, p. 69). Archetype and gesture "are things which have to grow and develop" (p. 70), but warns that "If you have prepared your part based on clichés, nothing will be changed" (p. 71). The critical point of the Psychological Gesture, he says, "is your own secret" (p. 72). It is not technique for its own sake, but rather a freeing process inspiring a sense of fantasy through gesture. Mala Powers explains that Psychological Gesture

> is a movement that embodies the psychology and Objective of a character. Using the actor's entire body, and executed with the utmost intensity, it gives the actor the basic structure of the character and at the same time can put the actor into the various moods required by the script. (p. xxxviii)

Exercise 31: Psychological Gesture 2

This exercise is an extension of Chekhov's Psychological Gesture. Find a painting or a photograph of a person you feel best personifies your character. It doesn't have to literally be like your character; even an abstract painting works, as long as you have faith that it will work for you. Do this only after you have studied your role sufficiently.

Look at the image of the person and strike a pose that resembles the image. Note the physical pose – assume it, embody it and breathe life into it. Your pose should be easy and relaxed, not stiff, with your eyes alert and able to look around you as you pose. Work from the spine and from your breathing (your hara, as described in Chapter 1).

What is your relationship to the space around you? What atmosphere is being created by your pose? Are there others in the painting – if so, how do you relate to them?

Justify the pose – how did you get here, why are you posing like this, and what are you trying to accomplish (your action)?

Ask yourself: what would I be if I were this person? What are the person's goals in life?

Now move about, using different tempo-rhythms. Where is the character's center? How are you relating to space? Other people? What is inspiring you about this body, this posture, this physical motion?

Homework

The following things should be considered when reading the play and before rehearsing. But don't execute them mechanically – because "the teacher says so." Bring your imagination and passion to the work. Make it personal.

Justify every word, action and relationship in the text. Keep your spontaneity and belief in what you are saying as if it is for the first time, but be aware of why you are saying and doing everything. You can change as you perform, but you need to know why you are here, where you came from, where you are going, and what motivates you to act.

Discover your motivation through objectives and actions. What have you come onstage to do? To whom are you doing it? What is the reason for doing it? Think it through and be prepared to change your mind during rehearsal. Your first choice is often a good one, but it should also lead you to deeper and richer choices.

What you covet – your objective – must have urgency. You must want it *now*. Not tomorrow, not later in the day, but at the very moment you enter. Ask yourself what the consequences will be if you do not obtain the objective? What is the obstacle preventing you from obtaining the objective? Remember that every inquiry is done with ease, breathing, relaxation and concentration.

What supports the objective? What is the subtext, the interstitial scene, the unspoken words or sounds that you say to excite you? You must have a non-verbal interior mantra beneath the text that you experience at every moment onstage. Consider scenes that are not in the script but are mentioned or implied. Prepare to act them out in rehearsal or by yourself.

Avoid generalizations. Make *specific choices* relative to the given circumstances of the story that have *meaning for you*. This includes the period of the story, the time of day, the economic conditions of your character, any physical identifiers noted in the story, social fashion, and status. If the story doesn't provide these things, you must fill in the blanks.

In defining the given circumstances, you must personalize and physicalize your life in this situation by living "as if" you are a human being among the given circumstances. You must give over to the world of the play with your imagination, energy, mind and body. Look for the unusual, the surprising, the spontaneous, what is happening at the very moment you are performing.

Work truthfully. Don't indicate anything. Trust yourself and your faith in what you believe. Allow the events and experiences to affect you onstage. Keep your mind and body open and alert. Engage with each actor.

Trust your impulses and inner imagery, but also allow yourself to be surprised by your own behavior. This will allow you to change and be affected by the events in the scene. You are improvising. Let every word or gesture by other actors affect you. Don't let anything they do go by unnoticed. Remember, the audience will see what they do, so you'd better be in synchrony with everyone and everything around you.

What is occurring the moment before the scene takes place? Where exactly are you coming from? Are you lying about anything? Make the choices vivid, exciting, imaginative.

What animal represents your character? How can you incorporate this into your movements? What other physical choices can you make? Does your character have an accent? Wear glasses? Dress a certain way? Have a certain self-image?

You also must consider "style," by which I mean a play's language, such as is often found in non-contemporary plays. Michael Saint-Denis said "One must love style. Style is liberation from the mud of naturalism" (p. 67). Style is the form of expression, an ability to bring the mind and body to life through a new way of speaking and moving. Style means moving into venues such as classical plays, and the only way to exercise style is to practice it – experience the words and movements so that they become a "living through" process. Imagine how powerful a performance could be if the actor appears human and natural in a Shakespearean role. All the more reason to work on truthful behavior in Shakespeare or other so-called classical authors – the demands are greater, therefore your efforts must be greater. The work in style is more difficult – but shouldn't that be your goal? You should no more make pedestrian choices in contemporary plays than in classics. Take pride in your artistry and take the responsibility of exercising your voice, body and emotional life – bringing to the stage the broadest imagination you can acquire. You must absorb the role's social standing, class status, life's work, surroundings and given circumstances, in every instance. Go through the entire play, Stanislavsky says, "Understanding that you must behave like the character in the given circumstances and according to his social standing. We call this merging with the role *the sense of oneself in the role and the role in oneself*" (*Actor's Work on a Role*, p. 60).

Rehearsal

The following is a recommended procedure for developing a scene and a play. It is an outline, a brief summation of procedures, and one that should be modified and added to as you see fit. Using the tools provided throughout this book as a foundation for the development of your role, work through each step methodically and carefully. Consider the role deeply, thoughtfully and patiently; find the humor in the script and its situations; keep in mind your character's humanity and vulnerability; and remember that your art is in the choices you make.

Analyze the text by considering the given circumstances of the play. Consider the socioeconomic background of the characters and the situations; what are the sources of income, how do the characters eat, pay rent and so on. Ask what the physical manifestations are: historical time and place, the weather and so on. What are the conflicts and issues? Determine the objectives, actions and obstacles. What is at stake? What will happen to you if you don't obtain what you want? Are there any physical or vocal conditions to consider? Accents? Disabilities? Follow the facts of the play and discern why they exist and how they occurred. As you work, kill the critic in you! Be ready to work with an open mind and heart. As Michael Chekhov said, "We have to be open to all the impressions which are coming to us during the rehearsals" (*Lessons for the Professional Actor*, p. 111).

Find the passion: What is the most exciting thing about the play that moves you? As Vakhtangov said, agitate from the essence – from the central idea and emotional inspiration you find in the role. Agitate from your soul, and not from prescriptive notions of what the scene should be like.

Relaxation, concentration and breathing: In every rehearsal it is essential to warm up the mind and body for creative purposes. Use breathing work and Feldenkrais/Alexander Technique methods. Begin by lying on the floor; this helps the actor to literally "get grounded," to sense the ground beneath her. It is crucial for performers to locate the breathing halfway between the naval and groin. Remember, too, that the jaw is a central point of tension. Work toward sensing both place (space) and gravity (feet, grounding and so on). Get present in your body. Kill the censor in yourself. Relax your knees. Breathe!

Sense memory: It is important to exercise the senses, to prepare them for work in the same way as you activate your body to receive stimuli. Touch, taste, smell, sound and sight must be stimulated and alive. Drink an imaginary cup of coffee, liquor, tea, soup or a cool drink on a hot day. Imagine the weather: Extreme heat, extreme cold, humid, dry and so on. Sense colors, textures, shapes, forms.

Read behavior in your fellow actor: How they move, tone of voice, their mood. Experience the repetition exercise; repeat phrases. Look for what is beneath the phrase.

While still using the repetition exercise, actors try to beckon each other to their side of the room with the phrase "come to me." The simple "objective" is to get the partner to cross an imaginary line, which is determined in the space. Improvise using a subtext "I want" or mantra to be spoken aloud. While on your side of the room, the repetition phrase is dropped, and in its place the actors develop an "I want" phrase. For example, "hug me," or "appreciate me," or "take me away from here." This becomes a mantra. The idea is to continue to read behavior, but now there is something at stake. The "I want" still uses the idea of drawing the other actor in.

Incorporate weather, age and any other physical manifestations that are appropriate to the scene. It is important to continue to relate to and play off the partner while simultaneously embodying physical attributes that are either from external sources (weather, time of day, locale) and characterizations (animal imagery, physical attributes of the character and so on).

Incorporate a secret, a lie, a photo that moves you, an image that excites you.

Incorporate interstitial scenes that inform your history and your relationships.

Incorporate the six basic actions: Beg or plead; seduce; dominate; destroy; celebrate; and accuse. Try all six; try others. This helps to develop a variety of actions and increases the depth of your performance. Try other actions.

Incorporate the Psychological Gesture. Embody the physicality of the role; that is, finding the quintessential gesture that expresses the full extent of the needs and desires of the role.

Incorporate what occurs just before you enter. Make your first beat (your first action) in the scene actually your second, with the first beat and action occurring offstage, just before you enter.

Actors repeat the beginning of the scene, using the actions, so that the scene begins strongly. Begin to incorporate "as if," – that is, working as if you are the character, in this situation, and justified in believing that you are in the here and now.

Launch into the scene itself, working truthfully, improvisationally and moment-to-moment. Don't be afraid to stop, start again, consider what it is you're saying and why. *Try out ideas and invest your imagination.*

CONCLUSION

It is easy to lose sight of our artist goals; from lack of attention, bad habits infect our work; and the daily grind erodes our talent. Actors, Stanislavsky said, "bring all the dirt of their daily lives into the theatre – gossip, intrigue, tittle-tattle, slander, envy, petty vanity. The result is not a temple of art but a spittoon, a rubbish heap, a cesspit" (*Actor's Work*, p. 557). Such behavior is wrong but understandable: actors receive little in the way of monetary reward; society rarely takes them seriously; and they often commercialize their gifts. They become cynical, lazy and despondent. They must work to overcome these obstacles. To grow as an actor requires a willingness to return to the basics at each and every rehearsal and performance, and to train oneself to observe inwardly and outwardly the human condition. "How do singers, pianists, dancers start their day?" Stanislavsky asked. Singers do vocal exercises; pianists play scales; dancers work their pliés at the ballet *barre*; and writers write every day, so as not to lose the habit of writing. For these artists, practice "happens every day, winter or summer, and a day missed is a day lost, a step backwards artistically" (*Actor's Work*, pp. 566, 567). Actors, too, must incorporate rigorous, daily discipline – working on sense memory, physical tasks, and exercises related to breathing, voice, movement, relaxation and concentration.

The systematic approach taken in this book can be followed chronologically, using each chapter as a stair-step approach to your creative development. But remember, there is no formula to being a better actor, no simplistic means to an end. The work is always process and discovery, trial and error, exploration and creative attempts to build imaginatively a human being. You must never neglect your body and voice: the exercises in the early chapters of this book are just some of the many ways to develop dexterity, vocal range, and physical plasticity and elasticity. Take dance classes, singing lessons; work on fencing, acrobatics, yoga; and cultivate all forms of breathing work. These daily routines are critical to your growth as an actor. *Do everything with full, committed breathing.* Practice relaxation and concentration daily. Sense and emotion memory must also be practiced every day, because if it is neglected it will atrophy. Practice one-action/one-objective exercises daily, especially in a classroom setting, where you can receive feedback and experience the exercise before an audience. Practice the repetition exercise so that reading other peoples' behavior becomes a part of your good working habits. Exercise your imagination by really observing things and putting yourself in the situations you see. This doesn't mean going into a trance, but rather observing with heightened concentration, paying attention to details, seeing reality more clearly, taking nothing for granted, and then imagining why things are the way they are. Actors are creators of make-believe and, like children, must have a willingness and accessibility to every situation. Read scripts daily, continuously, and as an actor – which means finding in the role the ruling idea that inspires you. Find ways to improvise, always looking to enrich your characters, making them more fully rounded and three-dimensionally human. Find the passion that reminds you of why you are in this noble profession – not the commercial success or the accolades, but the inner need to convey the human condition to an audience.

You must be vigilant and guard against two things that plague actors. First, the need to produce results quickly often rushes actors into glib choices and superficial performances. They lose patience; in their desperate efforts to "get work" they rush headlong into results without careful deliberation or the patience needed to shape a human being out of imagination, observation and experience. Stanislavsky reminds us that "the creative process of experiencing and embodiment is not sudden, using one method, but gradual, in several steps and stages." The process of creating a human being begins in the imagination, what Stanislavsky says is "our sleepless night," into the "calm of the study, then in closed rehearsals, then, for a small audience of strangers, then in a series of public dress rehearsals and, finally, in countless performances. And every time it is done anew" (*An Actor's Work on a Role*, p. 175).

Second, there is the strong desire to be "liked." Actors face multiple rejections; they have fragile egos that get bruised easily; and they endure a society that places little value on what they do. So likeability becomes actors' "objective": it infects their actions and objectives, even in the characters they play. The author Jonathan Franzen observes that "If you dedicate your existence to being likable, however, if you adopt whatever cool persona is necessary to make it happen, it suggests that you've despaired of being loved for who you really are." A result is avoiding risks, because "to expose your whole self, not just the likable surface, and to have it rejected, can be catastrophically painful. The prospect of pain generally, the pain of loss, of breakup, of death, is what makes it so tempting to avoid love and stay safely in the world of liking." Pain, however, is part of being alive, and the characters actors perform, even in comedies (perhaps even more so in comedies) experience pain, loss, rejection, humiliation and sadness. They, of course, experience other emotions; but if you spend your life hiding your pain and shortcomings you will run up against the greatest obstacle of being an actor: the fear of showing your audience precisely who you are.

Anything that obscures or prevents the ability to connect actors' lives with the roles and performance must be undone. But is it not enough for the actor merely to "feel" it; such pedestrian attitudes turn acting into mundane reality. Actors are artists who convey a heightened reality; their artistic choices must reflect a great sensibility. Actors are representatives of the human condition and therefore bear a tremendous responsibility to illuminate humans in all their mysterious extremes – their foolishness and heroism, their shortcomings and strengths. Actors bring life, but as Maria Ouspenskaya reminds us, the "stage should be better than life. If we just photograph life, it is realism for realism's sake, and nobody will be interested." Instead, we must "exercise the inner instrument all the time to jump above everyday life. Learn to get into an exciting state of mind and heart. It will make all the difference in the world in your performances for you and for the audience" (p. 2.4:4). Actors must rise above an enormous wave of pressure in order to demonstrate their humanity. The poet Rainer Maria Rilke maintains that

> If your daily life seems poor, do not blame it, blame yourself, tell yourself that you are not poet enough to call forth its riches; for to the creator there is no poverty and no poor indifferent place. And even if you were in some prison the walls of which let none of the sounds of

the world come to your senses – would you not then still have your
childhood, that precious, kingly possession, that treasure-house of
memories? (pp. 19–20)

As artists, Rilke adds, actors must "take whatever comes with great
trust, and if only it comes out of your own will, out of some need of
your innermost being, take it upon yourself and hate nothing" (p. 35).
Actors embark on a journey of self-discovery and observation, bringing to their art their own ideas and emotions. Actors empathize
with others because they bear the responsibility of demonstrating
human strengths and flaws. Actors never stop learning, seeing, feeling, growing; if they do, they stop acting. There are deeper, richer
choices to make; imaginative choices that unleash bizarre possibilities; and never forget that *passion* brought you to acting – passion
that ought to be continually renewed. Actors must, in Stanislavsky's
words "restock [their] minds" and why it is so important for an actor
to "study, read, observe, travel, be up-to-date with social, religious,
political matters. These are the handful of ideas he throws into the
sack of his superconscious" (*An Actor's Work on a Role*, p. 167). Acting
is a journey of a lifetime, and the life's journey is what matters.

BRIEF BIOGRAPHIES OF KEY ACTING TEACHERS

The following are sketches of the most influential teachers during the twentieth century, and of schools where students can further their knowledge of each teacher's method. Books mentioned below are listed fully in the bibliography.

Konstantin Stanislavsky (1863–1938) was the single most influential acting teacher of the twentieth century. Along with his artistic partner, **Vladimir Nemirovich-Danchenko** (1858–1943), he founded the Moscow Art Theatre in 1898, where his work can still be studied. His records of teaching can be read in his autobiography, *My Life in Art*, as well as his series of books and articles on acting (*An Actor's Work*, and two translations of the same work in English: *An Actor Works on the Role* and *Creating a Role*). Stanislavsky's groundbreaking work developed along two fronts: first, he advocated heightened awareness of the actor's sensory and emotional life through exercises; and second, he was one of the first directors to develop a lengthy rehearsal period where the actor lives through the life the character. The basic training of the actor begins with sense and emotional depth, along with training voice and movement; next, the actor learns how to read a script to ferret out objectives and action; and finally the actor embodies the role by experiencing the character's life. The actor lives the life of the role outside the text through improvisation (what I have referred to in this book as "interstitial scenes"), so that the actor creates a three-dimensional human being – someone with a past, present and future. In 1911–12 Stanislavsky founded the First Studio (later known as the Second Moscow Art Theatre), intended to develop his System of actor training. The studio spawned some of the most significant acting teachers of the twentieth century, among them the first leader of the studio, Stanislavsky's assistant and spiritual guide, **Leopold Sulerzhitsky** (1872–1916). It was Sulerzhitsky who, among others, exposed Stanislavsky to Eastern techniques of acting (yoga), as well as the necessity of delving into the depth of the actor to unearth the subconscious connections to the self and the role. Another member of the first studio, **Vera Soloviova** (1891–1986), with her husband Andrius Jilinsky and Tamara Daykarhanova, established schools of acting throughout the United States (primarily in Los Angeles). Additional members of the studio were Boleslavsky, Ouspenskaya, Vakhtangov and Chekhov (see below), who disseminated Stanislavsky's work during the twentieth century. More recent directors and teachers of Stanislavsky have been (among many others) Anatoly Smeliansky, Yuri Liubimov, Anatoly Efros, Grigori Kristi, Anatoly Vasiliev, Herman Sidakov, Rosa Tolskaya and Igor Lisov, the last three of whom were participants in the DVD *Beyond the Method* (ASTI 2006).

Richard Boleslavsky (1889–1937) and **Maria Ouspenskaya** (1876–1949) founded the American Laboratory Theatre in the 1920s, attended by Lee Strasberg and Harold Clurman among others. Boleslavsky's 1933 book, *Acting: The Six Basic Lessons*, established the fundamentals of the American Method style of acting. His work stressed "affective memory," which was carried on in the USA by Lee Strasberg.

Evgenii Vakhtangov (1883–1992) was one of the first actors to use Stanislavsky's System successfully. Also influenced by **Vsevolod Meyerhold** (1874–1940), he combined Stanislavsky's ideas of truthful behavior and emotion recall with Meyerhold's heightened theatricalism, creating when he called "fantastic realism." Two of Vakhtangov's greatest contributions were the idea of *justification* – not only of the characters being performed, but also justifying why you are an actor, why you are in the theater, and why you are performing in this or that play. Motivation for Vakhtangov was not a pedestrian choice ("I'm going to drink water because I'm thirsty"), but something grounded in a deeply-felt purpose. The play, production and the reasons for being an actor are part of the actor's work on motivation, justification and personalization. Second was his emphasis on "scenic faith" – the ability of the actor to believe in the situation and immerse herself in the given circumstances. His work influenced Lee Strasberg, Stella Adler, Sanford Meisner, Uta Hagen and Paul Mann, among many others, and his works in English have been superbly edited by Andrei Malaev-Babel.

Michael Chekhov (1891–1955), nephew of the playwright Anton Chekhov, Stanislavsky's student and close friend of Vakhtangov. Stressing (among other things) imagination and physicalization, he developed exercises that included the "psychological gesture," where the actor works to discover an inner movement which encapsulates the character's objective; emphasized the body's center of energy, teaching the actor from where his/her source of energy emanates and radiates; and devised a series of movements designed to free the body and imagination. He wanted to shift Stanislavsky's emphasis from the actor's inner life to the imagination, and accentuate the way that the imagination informs physical expression. He established studios, first in the United Kingdom (Dartington Hall) and then in the United States. His work is carried on by MICHA (The Mikhail Chekhov Association), the center for the development of Chekhov's technique, and among the leading proponents were Beatrice Straight and Deidre Hurst du Prey (his original students) and later Mala Powers, Alma Law, Joanna Merlin, Ted Pugh, Lenard Petit, Franc Chamberlain and Marion Seldes.

Maria Knebel (1898–1985), Chekhov's student who developed the concept of "analysis through action," which combines inner justification and personalization with physicalization of activity and acting. Knebel insisted on an "improvisatory state of mind in the role" (quoted in Carnicke, "Knebel Technique," p. 106), where the actor lives through the role from the depth of her emotions and actions, finding fresh experiences in each performance. Knebel's emphasis was on the fusion of actor and role, where the actor sustains personalization and affective memory but combines it with immersion in the work of "experiencing" the life of the character spontaneously.

Lee Strasberg (1901–82), was the leading figure of what is known as the American Method. Founder, with Harold Clurman and Cheryl Crawford, of the Group Theatre (1931–40), Strasberg worked as a director and later as the head of the Actors Studio. He stood by the view that Stanislavsky never abandoned the use of "affective memory," but this position raised considerable controversy in actor training. Despite the efforts to downplay or disregard affective memory, and despite Strasberg's dogmatic adherence to it, new evidence is proving that Strasberg was essentially correct. Additionally, Strasberg advocated animal exercises, private moments, action and adjustments to other actors. In the United States his work has been carried on by Ed Kovens, Dwight Edward Easty, Loraine Hull, Lola Cohn, Doug Moston, Robert Ellermann and others at the Actors Studio and the Lee Strasberg Theatre and Film Institute (Los Angeles and New York).

Stella Adler (1901–92), a daughter of the great Yiddish acting family, Adler was one of the founding members of the Group Theatre. She advocated imagination, belief in the given circumstances, and script analysis. After visiting with Stanislavsky in Paris, she broke with Strasberg in 1934, claiming that Strasberg had corrupted Stanislavsky's work by overemphasizing affective memory. Her contretemps with Strasberg has unfortunately split actor training into two camps – those for Strasberg and those against. Regardless of their personal hostilities, however, Adler's work on imagination, immersion into the life of the role and commitment to bold actor choices established her as one of the great acting teachers of the twentieth century. She was the Head of Acting at the Yale School of Drama and later established her studio in New York. Her work is continued by the writings of Joanna Rotté and can be studied at the Stella Adler Conservatory in New York and Los Angeles.

Sanford Meisner (1905–97), also one of the original members of the Group Theatre, Meisner became the director of the Neighborhood Playhouse, which still carries on his work. At the Playhouse he developed his signature Repetition Exercise, the Reality of Doing, and other significant contributions. Meisner, like Adler, rejected Strasberg's emphasis on affective memory, replacing it with ways to find personal connections with other actors. Like Adler and Strasberg, he has trained many gifted actors. His work can be referenced in the writings of CC Courtney, William Esper, and Larry Silverberg, among others, as well as practiced at the Neighborhood Playhouse.

Paul Mann (1913–85), student of Chekhov and a member of the Group Theatre, he was an acting teacher at the Negro Ensemble Company, Director of Actor Training at the Repertory Theatre of Lincoln Center, and founder of the Paul Mann Actor's Workshop. Following Vakhtangov and Knebel, his emphasis was on combining affective-emotion memory with analysis through action. He stressed an emotional connection to actions, finding that the way to combine affective memory and action was to make actions always responsive to personal investment and passion. Among his students were Earle Gister (former Head of Acting at the Yale School of Drama), director and actress Barbara Loden, and the acclaimed director of Lorraine Hansberry and August Wilson, Lloyd Richards (former Artistic Director of the Yale School of Drama).

Uta Hagen (1919–2004), actress and teacher, who, with her husband Herbert Berghof (a student of Strasberg) established the HB Studio in New York, which continues to carry on her work. A teacher of many great actors, she introduced the ideas of substitution, endowment, sense and emotion memory as a way of creating inspiring motivation.

Robert Lewis (1909–97), former Head of Acting and Directing at the Yale School of Drama, he too taught some of the most creative actors of the twentieth century. His books, *Method – Or Madness?* and *Advice to the Players*, sought to modify Strasberg's emphasis on affective memory without abandoning it.

Sonia Moore (1902–95) established the American Center for Stanislavsky Theatre Art. In her two major books, *The Stanislavski System* and *Stanislavski Revealed*, and her translations of essays in *Stanislavski Today*, Moore presented a diversity of opinions on Stanislavsky's work. She was the leading advocate in the United States for the "method of physical action," a working technique that emphasized physical tasks and activities over emotion recall. For a study of her work, see Suzanne Trauth and Elizabeth Stroppel, *Sonia Moore and American Acting Training*.

Jerzy Grotowski (1933–99), Polish director and founder of the theatre laboratory, his innovative work on "poor theatre" built on Stanislavsky but emphasized the purity of the actor through physical actions, a stripping away of bourgeois activity (*via negativa*), and work on "objective drama" (finding the cultural roots of activities). His book, *Towards a Poor Theatre*, is the veritable bible for the radical avant-garde, and his work on action can be further studied in Thomas Richard's *At Work with Grotowski on Physical Actions*.

Declan Donnellan (1953–) founded the Cheek by Jowl Theatre Company. His work with actors stressed imagination and the other actor as object of attention: "You can never know what you are doing," he writes, "until you first know what you are doing it to. For the actor, all 'doing' has to be done *to* something. The actor can do nothing without the target" (p. 17). The clues to the imagination for Donnellan are not necessarily in the internal past of the actor, but in the outwardly directed object of attention, what he calls the "target" – hence his book, *The Actor and the Target*. The object is perceived in space and the actor uses the immediacy of this observation to inspire a spontaneous impulse. This method is similar to Meisner's Repetition Exercise, where the impulse is stimulated by "a reality of doing" to another person or thing rather than a reliance on an emotional past.

Anne Bogart (1951–), theater director and founder (along with choreographer Mary Overlie and director Tina Landau) of the acting technique known as "Viewpoints." Viewpoints consists of six fundamental ways of approaching a role: through space, shape, time/tempo, emotion, movement, and story (narrative). Viewpoints is practiced at the Saratoga International Theatre Institute (SITI), and rooted in the work of the Japanese actor and director, **Tadashi Suzuki** (1939–).

Phillip Zarrilli (1947–), acting teacher and director who works to combine Eastern and Western performance practices. His book, *Psychophysical Acting: An Intercultural Approach after Stanislavski*, attempts to merge Western techniques derived from Stanislavsky with yoga, Indian Kathakali dance-drama, Japanese *butoh* dance-drama, and other Asian techniques. Zarrilli fundamentally defines the problems of the Western actor as excessive reliance on Cartesian dualism – a separation of mind and body – which leads to acting that is either "overly-intellectualized or becomes overly subjective" (p. 76). Western acting is too compartmentalized, he insists, and proposes a more physically-based acting training that makes no distinction between mind and body.

BIBLIOGRAPHY

Asterisk (*) denotes recommended books for beginners.

Adler, Stella, The Reality of Doing, in Munk, 1965, pp. 210–27

—— *The Technique of Acting*, New York: Bantam, 1988*

—— *On Ibsen, Strindberg, Chekhov* (B. Paris, ed.), New York: Vintage, 1999

Alberts, David, *The Expressive Body: Physical Characterization for the Actor*, Portsmouth, NH: Heinemann, 1997*

Alice, Mary, Always Have a Secret, *Eight Women on the American Stage* (R. Harris, ed.), Portsmouth, NH: Heinemann, 1997, pp. 67–81

Appel, Alfred, *Jazz Modernism*, New York: Alfred Knopf, 2002

Archer, William, *Mask or Faces?*, in Diderot, *Paradox*, 1957

Baraka, Amiri [LeRoi Jones], *Blues People*, New York: Morrow Quill, 1963

Barthes, Roland, *Mythologies* (A. Lavers, trans.), New York: Hill & Wang, 1972

—— *Image, Music, Text* (S. Heath, trans.), New York: Hill & Wang, 1977

—— *Camera Lucida: Reflections on Photography* (R. Howard, trans.), New York: Hill & Wang, 1981

Batson, Susan, *Truth: Personas, Needs, and Flaws in the Art of Building Actors and Creating Characters*, New York: Rugged Land, 2007*

Belgrad, Daniel, *The Culture of Spontaneity*, Chicago: University of Chicago Press, 1998

Benedetti, Jean, *Stanislavski: An Introduction*, New York: Theatre Arts, 1989

—— *Stanislavski & the Actor*, New York: Routledge, 1998

—— Translator's Foreword, in Konstantin Stanislavsky, *An Actor's Work*, 2008, pp. xv–xxii

Benedetti, Robert, Zen in the Art of Actor Training, *Master Teachers of Theatre* (B. Hobgood, ed.), Carbondale, IL: Southern Illinois University Press, 1988

—— *The Actor at Work* (8th edn), Boston: Allyn & Bacon, 2001*

—— *The Actor in You* (2nd edn), Boston: Allyn & Bacon, 2003*

Boleslavsky, Richard, *Acting: The First Six Lessons*, New York: Theatre Arts, 1933

—— The Creative Theatre (trans. and ed. M. Berry, retyped from the original typescript by J. Roberts); quoted here from *Acting: The First Six Lessons* (R. Blair, ed.), London: Routledge, 2010 (The original manuscript is in the New York Public Library at Lincoln Center.)

Bogart, Anne, *Viewpoints*, Lyme NH: Smith Kraus, 1995*

Bradley, Margaret, Emotional Memory, *Emotions: Essays on Emotion Theory* (S. H. M. Van Goozen *et al.*, eds), Hillsdale, NJ: Lawrence Erlbaum Associates, 1994, pp. 97–134

Brando, Marlon, Playboy Interview, *Playboy*, interviewed by Lawrence Grobel, January 1979, p. 112

Brecht, Bertolt, *Brecht on Theatre* (trans. J. Willett), New York: Hill & Wang, 1964

Brook, Peter, *The Empty Space*, New York: Atheneum, 1968

—— *The Open Door: Thoughts on Theatre and Acting*, New York: Pantheon, 1993

Bruehl, Bill, *The Technique of Inner Action*, Portsmouth, NH: Heinemann, 1996*

Brustein, Robert, *Letter to a Young Actor*, New York: Peraeus, 2005

Caldarone, Marina and Maggie Lloyd Williams, *Actions: The Actors' Thesaurus*, Los Angeles: Drama Publishers, 2004*

Carnicke, Sharon M., *Stanislavsky in Focus*, London: Harwood, 1998

—— The Knebel Technique: Active Analysis in Practice, in *Actor Training* (A. Hodge, ed.), 2010, pp. 99–116

Carnovsky, Morris, *The Actor's Eye*, New York: PAJ, 1984

Chaikin, Joseph, *The Presence of the Actor*, New York: Atheneum, 1984

Chamberlain, Franc, *Michael Chekhov*, London: Routledge, 2004

Chubbuck, Ivana, *The Power of the Actor: The Chubbuck Technique*, Los Angeles: Gotham, 2005*

Chekhov, Anton, *Uncle Vanya* (trans. M. Frayn), London: Methuen, 1987

Chekhov, Michael, *To the Actor*, New York: Harper & Row, 1953

—— Stanislavsky's Method of Acting, in Cole, 1955, pp. 128–40

—— Michael Chekhov, *The Drama Review*, 27(3), 1983 (edition devoted to Chekhov)

—— *Lessons for the Professional Actor*, New York: PAJ, 1985

Churchill, Caryl, *Plays: 2*, London: Methuen, 1990

Clausewitz, Carl von, *On War*, (trans. M. Howard and P. Paret), Princeton, NJ: Princeton University Press, 1976

Clurman, Harold, From the *Fervent Years*, in Stanislavsky, K. *Stanislavsky*, 1963, pp. 185–8

Cohen, Lola (ed.), *The Lee Strasberg Notes*, London: Routledge, 2010

Cohen, Patricia, Long-Delayed Opening for History of (and by) Joseph Papp, *New York Times*, November 6, 2009, pp. C1, C6

Cohen, Robert, *Acting One* (3rd edn), London: Mayfield, 1984*

Cole, Toby (ed.), *Acting: A Handbook of the Stanislavsky Method*, New York: Crown, 1955

Courtney, C. C., The Neighborhood Playhouse, in Krasner, *Method Acting Reconsidered*, 2000, pp. 291–5

Crouch, Stanley, *Considering Genius: Writing on Jazz*, New York: Basic Books, 2006

Daw, Kurt, *Acting: Thought into Action*, Portsmouth, NJ: Heinemann, 1997*

Day-Lewis, Daniel, The New Iron-Tier's Man, *New York Times Magazine*, November 11, 2007, pp. 60–5, 90, 94–9

Diderot, Denis, *The Paradox of Acting*, New York: Hill & Wang, 1957

Diehl, Nancy, Probing Questions: Can Animals Really Smell Fear?, March 16, 2005. Available at: http:www.rps.psu.edu/probing/smell.html

Donnellan, Declan, *The Actor and the Target*, New York: TCG, 2002*

Dunbar, Paul Laurence, We Wear the Mask, *Selected African American Writing from 1760 to 1910* (Arthur P. Davis *et al.*, eds), New York: Bantam, 1971

Edwards, Christine, *The Stanislavsky Heritage*, New York: New York University Press, 1965

Ellermann, Robert, Russian Dolls, Unpublished manuscript, 2009

Easty, Edward Dwight, *On Method Acting*, New York: Ivy Books, 1981

Esper, William and Damon DiMarco, *The Actor's Art and Craft*, New York: Anchor, 2008*

Feldenkrais, Moshe, *Awareness through Movement*, New York: Harper & Row, 1972

Freud, Sigmund, *The Freud Reader* (P. Gay, ed.), New York: W. W. Norton, 1989

Giddens, Gary, *Lady Gets Her Due: Billie Holiday Companion* (L. Gourse, ed.), New York: Schirmer, 1997, pp. 90–9

Gillett, John, *Acting on Impulse: Reclaiming the Stanislavsky Approach*, London: Methuen, 2007*

Gillette, William, Illusion of First Time in Acting, *Papers on Acting* (B. Matthews, ed.), New York: Hill & Wang, 1958, pp. 124–35

Gorchakov, Nikolai, *Stanislavsky Directs* (trans. M. Goldina), New York: Limelight, 1985

Gordon, Mel, *Stanislavsky in America*, London: Routledge, 2010

—— *The Stanislavsky Technique: Russia*, New York: Applause, 1987*

Gottschild, Brenda Dixon, *Digging the Africanist Presence in American Performance*, Westport, CT: Greenwood Press, 1996

Grotowski, Jerzy, *Towards a Poor Theatre*, New York: Clarion, 1968

Guskin, Harold, *How to Stop Acting*, New York: Faber & Faber, 2003*

Guthrie, Tyrone, *On Acting*, New York: Viking Press, 1971*

Hagen, Uta, *Respect for Acting*, New York: Macmillan, 1973*

—— *A Challenge for the Actor*, New York: Schribner's Sons, 1991*

Healy, Patrick, Better Acting Through Chemistry, *New York Times*, Arts & Leisure Section, May 23, 2010, pp. 1, 4

—— A Reluctant Redgrave, On 'Daisy' and More (interview with Vanessa Redgrave), *New York Times*, February 16, 2011, pp. CI, C2

Hirsh, Foster, *A Method to Their Madness*, New York: Da Capo, 1984

Hodge, Allison, *Actor Training* (2nd edn), London: Routledge, 2010*

Hornby, Richard, *The End of Acting*, New York: Applause, 1992

Hull, S. Lorraine, *Strasberg's Method*, Woodbridge, CT: Ox Bow Press, 1985

Johnston, Keith, *Impro*, New York: Routledge, 1989*

Katselas, Milton, *Acting Class: Take a Seat*, Beverly Hills, CA: Phoenix Books, 2008*

Kazan, Elia, *A Life*, New York: Alfred Knopf, 1988

Knebel, Maria, The Nemirovich-Danchenko School of Directing, in Sonia Moore (ed.), *Stanislavsky Today*, 1973.

—— *On the Action Analysis of Plays and Roles* (3rd edn) Moscow: Isskustva, 1982, trans. Mike Pushkin and ed. Bella Merlin, 2002

Kogan, Sam, *The Science of Acting*, London: Routledge, 2010*

Kovens, Ed, *The Method Manual*, New York: Lulu.com, 2006*

Krampner, Jon, *Female Brando: The Legend of Kim Stanley*, New York: Back Stage Books, 2006

Krasner, David (ed.), Introduction, *Method Acting Reconsidered*, New York: St. Martin's Press, 2000, pp. 3–39

—— Method Acting, *Actor Training* (A. Hodge, ed.), Routledge: 2010, pp. 144–63*

Lecoq, Jacques, *Theatre of Movement and Gesture* (David Bradby, ed.), London: Routledge, 2006

Lee, Al and Don Campbell, *Perfect Breathing*, New York: Sterling, 2008

Levin, Irina and Igor Levin, *The Stanislavsky Secret*, Colorado Springs, CO: Meriwether Publishing, 2002*

Lewis, Robert, *Method or Madness*, New York: French, 1958

—— Interview, *Educational Theatre Journal*, 28(4), December 1976, pp. 483–89

—— *Advice to the Players*, New York: TCG, 1980

Longwell, Dennis, *Sanford Meisner on Acting*, New York: Vintage, 1987

Lugering, Michael, *The Expressive Actor: Integrating Voice, Movement, and Acting Training*, Portsmouth, NH: Heinemann, 2007*

Mamet, David, *Theatre*, New York: Faber & Faber, 2010

Manderino, Ned, *All About Method Acting*, Los Angeles: Manderino Books, 1985

Mann, Paul, Theory and Practice, *The Drama Review*, 9(2), Winter 1964, pp. 84–96

Marowitz, Charles, *Stanislavsky and the Method*, New York: Citadel, 1964

—— *The Other Way: An Alternative Approach to Acting and Directing*, New York: Applause, 1999

McGaw, Charles and Larry D. Clark, *Acting Is Believing: A Basic Method* (5th edn), New York: Holt, Rinehart and Winston, 1987*

Meisner, Sanford, *Theatre Arts on Acting* (L. Senelick, ed.) London: Routledge, 2008

Merlin, Bella, *Konstantin Stanislavsky*, London: Routledge, 2003

—— *The Compete Stanislavsky Toolkit*, Hollywood, CA: Drama Publishers, 2007*

Moore, Sonia, *The Stanislavski System*, New York: Penguin, 1960

—— (ed.), *Stanislavski Today*, New York: American Center for Stanislavski Theatre Art, 1973

—— *Stanislavski Revealed*, New York: Applause, 1991

Moss, Larry, *The Intent to Live: Achieving Your True Potential as an Actor*, New York: Bantam, 2005*

Moston, Doug, *Coming to Terms with Acting*, New York: Quite Specific Media Group, 1993*

Munk, Erika (ed.), *Stanislavski and America*, New York: Hill & Wang, 1965

Nicola, James, *Playing the Audience: The Practical Actor's Guide to Live Performance*, New York: Applause, 2002*

Nilus, Tom, Viewpoints, *American Theatre*, January 1995, pp. 30–4, 70–6

O'Brien, Nick, *Stanislavski in Practice: Exercises for Students*, London: Routledge, 2011*

Oida, Yoshi, *An Actor Adrift*, London: Methuen, 1992

O'Neill, Rosary, *The Actor's Checklist: Creating the Complete Character*, Belmont, LA: Wadsworth, 2002*

Ouspenskaya, Maria, Notes on Acting, *American Repertory Theatre Magazine*, 2 (Nos 1, 2, 3, October, November, December) 1954

Owen, Mack, *The Stage of Acting: A Practical Approach for Beginning Actors*, New York: HarperCollins, 1993*

Paget, Brigid, *Essential Acting*, London: Routledge, 2009*

Parke, Lawrence, *Acting Truths and Fiction*, Hollywood, CA: Acting World Books, 1995*

Perry, John, *Encyclopedia of Acting Techniques*, Cincinnati, OH: Better Way Books, 1997*

Petit, Lenard, *The Michael Chekhov Handbook for the Actor*, London: Routledge, 2010*

Phillips, Gordon, *Take It Personally: On the Art and Process of Personal Acting*, New York: Applause, 2000*

Pitches, Jonathan, *Science and the Stanislavsky Tradition of Acting*, London: Routledge, 2006

Plato, *The Collected Dialogues* (E. Hamilton and H. Cairns, eds) Princeton, NJ: Princeton University Press, 1989

Poitier, Sidney, *Measure of a Man*, San Francisco: Harper, 2000

Powers, Mala, Preface: Michael Chekhov's Chart for Inspired Acting, *Michael Chekhov: On the Technique of Acting* (M. Gordon, ed.), New York: Harper Collins, 1991, pp. xxxv–xliv

Quinto, Zachary, Career Zigzag, Changing Coasts and Galaxies, *New York Times*, Arts & Leisure Section, October 24, 2010, pp. 6, 9

Redfield, William, *Letters from an Actor*, New York: Viking, 1967

Redgrave, Michael, *The Actor's Ways and Means*, New York: Theatre Arts, 1979

Richards, Thomas, *At Work with Grotowski on Physical Actions*, New York: Routledge, 1995

Richardson, Don, *Acting without Agony: An Alternative to the Method*, Boston, MA: Allyn & Bacon, 1994*

Rilke, Rainer Maria, *Letters to a Young Poet* (trans. M. D. H. Norton), New York: W. W. Norton, 1954

Rogoff, Gordon, Lee Strasberg: Burning Ice, in Munk, 1965, pp. 257–79

Rotté, Joanna, *Acting with Adler*, New York: Limelight, 2000*

Ruffini, Franco, Stanislavski's System, *A Dictionary of Theatre Anthropology* (E. Barba and N. Savarese, eds) London: Routledge, 1991, pp. 150–3

Saint-Denis, Michael, *Theatre: The Rediscovery of Style* (J. Baldwin, ed.) London: Routledge, 2009

Schoenberg, Loren, Great Moments in Jazz, Rediscovered After 70 Years, *New York Times*, August 17, 2010, pp. C1, C7

Shurtleff, Michael, *Audition*, New York: Bantam, 1978*

Shyer, Laurence, *Robert Wilson and His Collaborators*, New York: TCG, 1989

Silverberg, Larry, *The Sanford Meisner Approach*, Lyme, NH: Smith Kraus, 1994*

Soloviova, Vera, The Reality of Doing, in Munk, 1965, pp. 210–27

Sontag, Susan, *On Photography*, New York: Delta, 1977

Spolin, Viola, *Improvisation for the Theater* (3rd edn), Evanston, IL: Northwestern University Press, 1983*

Stanislavsky, Konstantin, *On the Art of the Stage* (trans. D. Magarshack) London: Faber & Faber, 1950

—— *Creating a Role* (trans. E. R. Hapgood), New York: Theatre Arts, 1961

—— *K. Stanislavsky, 1863–1963*, Moscow, Progress, 1963

—— *Selected Works*, compiled by Oksana Korneva, Moscow: Raduga, 1984

—— *An Actor's Work* (trans. J. Benedetti), London: Routledge, 2008a

—— *My Life in Art* (trans. J. Benedetti), London: Routledge, 2008b

—— *An Actor's Work on a Role* (trans. J. Benedetti), London: Routledge, 2010

Strasberg, Lee, Acting and Actor Training, *Producing the Play* (J. Gassner, ed.) New York: Dryden, 1941, pp. 128–62
—— Lee Strasberg, in Stanislavsky, *K. Stanislavsky*, 1963, pp. 212–13
—— Introduction, in Diderot, *Paradox*, 1957, pp. ix–xiv
—— *Strasberg at the Actors Studio* (R. H. Hethmon, ed.), New York: TCG: 1965
—— *A Dream of Passion*, New York: Plume, 1987
Sun Tzu, *The Art of War* (trans. D. Galvin), New York: Barnes & Noble, 2003
Toporkov, Vasily Osipovich, *Stanislavski in Rehearsal: The Final Years*, New York: Theatre Arts, 1979
Vakhtangov, Evgenii, Preparing for the Role (trans. B. E. Zakhava), in Cole, *Acting*, 1955, 141–51
—— *Diaries* (trans. D. Bradbury), Moscow: Progressive, 1982
—— *The Vakhtangov Sourcebook* (trans. and ed. Andrei Malaev-Babel), London: Routledge, 2011
Vineberg, Steve, *Method Actors: Three Generations of an American Acting Style*, New York: Schirmer Books, 1991
Whyman, Rose, *The Stanislavsky System of Acting*, Cambridge, UK: Cambridge University Press, 2008
Wilde, Oscar, The Decay of Lying, *The Major Works* (I. Murray, ed.), Oxford, UK: Oxford University Press, 1989, pp. 215–39
Wright, Nicholas, *Mrs Klein*, London: Nick Hern, 1988
Zarrilli, Phillip, *Psychophysical Acting*, London: Routledge, 2009

acting 1–9
  'good acting' 9–13
  training of actors 2–3, 13–18
  see also individual topics
action 119–27
  analysis through action 103–4, 199
  finding beats 130–1
  learning new actions through new
    instinct 128
  mirror/action exercise 128–9
  six basic actions exercise 125–6
  see also physical dynamics;
    physicalization
Actors Studio 13, 133, 199
Adler, Stella 11, 13, 73, 79, 92,
    121, 133, 157, 164, 166, 179,
    182, 200
affective (emotion) memory 60–72,
    87, 104, 194, 199
  emotion memory exercises 60–1, 62
  jack-in-the-box experience and
    79–84
  waiting exercise 63
aims of acting 5
Alberts, David 83
Alexander Technique 15, 28–9
Alice, Mary 77
American Academy of Dramatic
    Arts 14
American Center for Stanislavsky
  Theatre Art 201

American Laboratory Theatre 198
analysis through action 103–4, 199
Anderson, Pamela 15
animals
  acting with 144–5
  animal imagery 48–50
  exercise 50–1
Appel, Alfred 139
Archer, William 170
art
  acting as 2, 70
  painting by numbers 89–90
attention-seeking 11
attitude 64
auditions 43–4, 116, 126
  waiting for 63

Baraka, Amiri 138
Barry, B. H. 14
Barthes, Roland 87, 88
Batson, Susan 136
beats 130–1
Beiderbecke, Bix 136
Belgrad, Daniel 135
believability 152, 154
Benedetti, Jean 36, 134, 154, 177
Benedetti, Robert 2, 57–8
Bennett, Fran 14
blackface 137
Bogart, Anne 69, 70, 202
Boleslavsky, Richard 11, 17, 153, 198

Bradley, Margaret   62
Brando, Marlon   8–9, 42, 133, 136, 137,
      139, 140, 145, 153
breathing   21–4, 179, 194
   breathing awareness exercise   25–7
   see-saw breathing exercise   30
   sense and emotion memory and   62,
      63–4
Brecht, Bertolt   9, 78
   Baal   85–7
Brook, Peter   4, 32, 48–9, 68
Bruehl, Bill   103, 106
Brustein, Robert   8

Caldarone, Marina   122
Campbell, Don   22, 98
Carnegie Mellon University   14
Carnicke, Sharon   151
Carnovsky, Morris   49
Carra, Larry   14
Cazale, John   15
Chaikin, Joseph   13, 56
Chamberlain, Franc   179–80, 185,
      186
character   121
   culture and   181–2
   motivation   107, 188, 198
   objectives   105, 107, 180–1, 188
   psychological gesture and
      characterization   185–6, 199
      exercises   186–8
   stepping into character
      exercise   185–6
Cheek by Jowl Theatre Company   201
Chekhov, Anton   5, 69, 70
   The Cherry Orchard   70–1
   The Three Sisters   57
   Uncle Vanya   163–6
Chekhov, Michael   7, 10, 17, 40–4, 50,
      69, 92, 184–5, 186–7, 191, 199
chemistry   100–1
children, acting with   144–5
Churchill, Caryl, *Top Girls*   160–3
Cieslak, Ryszard   56
Clausewitz, Claus von   120
clichés   29–30
Clift, Montgomery   136
clowns   69
Clurman, Harold   65
Cohen, Robert   24
Coltrane, John   135, 136
combining techniques   72–3
come to me exercise   147–8
commedia dell'arte   172
communion   98

concentration   30–5, 194
   concentration and personalization
      exercise   31
   concentration in motion
      exercise   34–5
   mirror exercise   32–3
   observation and imagination
      exercise   33–4
Courtney, C. C.   96
creativity   2–5, 8, 17, 18, 79, 179, 194
   actions and   127
   affective memory and   66, 68, 69, 89
   concentration and   30, 35
   creative circle   64
   creative initiative   44–5
   good habits and   51
   imagination and   153
   improvisation and   136, 137, 144
   justification and   86, 157
   living through and   155–6
   mantras and   147–8
   psychological gesture and   183, 185,
      186
   relaxation and   24, 27–8, 35
   ruling ideas and   153
   trigger mechanism   100–1
Crouch, Stanley   138
culture   181–2

Dartington Hall   199
Davis, Miles   136
Davis, Viola   159
Day-Lewis, Daniel   153
De Niro, Robert   134, 175–6
Dean, James   133, 136, 139–40
deception *see* lying
denial   169
desires   181
diaphragm   24
Diderot, Denis   167, 170
Diehl, Nancy   22
disability   140–1
discipline   193–4
Donnellan, Declan   43, 92, 100, 101,
      124, 201–2
Draper, Paul   14
Dunbar, Paul Laurence   170

eating soup exercise   55–6
Edwards, Christine   185
Einhorn, Susan   93
Ellermann, Robert   50, 65
embodying   153
emotions   94, 195
   breathing and   22–4

emotion (affective) memory   60–72,
    87, 104, 194, 199
    emotion memory exercises   60–1,
        62
    jack-in-the-box experience
        and   79–84
    waiting exercise   63
    tone of voice and   99–100
entrances with a lie   176–8
    exercise   177
Esper, William   96
exercises
    animal imagery exercise   50–1
    breathing awareness exercise   25–7
    Chekov's movement exercises   40–1
    come to me exercise   147–8
    concentration and personalization
        exercise   31
    concentration in motion
        exercise   34–5
    creating images exercise   42–3
    eating soup exercise   55–6
    emotion memory exercises   60–1, 62
    entrances with a lie exercise   177
    interstitial scenes   166
    mirror exercise   32–3
    mirror/action exercise   128–9
    nursery rhyme exercise   145–6
    observation and imagination
        exercise   33–4
    one action/one objective
        exercises   107–10, 116–18, 194
    packing exercise   59
    photographs exercise   89
    psychological gesture
        exercises   186–8
    relaxation awareness exercise   27
    repetition exercise   95–9, 101
    sense memory exercise   54–5
    six basic actions exercise   125–6
    stepping into character
        exercise   185–6
    swinging side-to-side exercise   45–8
    vocal range and flexibility
        exercise   37–8
    waiting exercise   63
experience   78
    jack-in-the-box   79–84

fear, breathing and   22–3
Feldenkrais, Moshe   15, 21, 25, 26–7,
    30, 35, 67, 128
Feldenkrais Technique   28, 29
film acting   8
Fitzgerald, Ella   141, 142

flashbulb memory   62
Foster, Gloria   56
Franzen, Jonathan   195
Freud, Sigmund   66
Fugard, Athol: Sizwe Banzi is
    Dead   15

Gabler, Milt   139
generality   44
gesture, psychological   185–6, 199
    exercises   186–8
Giddens, Gary   143
Gillett, John   154
Gillette, William   132, 133
Ginsberg, Allen   136
Gister, Earle   15, 72
'good acting'   9–13
Gordon, Mel   154
Gosling, Ryan   159
Gottschild, Brenda Dixon   134
Graczyk, Ed: Come Back to the Five
    and Dime, Jimmy Dean, Jimmy
    Dean   31
Grotowski, Jerzy   5, 15, 16, 29, 50, 141,
    201
Group Theatre   199, 200
Guskin, Harold   7, 21, 144

habits   29–30, 156–7
    creating good habits   51–2
Hagen, Uta   13, 99, 119, 176, 201
HB Studio   13, 201
Healy, Patrick   159
Hicks, Israel   14
Hoffman, Dustin   90–1, 134
Holliday, Billie   132, 134, 136, 139, 140,
    141–5
homework   188–90
hooks   179, 181
Hopkins, Anthony   155–6
Hornby, Richard   173
hustling   171–2

imagination   35, 45, 78–9, 194
    creating images exercise   42–3
    observation and imagination
        exercise   33–4
    photographs and   85–92
        exercise   89
imitation of animals   48–50
    exercise   50–1
improvisation   110, 132–4, 194
    basics of jazz acting   137–41
    Billie Holliday as jazz actor   141–5
    jazz acting in 'time'   134–7

improvisation – *continued*
  mantras   146–7
    come to me exercise   147–8
    nursery rhyme exercise   145–6
initiative   45
inner monologue (mantras)   146–7
  come to me exercise   147–8
instincts   29–30, 96, 156–7
  learning new actions through new
    instinct   128
interstitial scenes   197
  living through   157–9
    '*Death of a Salesman*'   166
    'down by the river'   160–3
    exercise   166
    'Vanya's dream'   163–5
Ionesco, Eugène   5

jack-in-the-box, experience and
  79–84
jazz   132
  jazz acting   134–7
    basics   137–41
    Billie Holliday as jazz actor   141–5
Johnstone, Keith   89, 133, 144
Josephson, Barney   143
journeymen actors   11
Justice, Milton   166
justification   86, 198
  living through interstitial
    scenes   157–9
    '*Death of a Salesman*'   166
    'down by the river'   160–3
    exercise   166
    'Vanya's dream'   163–5

Kani, John   15
Katselas, Milton   8, 11–12, 43, 45, 84
Kazan, Elia   133, 140
Kerouac, Jack   133, 136
Klein, Franz   136
Knebel, Maria   17, 65, 68, 102, 104, 120,
  148, 153, 157, 199
Kogan, Sam   141
Kooning, Willem de   136
Kovens, Ed   60
Krampner, Jon   124
Krupa, Gene   137

laughter   104
Lawner, Morty   15
Lecoq, Jacques   39, 172
Lee, Al   22, 98
Lee Strasberg Institute   13
Leo, Melissa   71–2

Leon, Kenny   159
Levy, John   142–3
Lewis, Robert   84, 201
likeability   195
living through   151–7, 190
  interstitial scenes   157–9
    '*Death of a Salesman*'   166
    'down by the river'   160–3
    exercise   166
    'Vanya's dream'   163–5
Loden, Barbara   15, 31
lying   167–77
  entrances with a lie   176–8
  exercise   177

Mailer, Norman   136
Mamet, David   3, 48, 109, 118
Manderino, Ned   50
Mann, Paul   15, 43–4, 72, 73, 107, 159,
  200–1
Manoogian, Haig   14
mantras   146–7
  come to me exercise   147–8
Marjenin, Franz   15
Marowitz, Charles   181
masks   169–70, 172–3
Massey, Raymond   140
McGarry, Jackson   44
McRae, Carman   139
Meisner, Sanford   9, 13, 78, 91, 95, 96,
  99, 133, 200
Meisner Technique   15
Merlin, Bella   155, 181
Method approaches to acting   9, 14,
  109, 133, 173, 198, 199
Meyerhold, Vsevolod   17, 198
Mikhail Chekhov Association
  (MICHA)   199
Miller, Arthur: *Death of a*
  Salesman   166
minstrelsy   137
mirror exercise   32–3
mirror/action exercise   128–9
Monich, Tim   15
Monson, Ingrid   143
Moore, Sonia   146–7, 201
Moscow Art Theatre   197, 198
Moss, Larry   12, 56, 155–6, 180
Moston, Doug   60, 121
motivation   107, 188, 198
Murray, Albert   138

narcissism   12, 156
Negro Ensemble Company   200
Neighborhood Playhouse   13, 200

Nelis, Tom 69, 70
Nemirovich-Danchenko, Vladimir 197
Newman, Paul 171–2
Nicola, James 105
Ntshona, Winston 15
nursery rhyme exercise 145–6

objectives
characters 105, 107, 180–1, 188
one action/one objective
exercises 107–10, 116–18, 194
observation 78, 92–102
observation and imagination
exercise 33–4
repetition exercise 95–9, 101
Oida, Yoshi 24, 25, 32, 121
Olivier, Laurence 8–9, 90–1
O'Meally, Robert 139, 143
one action/one objective
exercises 107–10, 116–18,
194
Ouspenskaya, Maria 17, 77, 160, 195,
198
Overlie, Mary 69

Pacino, Al 15, 134, 173
packing exercise 59
pain 195
painting by numbers 89–90
Papp, Joseph 69
Parke, Lawrence 8, 83
Parker, Charlie 137
Parks, Bob 14, 15
Pasquin, John 14
passion 11–12, 105, 194, 195–6
Penn, Sean 134
personalization 31–2, 53, 57–8, 156
concentration and personalization
exercise 31
emotion (affective) memory 60–72,
87, 104, 194, 199
emotion memory exercises 60–1,
62
jack-in-the-box experience
and 79–84
waiting exercise 63
sense memory 53–60, 194
packing exercise 59
Pesci, Joe 175–6
Petit, Lenard 41
photographs, imagination and 85–92
exercise 89
physical dynamics 39–45
animal imagery 48–50
exercise 50–1

Chekov's movements exercise 40–1
swinging side-to-side exercise 45–8
physicalization 103–7, 109–16
one action/one objective
exercises 107–10, 116–18, 194
plasticity 39
Plato 167–8, 169, 176
Poitier, Sidney 72–3
poker face 173
Pollock, Jackson 136
"poor theatre" 201
Powers, Mala 187
prana 17, 35, 98
predictability 184
presence 56–7
psychological gesture and
characterization 185–6, 199
exercises 186–8

quality acting 9–13
Quinto, Zachary 151

rationalization 115
Redfield, William 8
Redgrave, Michael 25, 133
Redgrave, Vanessa 99
rehearsal 154–5, 156, 190–2
relaxation 24–5, 27–30, 35, 194
relaxation awareness exercise 27
repetition exercise 95–9, 101
rhythm 138
Ribot, Théodule 60
Richards, Lloyd 72, 73, 77
Richards, Thomas 59
Rilke, Rainer Maria 195–6
risk avoidance 195
Rogoff, Gordon 173
Rotté, Joanna 92
Ruffini, Franco 151, 152
ruling ideas 179–80, 181
rushing 194
Russia, acting in 17

Sacks, Oliver: The Man Who Mistook
His Wife for a Hat 32
Saint, Eva Marie 140
Saint-Denis, Michael 189
Saratoga International Theatre Institute
(SITI) 202
scenic faith 198
Schadenfreude 10
Schall, Ekkehard 56
Scott, George C. 50
scripts 10, 182, 188, 194
secrets 77, 87

see-saw breathing exercise   30
sense memory   53–60, 194
  eating soup exercise   55–6
  packing exercise   59
  sense memory exercise   54–5
  waiting exercise   63
sexuality   11
Shakespeare, William   5, 15, 36, 69, 190
  As You Like It   167
  Hamlet   37–8
  King Lear   101, 168
  Othello   168
  Romeo and Juliet   183
Shiffman, Frank   142
shock value   10
Shurtleff, Michael   126
Silverberg, Larry   91
Sinatra, Frank   136
singing
  breathing and   24
  jazz   132, 136, 139, 141–5
skills of acting   2
Skinner, Edith   14, 15
Soloviova, Vera   17, 123, 198
Sontag, Susan   88–9
specificity   44, 45
Spolin, Viola   103, 133
spontaneity   153
stage acting   7–8
  presence   56–7
Stanislavsky, Konstantin   4, 5, 6, 11,
  12, 16–18, 24, 28, 29–30, 33, 36,
  45, 51, 53, 58, 60, 63, 64, 66, 71,
  72, 83, 84, 86, 89, 94, 98, 103, 106,
  110, 111, 118, 120, 127, 133, 134,
  140, 143, 144, 147, 151, 152, 154–8,
  161, 163, 168, 169, 170, 176–7,
  181, 184, 190, 193, 194, 196
  biography   197–8
Stanley, Kim   15, 44, 50, 56–7, 73, 124,
  126, 133
Steiger, Rod   73
Stella Adler Conservatory   13, 200
stepping into character exercise   185–6
Stern, Marshall   137
Strasberg, Lee   4, 13, 16, 48, 53, 54, 62,
  70, 73, 78, 81, 121, 133, 139, 140,
  146, 173–5, 199–200
Streep, Meryl   134
style   189–90
Sulerzhitsky, Leopold   17, 98, 198
Sun Tzu   172, 174
Suzuki, Tadashi   202

Suzuki method   70
swinging side-to-side exercise   45–8
Swinton, Tilda   127

techniques of acting   3–4
  combining techniques   72–3
television acting   8
tone of voice   99–100
Toporkov, Vasily   70–1
training of actors   2–3, 4, 13–18
tricks   152, 154–5
trigger mechanisms   45, 61, 62, 64, 72,
  77–84, 87, 89, 100–1
Tucker, Bobby   141

units in scenes (beats)   130–1

Vakhtangov, Evgenii   7, 11, 17, 39, 63,
  72, 83, 86, 122, 135, 166, 179, 183,
  191, 198–9
Van Gogh, Vincent   31
Vaughan, Sarah   136
via negativa   141
Viewpoints   13, 69–70, 202
voice   36–9
  tone   99–100
  vocal range and flexibility
    exercise   37–8
Volkonsky, Sergei   36, 157

waiting exercise   63
Walker, Jewel   14
warm-up   27–8
Washington, Denzel   159
Whitaker, Forrest   171–2, 174
White, Ruth   56
Whyman, Rose   36
Wilde, Oscar   167
Williams, Heathcote: *The Local
  Stigmatic*   15
Williams, Maggie Lloyd   122
Williams, Michelle   159
Williams, Tennessee   5
  A Streetcar Named Desire   159
Wilson, August, *Fences*   159
Wilson, Robert   56
Wright, Nicolas: *Mrs Klein*   119

Yale School of Drama   200, 201

Zakhava, B. E.   82
Zarrilli, Phillip   21, 98, 202
Zazlov, Arnie   14